HEIDEGGER &

DERRIDA

Heidegger & Derrida

REFLECTIONS ON

TIME AND LANGUAGE

HERMAN RAPAPORT

UNIVERSITY OF NEBRASKA PRESS

LINCOLN & LONDON

First paperback printing: 1991
Most recent printing indicated by the last digit below:
10   9   8   7   6   5   4   3   2   1

Library of Congress Cataloging-in-Publication Data
Rapaport, Herman, 1947–
Heidegger and Derrida.
Bibliography: p.
Includes index.
1. Heidegger, Martin, 1889–1976.   2. Derrida, Jacques.
3. Time—History—20th century.   4. Deconstruction.   I. Title.
B3279.H49R34   1989   115'.092'2   88-4748
ISBN 0-8032-3887-8 (alk. paper)
ISBN 0-8032-8927-8 (pbk.)

In Memory of My Parents

Josef Max Rapaport

Betti Margarete Rapaport

But if time is to show an ambiguity
of *being* and the otherwise than being, its
temporalization is to be conceived not
as essence, but as Saying.

—Emmanuel Levinas,
   Otherwise Than Being
   or Beyond Essence

CONTENTS

ACKNOWLEDGMENTS

I wish to thank the State University of New York at Buffalo for awarding me a Butler Fellowship for the spring of 1983 and the University of Iowa for granting me an Old Gold Summer Stipend for the summer of 1986. Parts of this manuscript were researched and written during these times.

Moreover, I wish to thank Gerald Bruns, Sabine Gölz, Ned Lukacher, Donald Marshall, Andrew McKenna, Steven Ungar, and Gregory Ulmer for their encouragement and reflections. I am especially grateful to Stavros Deligiorgis for his extreme kindnesses in helping me with some of the particulars in the translations, though, of course, I take full responsibility for their adequacy. And I am very grateful, as always, to Alexander Gelley for his support and extremely helpful suggestions. I owe my wife, Susanne Rapaport, much gratitude for her help in proofing the manuscript and for the many other favors that no words can fully express.

INTRODUCTION

In this study I focus on what for me had always been a very obscure topic: Martin Heidegger's conceptions of time and their relationship to deconstruction. Anyone familiar with the critical writings on Heidegger will recall that far more has been written on just about every aspect of his philosophy than on what *Being and Time* suggests is the most pressing for modern thought: the question of temporality. Moreover, it has occurred to me that if one wanted to find some direct philosophical connections to an immediate predecessor whose works are crucial in determining the directions or latitudes that deconstruction has taken, one would necessarily be driven to come to terms with explicit and implicit claims made in Jacques Derrida's writings about Heidegger's handling of temporality and the degree to which that did or did not dismantle the history of ontological reflection. What I had not initially counted on was that such an approach might yield an interpretation which would span all the major phases of Derrida's philosophical career and help us better grasp even those essays which are not explicitly commenting on materials in Heidegger's work. What I discovered, somewhat to my surprise, is that the question of time is far more fundamental to a philosophical understanding of deconstruction than one might at first suppose.

My text is primarily philosophical in orientation, though I approach philosophy often from the standpoint of what may be called literary problematics. As someone trained in literary studies, I naturally gravitate to stylistic features and questions of language that have been of importance to literary scholars working in the field of critical theory, and at times I also bring in discussion of literary texts. However, I have also made it a point not to let literary wordplay dominate my analyses nor to let my style imitate a deconstructionist discourse too closely.

Having written a number of pieces in the past that are aggressively playful and performative, I wanted, in this study, to
write in a different mode, while, of course, not completely
losing sight of how both Heidegger and Derrida seriously play
with language in order to put distance between themselves and
a certain philosophical tradition.

A major problem I had to confront even in the early stages of
writing this book was how to handle the gravitational pull of
traditional intellectual history. One of my motivations in writing this study was, of course, to clarify the connections of
deconstruction to Heideggerian philosophy. At the same time,
it is obvious that deconstruction aggressively eludes the kind of
theoretical referentiality to precursors typical of many other
philosophical critiques—for example, the writings of Ludwig
Wittgenstein or Richard Rorty. Most troublesome, from this
perspective, is the meticulous deconstruction of intellectual
history performed by Derrida in *The Post Card*, wherein his
relation to Heidegger, another dismantler of this kind of history, is explicitly so disarticulated that it raises disturbing
ironies for the kind of project on which I have been working.
Thus I have had to consider the problem of how to write an
intellectual history about figures who have themselves annihilated the philosophical grounds upon which such a study
might be conceived.

That my study focuses on time has certain advantages with
respect to this problem. The main advantage is that instead of
treating the deconstruction of intellectual history as a univer-
salized aporia or double bind that cannot be historically negoti-
ated, I am able to consider it as a reinscription of a deconstructive set of temporal proximities which break with the
determinability of any one critical or philosophical temporal
model. Especially in relation to Heidegger's considerations of
time in his later writings, so important to Derrida's *The Post
Card*, it would be quite mistaken to think that Derrida's temporal or familial double binds ought to be considered as setting
a new "standard time," however unteleological, to which all
dimensions of intellectual history are to be subordinated or
limited. If one were to conclude from Derrida's dismantling of
the chronology underwriting traditional "intellectual history"
that such a history is no longer thinkable except from an un-

decidable set of problematics—for example, that of who is signing for whom in Plato or who is fathering what psychoanalysis by whom in Freud—one would, then, be encouraging a metaphysical recovery of time as a universal or cbjectified framework that has substituted one set of temporal aporias / (that of Oedipus) for another—for example, those of Aristotle, St. Thomas Aquinas, and perhaps even Heidegger. That Derrida himself shows the chronological aporias of an intellectual family romance to be as applicable to Socrates and Plato as they are to Freud and to Derrida himself should not suggest that an incipient universalization of genealogical temporality is being undertaken even as intellectual history in its traditional senses is being discredited and discarded. For in our considerations of the historical stances between Heidegger and Derrida it will become evident that even the genealogical or Oedipal critique of *The Post Card* is but part of a much more complex set of historical or temporal interrelations eluding not only *Geistesgeschichte* but the genealogical psychoanalysis of the double bind, while, at the same time, participating in them.

Throughout this study I focus on a number of latitudes wherein Derrida's texts are being positioned and repositioned along the lines of their turning toward and away from Heidegger in the context of the problematic of temporality which, as we recall, Heidegger abrogated in *Being and Time*. What is not well recognized is that Heidegger developed the problematic of time at great length in later studies and particularly with respect to language. In the paragraphs that follow, I will outline other ways in which my chapters relate through a brief overview of Heidegger, Derrida, and the question of temporality.

Destruction and Deconstruction

In the design for the argument of *Being and Time*, Martin Heidegger contemplates the question of Being in the context of two tasks which will divide the treatise. Part 1 is intended to be a discussion of "the interpretation of Dasein in terms of temporality, and the explication of time as the transcendental horizon for the question of Being," and part 2 is meant to be a demonstration of the "basic features of a phenomenological destruction of the history of ontology [*phänomenologischen Destruktion der Geschichte der Ontologie*] with the problematic of Temporality as our clue [*Leitfaden*]."¹ Exactly what Heidegger meant by "the destruction of the history of ontology" is not clear, though the program for part 2 sounds menacing enough. The suggestion is made that through a particular turn on the concept of temporality the ontological project of part 1 will be sublated, supported, and at the same time purified with an even more rigorous critique of ontology. Certainly Albert Hofstadter has this in mind when in his introduction to the English translation of Heidegger's *Basic Problems of Phenomenology* he makes the following remarks on ontology and temporality.

> In ancient ontology being is understood as presence, which is itself understood in terms of this common time, the time which on the surface seems so important in everyday life and productive activity, although the truth is that there is a profounder, more original, truer time at its foundation, which it has forgotten. Heidegger devotes much effort to the analysis of Aristotle's treatise on time and to the phenomenological examination of its definition of time, pressing on toward the original time—temporality as ecstatic-horizonal and eventually as ecstatic-horizonal Temporality—from which, as horizon, a more authentic realization of the meaning of being can be attained. Here, too, then, we find the *destruction of a fundamental part of traditional ontology and its de-construction, down to its original rooting in Temporality.*²

At the end of this English edition of *Basic Problems of Phenomenology*, however, an afterword appears by F. W. von Herrmann, the German editor of this volume, and oddly enough, Herrmann entirely contradicts Hofstadter's assessments. "This lets us see *that* and *how* the treatment of the question of being and of the analytic of *Dasein* pertaining to it arises from a more original appropriation of the Western tradition, of the orientation of its metaphysical-ontological inquiry, and not actually from motives germane to existential philosophy or the phenomenology of consciousness."³ Given Herrmann's view, anyone who would imagine Heidegger a deconstructionist in the earlier phases of his career would evidently be guilty of a profound and basic misunderstanding. And indeed, this difference of opinion between Hofstadter and Herrmann typifies a conflict of interpretations which underwrites much Heidegger scholarship and also figures, to some degree, in readings of Derrida.

Rodolphe Gasché, in *The Tain of the Mirror: Derrida and the Philosophy of Reflection,* for example, implicitly lends support to Herrmann when in explaining the meaning of Heidegger's term "destruction" he quotes *Basic Problems of Phenomenology,* presupposing that this text and *Being and Time* are so conceptually congruent that one text can accurately gloss the other. The passage Gasché quotes from reads as follows.

> It is for this reason that all philosophical discussion, even the most radical attempt to begin all over again, is pervaded by traditional concepts and thus by traditional horizons and traditional angles of approach, which we cannot assume with unquestionable certainty to have arisen originally and genuinely from the domain of being and the constitution of being they claim to comprehend. It is for this reason that there necessarily belongs to the conceptual interpretation of being and its structures, that is, to the reductive construction of being a *destruction*—a critical process in which the traditional concepts, which at first must necessarily be employed, are de-constructed [*kritischer Abbau*] down to the sources from which they were drawn. Only by means of this destruction can ontology fully assure itself in a phenomenological way of the genuine character of its concepts.[4]

This lengthy passage, in which Gasché's quotation (the last two sentences) takes place, immediately discloses that in comparison with *Being and Time*'s much more aggressive tone and boldness of purpose, *Basic Problems* is a more cautious and far less ambitious text, perhaps because it is still very closely attached to phenomenological method, whereas *Being and Time* has taken more distance from it.[5] Indeed, as I will demonstrate in some detail in chapter 2, *Basic Problems* is a conservative version of *Being and Time,* wherein opportunities for breaking with the history of ontology are, in fact, carefully avoided rather than explored as in the latter. Hence one could debate Gasché's definition of "destruction" in Heidegger's *Being and Time* as not being far more violent in intent than "the dismantling of tradition" for the sake of critical inspection of its foundations or the "systematic removal or dismantling of the concealments of the meaning of Being by the history of ontology." Indeed, the program for part 2 of the design for *Being and Time* could be read so that the temporal clue functioned not merely to inspect the foundations of tradition by careful dissection but violently to demolish the conceptual apparatus of metaphysics embedded in the history of ontology. When, as Gasché notes, Heidegger used the term *Zerstörung* at a conference in 1929 rather than the word *Destruktion,* the much more violent connotations of *Zerstörung* may have been more apt in disclosing what Heidegger had conceived when he projected the second part of the design for *Being and Time.*

That Gasché's definition of "destruction" is crucial for a particular understanding of "deconstruction" is self-evident, but its significance is not, since how one understands Heideggerian "destruction" establishes not just a particular relation between words but between the philosophies in general of Derrida and Heidegger. In Gasché's study, the result of defining Heidegger's term "destruction" in the context of *Basic Problems* has predictable results. It leads to a highly defined and static difference between a Heideggerian philosophy that appears conservatively tied to the tradition of metaphysics and a deconstructive philosophy that is considered much more adroit in challenging the history of ontology. "If, as Derrida writes in *Writing and Difference,* referring to the *Cartesian Meditations,* that 'in criticizing classical metaphysics, phenomenology accomplishes the most profound project of metaphysics,' then the same can be said of Heidegger's destruction of the Occidental tradition of ontology and of his focus on Being."[6] Gasché's conclusion is that even if "destruction" and "deconstruction" analogously disrupt the foundations of thought, they are very different concepts, because unlike "deconstruction" the Heideggerian notion of "destruction" leads to "an ever more fundamental notion of the essence of what is under consideration." Deconstruction, unlike destruction, searches for "ultimate foundations . . . exterior to metaphysics."[7]

Of course, Derrida himself has taken some definite positions on his relationship with Heideggerian philosophy, and when Gasché cites him for authority it has to be recollected that Derrida has, in fact, taken many *different* positions on whether deconstruction has close ties to Heidegger or whether it is something not to be confused with Heideggerian thought. Derrida participates, as it were, in an ongoing debate with explicit and implicit claims on the overall evaluation of Heidegger's corpus with respect to the question of his radicality as a thinker whose work destabilizes and undermines the presuppositions upon which Western philosophy has been established. Derrida's evaluation is distinctive in that instead of choosing between the two options that, for example, Hofstadter and Herrmann (or Gasché) delimit, it plays with their "difference" of opinion and thereby takes on many directions or perspectives which would appear to be merely incompatible.

For example, one can find passages in Derrida's work that are hostile to the association of Heideggerian thinking with deconstruction. In *The Post Card* Derrida criticizes those French translators who have made an identification between Heidegger's notion of destruction and Derrida's formulation of the term "deconstruction":

> *Abbauen*: the word that certain French Heideggerians recently have translated as "to deconstruct," as if all were in all, and always ahead of the caravan. It is true that this translation is not simply illegitimate once it has been envisaged (rather recently). Unless one manipulates an aftereffect [*l'après-coup*] precisely in order to assimilate, and in order to reconstruct that which is difficult to assimilate.[8]

In a similarly sarcastic vein, Derrida remarks, "One puts one's hand on a mark [or brand name], and reapplies everywhere."[9] These remarks are part of Derrida's insistence that deconstruction is *different* from Heideggerian philosophizing, that one cannot reduce Derridean terms to their sources of inspiration, if, indeed, such sources are to be located at all. A major position that Derrida implies with respect to Heidegger is that Heidegger never broached deconstruction as developed in such works as *Of Grammatology, Margins of Philosophy, Glas,* or *The Post*

Card, because Heidegger never truly embarked on part two of the philosophical itinerary outlined in *Being and Time*. In other words, Derrida contradicts Hofstadter's assumption that we may read the complete *Being and Time* by way of examining the volume and its supplements, *Basic Problems of Phenomenology* and *Kant and the Problem of Metaphysics*, as the completion of a single treatise that does, in fact, fulfill the itinerary written at the outset of *Being and Time*, wherein the history of ontology is subjected to a phenomenological destruction by means of a temporal clue. In denying Hofstadter's not untypical "revisionary" reading of Heidegger, the Derridean perspective would necessarily have to claim that the supplements to *Being and Time* are not, in fact, continuations of *Being and Time*'s more radical impulses but symptoms of Heidegger's failure to bring such philosophical aims to fruition.

Despite an antipathy to the blanket identification of Heideggerian thinking with deconstruction, there are also many instances in which Derrida elicits such comparisons and establishes such a Heideggerian lineage for deconstructive thought. In a recent interview with American critics published by the Society for Critical Exchange, Derrida related that "the word 'deconstruction' itself has a whole genealogy. It's an old French word which had fallen out of use, that I used for the first time, so to speak, in this particular sense. But I did so with the sense that I was translating and deforming a word of Freud's and a word of Heidegger's."[10] And, more recently, in *De l'esprit* Derrida directly translates Heidegger's term *Destruktion* into French as *déconstruction*.[11] These examples are surprisingly odd, given what we have just quoted from *The Post Card*, and they suggest that readers like Hofstadter are, indeed, expressing views which are from Derrida's perspective quoted above not entirely without merit. I cite these somewhat contradictory statements by Derrida in order to introduce my conviction that peculiar to Derrida's stance on Heidegger is that instead of choosing between the two options of a radical or conservative Heidegger delimited by scholars like Hofstadter and Herrmann, Derrida plays with the "difference" of such a choice and thereby allows himself to pursue simultaneous perspectives or directions which would appear to be merely incompatible or untenable. In this way he disarticulates the decidability of any intellectual "event" that would constitute the historical difference between deconstruction and Heideggerian thought.

Indeed, Derrida's remarks concerning the filiation of the word "deconstruction" belong to a much larger field of interpretations about Heidegger, suggesting that Heidegger's corpus approximates an archaeological site with heterogeneous strata. From Derrida's perspective contradictory positions about Heidegger may be asserted, since the "ground" of Heidegger's philosophy is an incompatible interplay of strata which are but what remains of specific philosophical moments. In this sense, the matter is not a question of choosing between positions such as those of Hofstadter or Herrmann but of recognizing the possibility of their simultaneity or synchronicity in Heidegger's work. Clearly, when Derrida excoriates the bandying of deconstruction as a "brand-name" applied to Heidegger, or what amounts to a slick packaging technique, what is largely at issue is the reduction that takes sides on the intellectual historical debate between scholars like Hofstadter and Herrmann, as if one were justified in assuming that from a Heideggerian orientation one could simply make such easy determinations. And when Derrida explains in the interview with the Society for Critical Exchange that deconstruction relates to words in Heidegger and Freud, he destabilizes the interlocutor's presupposition that deconstruction is something separate from other ways of thinking, that the "place" of deconstruction can be restricted or easily delimited. This, in fact, is the common denominator between the two "contradictory" passages above: Derrida's strong antipathy to restrict deconstruction to a place of its own (*le propre*).

Heidegger's Turns

W. J. Richardson is well known for having first made the distinction between a Heidegger I and a Heidegger II, and ever since there has been controversy about which Heidegger is radical and which is conservative.[12] Moreover, this controversy has concerned the identification of what Heidegger himself has called "the turn." Although the "turn" in Heidegger is not reducible to any given text, line, or idea, Heidegger scholars have debated several understandings of what this turn is and where it occurs in Heidegger. Indeed, the question of deconstruction's relation to Heideggerian thought depends largely on the extent to which Derrida not only reads these turns but evaluates them in terms of the Heideggerian "destruction" of the history of ontology. Anticipating later remarks, I should clarify that I think Derrida makes different evaluations of this "destruction" depending upon which turn he is examining. Hence any static distinction made between Derridean deconstruction and Heideggerian philosophy will quickly be perceived to be inadequate, since the relationships between these modes of thinking shift their positions or proximities over time. This is important, since most critical approaches to the relation between Derrida and Heidegger have tended to be spatially motivated as territorial determinations rather than temporal modulations. As another note of clarification, let me add that for me the Heideggerian turns are all to be read with respect to the temporal clue in the proposed second part of the design in *Being and Time*. This is not to be interpreted as a crude reduction but as a certain bracketing of other problematics for the sake of focusing on the question of temporality which, as I see it, takes place in time as time.

Before outlining how the turns are developed in my study, we ought to review briefly some of the citations of the turn by Heidegger interpreters critical to an understanding of deconstruction's relationship to Heideggerian thinking. In doing so we will move retrogressively from Heidegger's explicit announcement of the turn in the essay "The Turning" included in the volume *Die Technik und die Kehre* (1962). As is well known, this essay discusses how being turns into "the oblivion of its coming to presence" and argues that in the coming to presence of Being, Being "turns counter to the truth of its coming to presence." Moreover, this turning counter to the truth has to be considered with respect to language "within which man's essence is first able to correspond at all to Being, and its claim, and, in corresponding, to belong to Being." Heidegger infers that language as technical apparatus facilitates a "turning" in which "danger" comes to pass in "the turning of the oblivion of Being."[13] In *Heidegger and the Tradition,* Werner Marx acknowledges that this turn separates the "earlier" from the "later" Heidegger, though Marx doubts that the turn actually does much more than mystify and obscure what was more clearly laid out in *Being and Time*.[14]

In "The Letter on Humanism" of the mid-1940s, however, the turn in Heidegger already consisted in contemplating language as the "house of Being," a turn reflected, too, in *Holzwege* and *On the Way to Language*. Maurice Blanchot acknowledges this turn in *L'entretien infini*. "Writing only begins when language, returning to itself [*retourne sur lui-même*], disappears in its being shown and apprehended."[15] For Blanchot the Heideggerian turn is the turning of the language of metaphysics upon itself which results in the disarticulation of metaphysics. Similarly, in *Of Grammatology* Derrida acknowledges such a turn when he writes that Heidegger's question of Being is contextualized within a "system of languages and an historically determined 'significance,'" privileging assumptions through which Being appears. Heidegger analyzes these languages because he suspects "Western metaphysics, as the limitation of the sense of being within the field of presence, is produced as the domination of a linguistic form."[16] In examining this linguistic form, Heidegger deliberately does violence to metaphysics. Certainly, the French poststructuralist reception of Heidegger is largely based on this interpretation of the Heideggerian turn as a linguistic turn. However, it too is controversial even for thinkers sympathetic to such a reading of Heidegger. Paul Ricoeur, for example, maintains that the turn to language cannot be divorced from Heidegger's early formulations. "The question of Being and the self, of which we read in the introduction of *Being and Time*, keeps ruling the philosophy of the later Heidegger."[17]

In addition to such concerns, the linguistic turn is inherently part of a most difficult Heideggerian problem, the "ontological difference," or, difference between beings and Being. The essays "The Anaximander Fragment" [from *Holzwege*] and "Logos" [from *Vorträge und Aufsätze* (1954)] are especially important in considering "difference" from the perspective of language, and later texts such as *On the Way to Language* and *Identity and Difference* develop further various thoughts in the earlier works. However, long before *Holzwege*, Heidegger had broached the question of ontological difference in *An Introduction to Metaphysics* (1935) and *Vom Wesen des Grundes* [*Of the*

Essence of Reasons] (1928), not to mention sketches and notes associated with *Being and Time*. Derrida's well-known essay "La différance" could be viewed as a development of the ontological difference in the context of the linguistic turn made in "The Anaximander Fragment," as if to say that the ontological difference itself becomes a crucial moment in this turn at the point when Heidegger considers questions of language. However, Heidegger scholars, particularly in Germany, often put much more stress on the problematic of the ontological difference as something to which the considerations of language are subordinated, since the ontological difference becomes the means whereby a turn, itself planned at the outset of *Being and Time,* was to be made from being to Being.[18]

In his introduction to *On Heidegger and Language,* Joseph Kockelmans discusses the "ontological turn" in this way:

> Heidegger hoped that a careful analysis of man's Being would help him find a way to make our preontological understanding of Being explicit. In his later works he continued to struggle with the same basic problem but approached the question from the viewpoint of the different forms, or "expressions," in which Being manifests itself in the various epochs of Being's own history. . . . This "turn" in Heidegger's approach to the main problem took place between 1929 and 1935.[19]

A major place where scholars often situate this earlier "ontological turn" is in *The Essence of Reasons* when Heidegger discusses transcendence as *Überstieg.* "Im Überstieg kommt das Dasein allererst auf solches Seiendes zu, das *es* ist, auf es als es 'selbst.' Die Transzendenz konstituiert die Selbstheit" ("*In* surpassing, Dasein first attains to the being that *it* is; what it attains to is its 'self.' Transcendence constitutes selfhood").[20] *Überstieg* is "undecidable" and Maurice Blanchot therefore renames it *le pas au-delà:* the step (not) beyond. When Heidegger says "transcendence constitutes selfhood," he is not saying anything that would be compatible with mystics, American transcendentalists, or the like. For Heidegger views transcendence as an inhabiting of ontological difference through which the categories of metaphysics are violently demolished. The "difference" between being and Being is incapacitated in the very moment it prevails as a means through which the turn from being to Being is made.

But Heidegger himself seems to have abandoned this "turn," for in *An Introduction to Metaphysics* Heidegger had transposed the work on transcendence into a discourse about the language of metaphysics—polemos—which comprised an ab-original conflict wherein differences were affirmed even as the binding together that is *logos* was achieved. "It is this conflict that first projects and develops what had hitherto been unheard of, unsaid and unthought."[21] This "projection" of polemos is itself a transposition of the notion of transcendence as ontological difference into a linguistic context, a close examination of ancient Greek etymologies. Yet, is it here that the temporal clue mentioned at the outset of *Being and Time* would be discovered? Not judging from the end of *An Introduction,* where the time problematic is just as nascent and undeveloped as in many of the previous works. Thus once more the adequacy of the turn noticed by Heidegger scholars is enough in doubt to disqualify the notion that a turn has, indeed, been taken rather than merely announced.

Thomas Sheehan, in taking issue with many of the prevalent views about what constitutes Heidegger's turn, thinks that such a turn was in fact made in the early work of Heidegger and that it was explicitly worked out in the *Metaphysical Foundations of Logic,* which comprises lecture notes from 1928, only a year after *Being and Time* was published. At that time Heidegger wrote: "The temporal analysis is at the same time the turning-around [*Kehre*], where ontology itself expressly runs back into the metaphysical ontic in which it implicitly always remains. Through the movement of radicalizing and universalizing, the aim is to bring ontology to its latent overturning [*Umschlag*]. Here the turn-around [*Kehre*] is carried out, and it is turned over into the metontology."[22] Although Sheehan insists this is the place where the turn occurs, he recognizes it occurring, too, in *Being and Time* and, less convincingly, in Heidegger's thinking of the early 1920s. But certainly, it does not take much imagination to uncover it also in the design cited above in *Being and Time,* where the two fundamental moments of Heidegger's analysis are announced, the one constituting a turn with respect to the other.

The turn, then, inherently divides, parcels out, or iterates throughout much of Heidegger's corpus and works against finite distinctions that might separate an earlier from a later Heidegger. Hence, it "overturns" the usual chronological sense we have of the development of intellectual thought and de-constitutes what scholars would like to reduce to the history of Heideggerian thinking. Moreover, the turn becomes an iterated problematic always raising the issue of whether Heidegger's initial itinerary in *Being and Time* is ever satisfied, as if to say that the questions regarding Being and time must necessarily be posed from the vantage point of an aporia whose assertion and repetition may be offered the chance of being surpassed even as it is reinstated.

Indeed, although my project is not conceived primarily to evaluate Heidegger's successes or failures with respect to fulfilling the turn(s), I have come to the conclusion that these moments in Heidegger's work disclose a *metaleptic* or paronomasic movement (a going beyond even as one stays in the same place) that reveals a modality of time or history which radically resituates not only how we are to comprehend Heidegger but how we are to evaluate the "correspondences" of his various philosophical moments. To my knowledge, Derrida's writings on Heidegger are the only interpretations which respect this deconstitution of a teleological intellectual history of self-enclosed moments within the trajectory of philosophical meditation. And precisely when Derrida addresses issues of temporality which bear on Heideggerian thinking, we begin to realize exactly how radical Heideggerian thought is from the perspective of a historical sedimentation which works against the familiar notions of chronological development or historization.

Derrida's Turning the Turns

Of course, Derrida, like other readers of Heidegger, has been interested in the extent to which even in the iteration of a turn that turn is actually made. Although it might be reductive to assume, as some Heidegger scholars do, that the turn either occurs at one go or not, it remains an issue whether a particular turn will be made at all, a turn which would take us from part 1 to part 2 of the itinerary of *Being and Time*. The passage above from *The Metaphysical Foundations of Logic* certainly reformulates the "design" of Heideggerian analysis as metaphor, the turning or overturning. Yet the question is whether this turn is actually made in such lecture notes as *The Metaphysical Foundations of Logic, Basic Problems of Phenomenology*, or *History of the Concept of Time*. As we have noticed, Heidegger scholars debate the issue of the turn at every turn, and Derrida has asked this question with respect to a footnote in *Being and Time*, suggesting that such a turn is hardly achieved or even adequately addressed. As I will corroborate in a brief overview of the background lectures and notes surrounding the publication of *Being and Time*, Derrida's intuition derived from a reading of a footnote in Heidegger is quite correct. Yet, although the announced turn is not fulfilled during the 1930s, a "linguistic turn" later becomes noticeable, for example, in "The Letter on Humanism" of the mid-1940s. At various points in the letter, Heidegger glosses *Being and Time*. At one point he quotes himself as having written, "The 'essence' of Dasein lies in its existence." The subject of this sentence from *Being and Time* is clearly the essence of Dasein, which is to say, Dasein itself. But in "The Letter" Heidegger rereads this sentence in order to make a turn emphasizing existence. "The 'Being' of the *Da,* and only it, has the fundamental character of ek-sistence, that is, of an ecstatic inherence in the truth of Being."[23] It has become commonplace for Heideggerians to situate the famous turn at this juncture in which emphasis from the perspective of Dasein gives way to emphasis on the perspectives offered from Being. However, in "The Letter" Heidegger says, "language is the house of Being," and instead of providing an analysis of existential phenomena, such as the moods, which occurred in the earlier *Being and Time* as an accompaniment to the analysis of Dasein, he now turns to the question of language. This turn is reflected in the French structuralist overturning of Sartrean existentialism for the sake of an inquiry into practices of signification, and Derrida himself makes this turn in *Of Grammatology* when he discusses Heidegger within Saussurean contexts. Less obviously, however, the hint occurs that in the turn to language, the earlier turn predicted in the design of *Being and Time* is also brought toward completion, and this, of course, concerns temporality as a radical clue through which the history (chronology, temporality) of Western ontology is deconstituted or, as Derrida would have it, deconstructed. This is a "turn" which has not been generally recognized and without which one cannot adequately understand Derrida's own corpus of books and essays which begin reperforming the Heideggerian "turn" by the mid-1970s. Whereas the essays on Heidegger written during the late 1960s appreciate Heidegger's notions of "ontological difference" about which so much had been worked through by the Heideggerians themselves, it appears that the temporal turn through language made by Heidegger is not fully appreciated by Derrida until he comes to a reading of Maurice Blanchot who, I feel, has been an enormous influence in developing the implications of the linguistic turn noted in Heidegger's "Letter." In fact, the performance of this "turn" comprises Blanchot's literary achievements.

In "The Turning" (1950) of Heidegger, however, a later phase of Derrida's consideration of the handling of time in Heidegger is raised as a "correspondence." Here the linguistic turn of the 1940s gives way to an even sharper turn which Heidegger makes after his consideration of philosophy from the perspective of the truth of Being. This turn develops the notion of *Ereignis* or the appropriative-event-of-disclosure, wherein an event comes to be seen as a manifold in which various moments correspond. In the small essay "Zeit und Sein," Heidegger develops the notion of *Ereignis* at length, and it culminates in the very radical disarticulation of a temporality as we experience it in our day-to-day affairs. Of major importance in "Zeit und Sein" is the idea that Being is sent through an "event" whose moments both appropriate and expropriate "correspondences" so that in the arrival of Being there is what Heidegger calls a "turning away" from the truth of Being, a moment, in other words, in which Being is subjected to "demolition" or "destruction." Certainly, the turn announced at the beginning of *Being and Time* is brought very much to pass in the "correspondence" of "The Turning" to "Zeit und Sein."

For Derrida the realization of this turn influences both *The Post Card,* written in the late 1970s, and what amounts to an important turn in Derrida's own writing, "Of an Apocalyptic

Tone Recently Adopted in Philosophy," which appeared in the early 1980s. In *The Post Card* Derrida literalizes Heidegger's notion of "correspondence" as the postal system's technology, and he considers the "sending of Being" in the sense of an *envoi* or "dispatch" which is part of an "event" disclosing extremely radical notions about temporality. Here the "linguistic turn" in Derrida's *Of Grammatology* is carried over into a performative writing,—that is, the letters—wherein the even later "turnings" of Heidegger are inscribed as correspondence, technology, dispatch, relay, and postcard. The "correspondences" of Derrida, then, consider language as the medium wherein *Ereignis* is at once articulated and subverted; however, this is also where Derrida makes his own peculiar turn back to an existential position, since the "letters" Derrida writes are autobiographical, personal effects of the life of the writer.

This "turn" in Derrida is accompanied by an even stranger one, perhaps, which is the turn from ontology to theology. Already in *The Post Card* Derrida is thinking about the history of metaphysics or ontology from the later Heideggerian perspective and then translates it into religious or sacred history—for example, the meditation on the *Book of Esther* in the Old Testament. In "Of an Apocalyptic Tone" Derrida again thinks about dispatches, though as a dispatch from God to St. John the Divine and St. John's dispatches to the seven churches of Asia from Patmos. We recall that in "The Turning" Heidegger talks about the turn away from truth as well as the oblivion of Being that occurs in its coming to pass. Derrida's "dispatch" concerns "oblivion" or "demolition" as the "destiny" of the "sending of Being," a destiny disclosed in an "end" or manifestation of the oblivion of Being: the catastrophe called technology wherein the dangerous turn of Being is disclosed in modern history. This end is apocalyptic, as Derrida indicates, and in it there is made yet another turn which is specifically Derrida's: the turn from Christianity to Judaism by way of a reexamination of the philosophy of Emmanuel Levinas. We recall that in Levinas the "end" is thought from the "beyond" of Being, from the "end of the end of the end," which is to say, from the forestalling of apocalypse, its demolition, in its very arrival.[24] Indeed, by way of Levinas, Derrida will demonstrate that even the later and most radical turns of Heidegger prove to be inadequate, as not radical enough, since in the "event" that is the catastrophe or apocalypse something is held back, not given, *en retrait*.

Outline

The first four chapters of my study correspond to crucial Heideggerian "turns," and in the fifth chapter I consider the "time of the thesis." In chapter 1 I focus on a turn which occurs in Heidegger's "The Anaximander Fragment" from *Holzwege* that is crucial for understanding some of the continuities in the relation between deconstruction and Heideggerian philosophy. After a very brief introduction, I begin with remarks on Derrida's reading of "The Anaximander Fragment" in "Ousia et grammè," wherein we have perhaps one of the clearest examples of deconstruction's direct filiation to a passage in Heidegger whose ostensible subject is temporality. That the "attachment" is made very fleetingly in the essay, and that it occurs as a reading that largely ignores a close reading of Heidegger's essay, not to mention Anaximander's consideration of temporality, is particularly interesting, since, as I show, "The Anaximander Fragment" has more than a few characteristics bearing on the time question that anticipate much of what has been considered to be innovative in the deconstructive method. Throughout this chapter I emphasize the bearing of Heidegger's work on Derrida even when in Derrida's tactical disregard of Heidegger we see a performative imitation by Derrida occurring: that of recollection as strategic forgetting.

In chapter 2 I stress the dissimilarites between Heideggerian philosophy and deconstruction, starting with a close examination of the turn from Being to time missed in the early part of Heidegger's career. I demonstrate that the early career is very problematic because Heidegger had been writing several versions of *Being and Time* simultaneously and that these versions are not exactly interchangeable. The turn, therefore, is and is not being made simultaneously in a number of tracts. However, when Derrida criticizes a footnote in *Being and Time* in such a way that he exposes Heidegger's inability to make the turn outlined in the second part of the design in *Being and Time*, I show that, in fact, given the Heidegger materials published after Derrida's "Ousia et grammè" the intuitions of Derrida are, indeed, upheld. Still, given the enormous amount of writing that Heidegger had undertaken during the period, we will see that here, again, determining the status of Heidegger's project is a very complex issue which, quite evidently, exceeds the bounds of my study, though its most important consequence can already be glimpsed: a textual performance that prefigures the more radical notions of temporality of the 1950s. Also, this chapter provides a historical outline of some of Heidegger's positions on temporality during the early period, which are explained and put into correspondence with deconstruction.

In chapter 3 I consider the relation between language and temporality from the perspective of the famous Heideggerian linguistic turn announced in "The Letter on Humanism," but which is also reflected in the seminar *Heraklit*, a seminar given during the war years. In introducing Derrida's essays on Heidegger from the mid-1970s, I focus on Maurice Blanchot who, I feel, was very influential for Derrida during this time, and particularly with respect to reading Heidegger. In part I analyze a chapter from *La part du feu* in order to show that Blanchot, writing before "The Letter on Humanism" was published, clearly foresaw the famous turn in the "Letter" from having read Heidegger's work on Hölderlin. Part of my argument in this chapter is that Blanchot already saw that Heidegger had made the turn from an ontological to a temporal analytic through a consideration of language as metalepsis. That Derrida seems to have been influenced rather late by this view is reflected in "Pas." My claim is that whereas Derrida had estranged deconstruction from Heideggerian thinking in the late 1960s, there is in texts like "Pas" a rapprochement with a rhetoric of proximity that earlier had been dismissed. In chapter 3 I also discuss Derrida's "The Retrait of Metaphor" and "Restitutions." I conclude with an analysis of *De l'esprit* (1987), wherein metalepsis again plays an important role, particularly insofar as *l'esprit* is considered as a parceling out of terms that cannot be considered apart from the question of temporalization. In *De l'esprit,* however, one notices a decided if not hostile turning away from Heidegger in the 1980s, which will be investigated at greater length in the chapter that follows.

In chapter 4 I consider Heidegger's announced turn in his writings on technology during the 1950s in relation to Derrida's *The Post Card,* wherein the technology of the post office has very strong analogues with the late Heidegger. A key term in the chapter is "correspondence," a Heideggerian notion that is literalized by Derrida as meaning "dispatch" or "missive." In Heidegger's later work "correspondence" refers to a gathering together of words wherein a temporality takes place that is far more radical than any Heidegger had considered earlier in his career, a temporality associated with the term *Ereignis.* I also consider Derrida's "Of an Apocalyptic Tone Recently Adopted in Philosophy" and discuss how in the 1980s there is not only a turning to Heidegger and an acknowledgment of his very radical notion of temporality which developed in his late career but also a turning away from Heidegger, which is signaled by an interest in the temporality of Christian apocalypse and its relationship to Jewish religion. In this context I am particularly interested in Derrida's turning away from Heidegger and toward the philosophy of Emmanuel Levinas, who has considered temporality at length with respect to the question of Being. That Derrida is considering a Jewish philosopher and engaging religious history even while allowing his texts to resonate with Heideggerian concerns raises a number of interesting problems which surface much more strongly in the essay "Two Words for Joyce," the recent "Geschlecht" articles, and the short book *Shibboleth.* In these writings one can detect an antipathy between Jewish and German thinking which comes to the fore, something that has already appeared in very disturbing ways in Derrida's *Glas* with respect to the notion of the intercolumn as "Judas" and in the anti-Semitic passage by Jean Paul wherein Derrida weaves the notion of philosopher as traitor or one who turns away from. This is not meant to suggest that Derrida is finally taking an absolute distance from Heidegger but that he reinscribes deconstruction's turning to and away from Heidegger within historical or temporal contexts that again harass the decidability of an intellectual history that might strive for a fixed distance between Heidegger and Derrida.

Chapter 5 concludes this book with remarks on the time of the thesis in order to underscore a deconstructive philosophy on the taking of intellectual positions. I argue that position taking is inextricably bound with the strictures of temporality and that this undermines the sorts of comparative analyses best exemplified in the work of Jürgen Habermas, who is himself very familiar with philosophical backgrounds and attentive to the question of temporality pertaining to Derrida and Heidegger. That the question of temporality has to be grasped in terms of its own historical unfolding as a taking time with time is a point that intellectual historicizing easily elides.

ONE

TRANSLATING

THE ASSESSMENTS

OF TIME

errida has been extremely concerned with grounding his philosophical project within intellectual history, and his thought is meant to be a continuation of ideas, however much they may be modified, of thinkers like Aristotle, Hegel, Nietzsche, Husserl, and Heidegger. Indeed, Derrida's patient and meticulous readings of philosophy are also meant to push further conceptual relationships which threaten to fracture a text's continuity or totalizing claims. *Parergon* in Kant, *Aufhebung* in Hegel, and *Spur* in Heidegger are deconstructive terms which expose those places where texts fissure. Such fault lines indicate a division where the logic of philosophical tradition is itself at stake, because such traditional logical claims are indebted to a metaphysical philosophy which has its sources in Plato and Aristotle. However, if Derrida wishes to break with this tradition, he still wants to claim legitimacy as one of the most important contemporary heirs of philosophy.

In her introduction to *Dissemination,* Barbara Johnson has written that "deconstruction is a form of what has long been called a *critique.*" She defines critique as a discourse which "focuses on the grounds of [a] system's possibility." And she adds, "The critique reads backwards from what seems natural, obvious, self-evident, or universal in order to show that these things have their history, their reasons for being the way they are, their effects on what follows from them, and that the starting point is not a [natural] given but a [cultural] construct, usually blind to itself."[1] Johnson's reading of deconstruction presupposes the traditional assumption that ideas have "their history" and "reasons for being the way they are" and that ideas have effects on "what follows from them." This view supports the claim that deconstruction is part of a continuous intellectual history. Derrida himself makes this point when he writes: "This moment of doubling commentary should no doubt have its place in a critical reading. To recognize and respect all its classical exigencies is not easy and requires all the instruments of traditional criticism."[2] Derrida corroborates Johnson's perception that deconstruction is a critical method within the philosophical tradition, and Derrida also comments, "Without this recognition and this respect, critical production would risk developing in any direction at all and authorize itself to say almost anything."[3]

This chapter begins with an analysis of Derrida's writings of the late 1960s, largely from the viewpoint of those features which either explicitly or implicitly presuppose continuities with Heidegger's philosophy. My intention is not to develop an account that suffers from *clôture,* though I would not like to lose sight altogether of a developing and consistent argument. My approach throughout this book is to work through a number of *parages,* or latitudes, wherein texts are positioned and repositioned along the lines of their turning toward and away from one another. That is, I am concerned with the "correspondences" of philosophical texts as part of an open structure wherein affinities and resistances are dynamically situated and resituated. The main readings by Derrida which concern me in this chapter are "Ousia et grammè," "La différance," and "The White Mythology." In "Ousia et grammè" and "La différance" it is more than hinted that Heidegger had failed to make a "turn" from Being to time in his earlier treatises and that this failure can again be detected in Heidegger's works of the 1940s. However, Derrida also suggests much more marginally that Heidegger to the contrary also succeeded in dismantling the ontological grounds wherein the proposed turn to time could take place. What I first wish to develop, therefore, are the remarks by Derrida himself which situate philosophical features of deconstruction in continuity with the more radical aspects of Heideggerian thought.

The Difference of Difference

In "Ousia et grammè" Derrida considers not only Heideg-ger's resistance to deconstructing the history of ontology but discloses how Heidegger also outlines a "temporal clue" with the potential of deconstructing the question of Being as presencing. Derrida's specific intervention in Heidegger touches on "The Anaximander Fragment" and addresses Hei-degger's phrase "Lichtung des Unterschiedes" (illumination of difference). The crucial moment in Derrida's analysis occurs when Derrida first attempts to surpass Heidegger's metaphys-ical constraints, a moment when in articulating the interplay of differences in which metaphysics is suspended, Heidegger up-holds and annihilates metaphysics in the same breath. Heideg-ger writes:

> However, the distinction between Being and beings, as something forgotten, can invade our experience only if it has already unveiled itself with the presencing of what is present; only if it has left a trace which remains pre-served in the language to which Being comes. Thinking along those lines, we may surmise that the distinction has been illuminated more in that early word about Being than in recent ones; yet at no time has the distinc-tion been designated as such. Illumination of the distinc-tion therefore cannot mean that the distinction appears as a distinction. On the contrary, the relation to what is present in presencing as such may announce itself in such a way that presencing comes to speak *as this relation*.

> [Der Unterschied des Seins zum Seienden kann jedoch nur dann als ein vergessener in eine Erfahrung kommen, wenn er sich schon mit dem Anwesen des Anwesenden enthullt und so eine Spur geprägt hat, die in der Sprache, zu der das Sein kommt, gewahrt bleibt. So den-kend, dürfen wir vermuten, dass eher im frühen Wort des Seins als in den späteren der Unterschied sich gelichtet hat, ohne doch jemals als ein solcher genannt zu sein. Lichtung des Unterschiedes kann deshalb auch nicht bedeuten, dass der Unterschied als der Unterschied erscheint. Wohl dagegen mag sich im Anwesen als sol-

chem die Beziehung auf das Anwesende bekunden, so zwar, dass das Anwesen *als diese Beziehung* zu Wort kommt.][4]

The recovery of the distinction presencing/present is that which takes place only by attention to the trace of the distinction which has been obliterated when presencing appears as something present. In the oblivion of such a distinction Being achieves its destiny and not merely as lack but as a rich and prodigious event. "In it the history of the Western world comes to be borne out. It is the event of metaphysics."[5]

In discussing the passage on *Unterschied*, Derrida stresses the term "trace," or *Spur*, and in exaggerating it can accentuate difference and downplay the question of presence, Heidegger's main concern. Some sentences from "Ousia et grammè" readily show this change of emphasis: "Presence, then, far from being, as is commonly thought, *what* the sign signifies, what a trace refers to, presence, then, is the trace of the trace, the trace of the erasure of the trace." Or, "The trace of the trace which (is) difference above all could not appear or be named *as such*, that is, in its presence." Having paraphrased Heidegger by means of unconcealing the wearing and tearing of traces, Derrida adds, "The determinations which name difference always come from the metaphysical order."[6] Derrida means that just because the trace which is difference (the "is" being understood as under erasure) cannot appear or be *as such*, cannot make itself appear or be present in its presencings, this does not mean the determinations or inclinations which delimit the name difference are any less metaphysical. Having ascertained that Heidegger's tracings are all too metaphysical, no matter how purified of metaphysical categorizations, Derrida makes the step "beyond" Heidegger: "Beyond Being and beings, this difference, ceaselessly differing from and deferring (itself), would trace (itself) (by itself)—this *différance* would be the first or last trace if one could still speak, here, of origin and end."[7] Derrida's insight is to have recognized in the interplay of Heideggerian differences an *excess* which ruptures a metaphysical economy of terms. The excess of differences goes beyond the oppositions of presence and absence, emergence and decline, origin and end. Since the difference ceaselessly differs and defers, estranging and establishing itself within and without itself, we must acknowledge difference as the "effect" of Being and beings and also as something more primary, the first and last trace, if one could speak of origin and end. The difference of difference, then, supports and undermines mimetic recovery as that which is re-presented. In this sense Derrida realizes that Heidegger's passage points to a way beyond the metaphysics of representation. For the differences differ without cease, trace themselves by way of simulacra which make undecidable the proximity of difference to identity.

This is the extent, then, in Derrida's "Ousia et grammè" of the critical reading which "requires all the instruments of traditional criticism" for the sake of tracing a filiation between one body of thought and another. In Derrida's incisive and brief reading of Heidegger we see the point where "la différance" is located as an essential feature of an essay in *Holzwege*. This reading will be repeated at the end of an essay, entitled "La différance," where Heidegger's essay on Anaximander is oddly subordinated like a footnote to the very sophisticated theory of undecidability. Leaving for much later our reading of "La différance" and the questions it resolves, we want to know what accounts for the brevity of this auspicious moment in "Ousia et grammè" and the cursory reading of Heidegger's text "The Anaximander Fragment."

Curiously enough, although "The Anaximander Fragment" directly engages many issues extremely pertinent to Derrida's writings, Derrida, in large part, fails to address these matters in precisely that essay where he clearly delimits the filiation of deconstruction to Heideggerian thought. We have noticed that Derrida has selected only that place in "The Anaximander Fragment" where the question of ontological difference is raised in terms of the trace, implying that Heidegger's discourse broaches a most radically antimetaphysical perspective even as Heidegger is resisting this by means of dwelling on the question of presence. Derrida, in short, reperforms the Heideggerian text and in so doing exposes the radical temporal clue, "différance," which remained concealed to Heidegger. But this reperformance of Heidegger comes at the expense of a general interpretation of "The Anaximander Fragment," which, if undertaken, would almost certainly weaken Derrida's thesis that Heidegger remains only on the threshold of deconstruction, that it is Derrida who is entitled to lay claim to being the founder of deconstruction, something he maintains in *The Post Card* when he defensively attacks those Heideggerians who translate *Abbauen* as *déconstruire,* as if intellectual history can be reversed.

Time as Translation

In "The Anaximander Fragment" Heidegger discusses the translation and translatability of a pre-Socratic fragment whose original is lost but whose text is paraphrased as well as quoted by Plutarch, Hippolytus, and Simplicius, quotations or commentaries in themselves indebted to a lost paraphrase and quotation of Anaximander by Theophrastus. That the Anaximander passage concerns the origination and destruction of things according to necessity makes Heidegger's use of the passage quite intriguing with respect to the question of translation in which necessity involves both the question of origin or originality and of belatedness, secondariness, and destructiveness. Moreover, the issue of translation also suits Heidegger's aim of demonstrating how Being is disclosed as a network of supplementary marks whose original cannot be recovered but which has withdrawn and become concealed. Heidegger's interest presupposes an idea expressed elsewhere in *Holzwege,* the collection in which "The Anaximander Fragment" is contained, that through the destruction of works we intuit the unconcealment and concealment of Being. The Anaximander fragment, not unlike the ruins of a Greek temple discussed in Heidegger's "The Origin of the Work of Art," is a formation whose original relatedness to Being is unrecoverable though its traces can be detected through reflection on what the fragment of the work has meant throughout history or the assessments of time by means of which it is translated.[8]

Heidegger is well aware that he enters late into the history of paraphrases on the Anaximander fragment, and he cites Nietzsche and Hermann Diels, whose translations are, of course, interpretations or paraphrases in themselves. Heidegger therefore asks: "Can the Anaximander fragment, from a historical and chronological distance of two thousand five hundred years, still say something to us? By what authority should it speak?" Heidegger's question is not meant to be dramatic but addresses Anaximander's premonition of a destruction related to the question of temporality: "Do we stand in the very twilight of the most monstrous transformation our planet has ever undergone, the twilight of that epoch in which earth itself hangs suspended? Do we confront the evening of a night which heralds another dawn? Are we to strike off on a journey to this historic region of earth's evening?"9 Anaximander's fragment, "the oldest vouchsafed to us by our tradition," is at once about origin and, according to the assessments of time, about the end, the end of philosophy and of the Occident. The fragment and its ontological and temporal references become, for Heidegger, a clue which "systematically destroys the future and our historic relation to the advent of destiny."10 However, this systematizing is not rational in an Enlightenment sense; rather, it is a systematizing of the wearing of translations, of the tracework of one text upon another, the retraction and protraction of the meaning of being as relayed through a network of transferential inscriptions. In this sense, then, Heidegger broaches a notion of *écriture* similar to that which Derrida advances in the 1960s. Yet, in "Ousia et grammè" Derrida ignores Heidegger's "The Anaximander Fragment" in this context. Instead, he focuses only on that passage in which Heidegger is discussing the clarification of difference, or "Lichtung des Unterschiedes."

Of course, the passage Heidegger reads is divided or disseminative insofar as one has to read Simplicius, Hippolytus, and Plutarch side by side and then opt for various translations of them into modern languages. And Heidegger is extremely sensitive to the fact that the text he reads is not univocal, that it is at best residual, polyvalent, and perhaps even unreliable. Intuitively Heidegger is drawn to the text of Simplicius and after Nietzsche's translation cites the translation of Diels.

> The beginning and origin of existing things is the Apeiron (the limitless-undetermined). Out of which, however, becoming relates to existing things even though it also transpires in what lies beyond; passing into obligation, for they pay just penalty and retribution to each

other for their injustice according to the disposition of Time.

[Anfang und Ursprung der seienden Dinge ist das Apeiron (das grenzenlos-Unbestimmbare). Woraus aber das Werden ist den seienden Dingen, in das hinein geschieht auch ihr. Vergehen nach der Schuldigkeit; denn sie zahlen einander gerechte Strafe und Busse für ihre Ungerechtigkeit nach der Zeit Anordnung.][11]

Heidegger's own translation follows.

along the lines of usage; for they let order and thereby also reck belong to one another (in the surmounting) of disorder.

[entlang dem Brauch; gehören nämlich lassen sie Fug somit auch Ruch eines dem anderen (im Verwinden) des Un-Fugs.][12]

In large part, "The Anaximander Fragment" is both a justification of Heidegger's translation and a means to develop thoughts on being which are precategorical and therefore not bound to concepts which are part of a metaphysics as developed by Plato and Aristotle. This is why Heidegger's translation deviates so much from those of his precursors. However, Heidegger's essay on Anaximander is also concerned with the question of time, and Heidegger's important contribution to the scholarship on the Anaximander fragment is precisely the idea that trans-scription and trans-lation are key to the uncovering of a radical temporal clue by means of which the history of ontology is dismantled as a continuous and coherent flow of events which are appropriable as something that is whole, revealed, rational. Most significant is the fact that "The Anaximander Fragment" does not discuss transcription so much as it *performs* transcription within the interpretive process of revision and rewriting. Indeed, for Heidegger the destiny of philosophy is the process of a trans-lation or trans-scription which must yield to the revelations and concealments of the assessments of time that inheres in the making present of that which was given at the beginning of thought. Heidegger's meticulous readings of Anaximander's words are not so much a philological exercise but the performance of a sentence's transcription. Itself a fragment, the sentence reveals the beginnings of philosophy as always already belated, not to mention as prophetically describing the wear and tear of words which act upon the fragment through time by way of trans-scribing the trans-scriptions, or of trans-lating the trans-lations. For Heidegger, as is well known, the tracks or traces which translation leaves historically recall the beginnings of philosophy. In fact, the meaning of Being is conveyed through time as error, that is to say, as those deflections which make up the abrasion and destiny of Being. This is the effect of trans-scription, of writing, and Heidegger writes, "Without errancy there would be no connection from destiny to destiny: there would be no history."[13]

In the context of the Greek paraphrases of Anaximander, errancy and abrasion are terms well established in the word *phthora,* which Heidegger defines in an abstract way when he writes: "*Phthora* means the departure and descent into concealment of what has arrived there out of unconcealment. The coming forward into . . . and the departure to . . . *become present* within unconcealment between what is concealed and what is unconcealed. They initiate the arrival and departure of whatever has arrived."[14] *Phthora* is intimately related to genesis in Anaximander, since, as Heidegger says, the difference between creation and destruction is unbounded, a point Heidegger makes once more in "Over 'The Line'" when he explains the role of language in terms of nihilism: "The position of nihilism has, so it seems, already been given up in a certain way by the crossing of the line, but *its language has remained.*"[15] Language, or *Sprache,* is subjected to the erasures and crossings of the limits that demarcate "ontological differences." It moves over the line between existence and oblivion, though its "language," or jargon, remains behind, resisting or forestalling the totality of a crossing beyond, in the sense of a lag or residue. In its very evocation, disorder is brought into line, is given order. In "The Anaximander Fragment," *phthora* is read in terms of Heidegger's translation, "along the lines of usage." For *phthora* is the wearing and tearing, or destruction, which accompanies the founding, genesis, creation, or production. "For they let order and thereby also reck belong to one another (in the surmounting) of disorder." This sentence from Anaximander, translated by Heidegger, is, of course, an implicit gloss on the familiar translation, "according to necessity; for they pay penalty and retribution for each other for their injustice according to the assessment of Time." *Phthora*, here, concerns the reck (Heidegger's term is *ruch*) through which disorder is surmounted, what one might call the unconcealment of nihilism, but not as an antithesis to being through which the belonging of order/disorder is disclosed so much as that which comprises being even in the moment of its erasure. For Heidegger what constitutes being as that wherein being is destined is itself the Anaximander fragment which is sent through its *phthora*, or reck, as language. Through this abrasion language as thought continues, the fragment survives, disorder is surmounted. This is what the more familiar translation of Anaximander calls "according to necessity" and what Heidegger wishes to consider "according to the lines of usage."

Heidegger's focus is largely upon the undialectical relationship of order/disorder, a relation which the more familiar translation presents as the question of "retribution" occurring according to the "assessments of Time." *Phthora*, like the term *usure* in French, involves paying back and not just abrasion. It is as if the fragment of philosophy has had to pay the penalty of being kept alive through the assessments that time as history makes upon it. Indeed, is such fragmentation evidence that penalty has been paid, that the majority of Anaximander's text has been taxed and forfeited? Heidegger's reading reflects how the forfeits of time mark a continuation and even a revelation of the text, as if only because of a treatise's fragmentation through time, we come to see those aspects of its relationship to Being that would remain concealed were it not for time's reck.

Yet, such a reading depends not merely upon the fragmentation of philosophy but upon its pluralization: the counterpointing of translations. Certainly fragmentation is accompanied by the dissemination of error, the proliferation of translations or transcriptions. Philosophy is not a return to any arche so much as it is a historical performance unconcealing relations to Being which in Heidegger's earlier works were subsumed under the term "Dasein." Interpretation far from being authorized by any origin is always parasitical, unsituated, the performance of the conflict of translations, each of which is inherently supplementary. It may not be accidental that Heidegger emphasizes *phthora*, since it discloses parasitism not only in the sense of abrasion but in its affinity with *phtheir*, which means louse or parasite.[16] At this point one could develop an interpretation of "The Anaximander Fragment" by way of Michel Serres's *The Parasite*, a study investigating information theory from the perspective of parasitical interruptions. But let me say in lieu of a lengthy digression on Serres that as far as modern classical scholarship is concerned, Heidegger's reading of Anaximander is at best para-sitical, a reading not taken as serious scholarship on Anaximander but understood as adopting Anaximander in order to advance preconceptions worked out prior to investigating the Greeks. Heidegger is often considered, then, as one who merely uses figures like Anaximander as hosts for a refined critique of ontology that the pre-Socratics themselves would not have recognized. And yet, Heidegger appears quite aware that such parasitism is always the condition under which any ancient text is to be received as trans-scribed or trans-lated. It is a question of the destiny of the letter, the destiny of writing, a destiny infiltrated by parasites who facilitate *phthora*.

In answering the question What is philosophy? Heidegger writes:

> This path to the answer to our question is not a break with history, no repudiation of history, but is an adoption and transformation of what has been handed down to us. Such an adoption of history is what is meant by the term "destruction" (*"Destruktion"*). The meaning of this word has been clearly described in *Being and Time*. Destruction does not mean destroying (*bedeutet nicht Zerstören*) but dismantling, liquidating, putting to one side (*sondern Abbauen, Abtragen und Auf-die Seite-stellen*) the merely historical assertions about the history of philosophy. Destruction means—to open our ears, to make ourselves free for what speaks to us in tradition as the Being of being (*Sein des Seienden*). By listening to this interpellation we attain the correspondence (*Entsprechung*).[17]

Translation and transcription are modalities of this destruction, a destruction or breaking up which allows one to pursue a path toward the bearing of a relationship of Being to being. In the transformation of what comes down to us, in its disturbance, we become capable of opening our ears to what is concealed in the legacy. It is in the destruction—what Derrida later will call deconstruction—of the handed down that a certain tuning and correspondence can take place. The philosopher is a parasite or interrupter of the "handed down," a destroyer of continuities, and yet this philosopher does not "break with history" or dismiss it.

Derrida's own historical attitudes are not distant from Heidegger's, a point acknowledged in *Positions.*

> Must I recall that from the first texts I published I have attempted to systematize a deconstructive critique precisely against the authority of meaning, as the *transcendental signified* or as *telos,* in other words history determined in the last analysis as the history of meaning, history in its logocentric, metaphysical, idealist [. . .] representation, even up to the complex marks it has left in Heidegger's discourse?[18]

And in *Of Grammatology,* he has written:

> A historico-metaphysical epoch *must* finally determine as language the totality of its problematic horizon. It must do so not only because all that desire had wished to wrest from the play of language finds itself recaptured within that play but also because, for the same reason, language itself is menaced in its very life, helpless, adrift in the threat of limitlessness, brought back to its own finitude at the very moment when its limits seem to disappear, when it ceases to be self-assured, contained, and *guaranteed* by the infinite signified which seemed to exceed it.[19]

Derrida recognizes, in following Heidegger, that no philosophical or literary text can simply step outside of a historico-metaphysical framework, since language will be brought back to its own finitude at the point when its boundaries or limits are worn and torn away. Destruction or deconstruction are not in themselves terms which prophesy the "end" of a historico-metaphysical temporal structure, a going beyond metaphysics, but terms which address the destiny of thought which through translation and reinscription allows us to consider and even perform those textual enactments of menacing limits whose effect is to counter the premises upon which an authority of the self-givenness of meaning is established. In terms of Anaximander this threat to the self-givenness of meaning ought to be considered as the assessments of time, revealed through the handing down of thought as reinscription. And through this reinscription the limits of thought are menaced even as in the delimitation of thought metaphysical recovery takes place. Derrida's interpretation of Heidegger's "The Anaximander Fragment" is quite clearly such a reinscription, and one that reveals the stress of translation. As *phthora* it necessarily takes place as *phtheira*, which is to say, in the place of an other's words.

And this is the fate of criticism which deconstruction would like to elude. Deconstruction in taking the form of what Barbara Johnson calls a "critique" still wants to elude its taking place in an other's words even as it depends upon them. But how does deconstruction go back to the place of the other's words without simply being subsumed under the genre of critique? Rodolphe Gasché in *The Tain of the Mirror* mentions that in Heidegger there is already a *Schritt zurück*, or "step back," which comprises "a return to a beginning . . . a beginning that never occurred as such, and that is the realm, 'which until now has been skipped over,' of the essence of metaphysics, which comes into view only by means of retrogression." Such a retrogression is a reflective movement that allows the "ontico-ontological difference, or the question of Being—[to] appear face to face with thought."[20] Hence in "The Anaximander Fragment" retrogression is under way in Heidegger's taking the translation of Anaximander a step forward, as if to go ahead is to go back. But such a taking place in an other's language is never anything else than a question of translation whose resistance to the language of an other is itself where the ontico-ontological difference is manifest as *écriture* (philosophy).

Heidegger's essay goes back to Anaximander only by going

forward as a translation that resists taking place in the language of an other. This suggests, then, that for Heidegger recollection is a steadfast refusal to go back *critically* in the sense that Barbara Johnson uses the term. Rather, recollection occurs in the meditation on how an ancient philosophical fragment has been worn and torn, on how recollection or retrospection is itself an effect of the sending of this fragment through time by means of metaleptic transferrence (i.e., translation), wherein the language of an other is both welcomed and resisted. What Heidegger stringently avoids is that his text take place in the place of Anaximander's fragment as if that fragment could be recovered and remembered as anything other than the *phthora* of its destining. And to that extent Heidegger takes his distance from critique which assumes the recovery Heidegger denies.

In Derrida's "translation" of Heidegger, reflection as retrogression occurs not in spite of but because of its resistances to recollect Heidegger, its refusal to speak in the words of precursors, even as they are being imitated otherwise. If Gasché stresses reflective recollection (*Andenken*) as "face-to-face" confrontation, it is a confrontation where the face-to-face is critically elided even if philosophically reinforced. Gasché's account of reflection is particularly important, because it defines retrogression already in Heidegger as

> the very movement of differentiating (*krinein*) between what shows itself in and by itself and what does not— *what is* in all its forms. As such a differentiation, a retrogression manages the radical space of the ultimate ground of what is. That ground is a "function," so to speak, of the regressive differentiation and dismantling of the tradition. More precisely, it is itself of the order of that dismantling retrogression, of an appearing through retreat; moveover, the operation of dismantling is itself grounded therein. This ground grounds when it is set free in the very act of returning to it. Such a ground, since it can never be given, cannot become the end point of a reflection. As one reaches out for it reflectively, it withdraws.[21]

Whereas Gasché addresses thought, I would prefer to apply his penetrating consideration of recollection as differentiation and stepping back as a translation of writings wherein going forward reflectively implies a dismantling of the tradition by allowing things to appear through a writing that is *en retrait* (in retreat even as it steps ahead) insofar as it steadfastly refuses to remember and hence pay its debts to the assessments of time.

Re-collecting Heidegger

Readers familiar with Derrida's work will have recognized in the discussion of *phthora* many of the main arguments of "The White Mythology," and certainly the parallels between Derrida's study of metaphor in Aristotle and Heidegger's translation of a text by Anaximander reflect a strong identification between Heideggerian philosophy and deconstruction. In fact, such parallels implicitly establish an understanding between the informed reader and Derrida that Heidegger has more than merely anticipated the main features of a deconstructive discourse. In this sense deconstruction fits into a philosophical context of thoughts which were rigorously developed in the late 1930s. "The White Mythology" could be read as a reenactment of a relation between text and temporality that has already transpired in Heidegger's analyses of the significance of translation in "The Anaximander Fragment." And this raises the interesting fact that in Derrida's reinscription of Heidegger's notion of *Unterschied* (difference) under the signature of difference, in not only "The White Mythology" but in "Ousia et grammè" and "La différance," Derrida performs Heidegger's philosophical strategy of trans-lation or trans-scription and inscribes deconstruction into that Heideggerian history. Moreover, it is in the translation of Heidegger's German into French that *Unterschied* succumbs to the metaleptic slippages of difference—*différance*. In itself, this slippage in French is a metaphorical transposition in which the abrasion of words—the removal of an "e" and substitution of an "a"—becomes evident, an abrasiveness of language which becomes one of the main topics of "The White Mythology."

A consequence of this linguistic "abrasion" is the differentiation of deconstruction from Heideggerian thinking. And, of course, in metaleptically engaging Heidegger's play of substitutions or translations, deconstruction will come to stand in place of that which it has worn against: "The Anaximander Fragment." This abrasion between discourses authorizes Derrida not to explicitly point out the parallels, for one of the main tasks of essays like "The White Mythology" is to put themselves in place of something which has gone before and in so doing to become metaphorical reenactments or performances both of what is called a white mythology—in this case, the presupposition that deconstruction could be reduced to its original, which is to say, Heidegger's philosophy—and of a deconstructive notion of metaphor that is not reducible to a specific referent. As reflection or recollection, "The White Mythology" metaphorically substitutes itself for what has already been said, in this case, Heidegger's "The Anaximander Fragment." In taking the place of Heidegger's essay, "The White Mythology" allows itself to forget it, just as the translations of Anaximander by Plutarch and others left the original in or as oblivion.

That "The White Mythology" performs a Heideggerian text such as "The Anaximander Fragment" is evident when one focuses, for example, on Derrida's interest in the term *usure* to signify a wearing and tearing of words in an economy of metaphorical substitutions, though *usure* also refers to the usury of language, the production of a surplus value by means of lending and borrowing words, a negotiation which concerns translation, transcription, transference. This is contextualized in terms of Anatole France's *The Garden of Epicurus,* though it is clear Derrida is also thinking about Nietzsche's writings on metaphor in *The Genealogy of Morals,* where culture is situated with respect to notions of indebtedness, usury, reciprocity, substitution, and metaphysical translation. The "white mythology" concerns the idealistic presupposition that beneath economies of words there exists a pure, unadulterated language which is only approximated by the usurous economies (*usure*). This is a mythology which does not exist in time and which can be said to be metaphysical. The white mythology is, according to Derrida, a fantasized scene inscribed in white ink, an invisible design covered over by a palimpsest. This design is an after world, a place of metaphysical speculation that evades the "assessments of time," a phantasm that negates writing as both temporal (historical) and spatial (writerly). For Derrida the question is how to move from this theology of writing to the philosophy of writing, a philosophy that in the Nietzschean sense can take account of the usury of day-to-day exchange, of that transference or translation which is always already corrupted even as it gathers value.

Most important is that through this *usure* (or *phthora*) we are to understand the temporalization and spatialization of meaning. Thus Derrida asks: "How are we to know what the temporalization and spatialization of meaning, of an ideal object, of an intelligible tenor, are, if we have not clarified what 'space' and 'time' mean? But how are we to do this before knowing what might be a *logos* or a meaning that in and of themselves spatio-temporalize everything they state? What *logos* as metaphor might be?"[22] Whereas Heidegger speaks of a fragment, Derrida speaks of transcription as metaphor, corroborating a Heideggerian reading of *logos* which is not, as Heidegger says, "the expressing of a word-meaning" (i.e., denotation) but "rather a letting-lie-before in the light wherein something stands in such a way that it has a name."[23] This suggests not a term but a manifold of relations whose constitution comes about through the *phthora* or *usure* of transcription, transference, carrying-over, or metalepsis. Meaning does not subtend these relations but is the effect or excess which arises from overdetermination. More important, it is through the transportation of words that the notions of space and time are related, for the effect of the history of philosophy is to posit notions of space (limits, boundaries, breaks, fragments, wholes, bodies, ensembles) and time (history, telos, founding, continuity, succession, the arche, and futuricity). Moreover, space and time are dependent upon the abrasions or errancies of words as they are transmitted through space and time, that is through the canon, the institution, scripture, culture, nationhood, and so on. These aspects of spatiality and temporality are themselves "figures" of speech through which writing must pass in order to become legible. Meaning is usually thought of as atemporal and nonspatial and therefore opposed to metaphor which is, according to Derrida, both temporal and spatial; yet, there can be no meaning which does not pass through the "figure" or figuration of history.

The Performance of Metaphor

If "The White Mythology" can be read as a metaphorical substitution that performs "The Anaximander Fragment," should we not become attentive to the question of the performative or performance itself? This question is crucial to our concerns, because instead of developing a criticism that takes place in an other's words, Derrida performatively translates or transfers the other's words into his own deconstructive discourse, allowing words like *usure* to function metaphorically for something else that cannot be recovered as an "original" or "originary" concept. In other words, a text such as Heidegger's "Anaximander Fragment" itself becomes a white mythology as far as deconstruction is concerned.

Several quotations from "The White Mythology" are relevant in respect to a performative reading of metaphor: "It is impossible to dominate philosophical metaphorics as such, *from the exterior,* by using a concept of metaphor which remains a philosophical product"; and, "The philosopher will never find in this concept anything but what he has put into it, or at least what he believes he has put into it as a philosopher."[24] Both of these remarks indicate rather strongly that for Derrida metaphor cannot be divorced from a notion of performance, since metaphors comprise a specific act wherein the difference between what is "proper" and what is "improper" is transgressed by an act of will. However, what is the "subject" of this act? Who or what wills?

In *Vorträge und Aufsätze,* Heidegger includes the essay "Who Is Nietzsche's Zarathustra?" ("Wer ist Nietzsches Zarathustra?") and focuses on the figure of the teacher who performs philosophy. The teacher's performance is a temporal transition from the prior through the now to what lies beyond, the future. And in discussing this performative aspect of Zarathustra's teaching, Heidegger writes, "Still, it remains to be considered whether the inquiry beyond Nietzsche's thinking can be a continuation of his thought, or must be a step backward."[25] Zarathustra's performance of philosophy does not transpire teleologically as academic intellectual history; rather, it breaks with this notion of time in articulating within it a proximity of moments which ruptures self-identity and the positing of a consciousness whose thought is unified in a manifold of compatible and teleological moments. To recall Gasché's remarks once more, Heidegger is considering the performance of the continuation of thought as the retrogression wherein philosophy undergoes dismantling.

> The manner in which Zarathustra pronounces the [fundamental features of time] points toward what he must henceforth tell himself in the foundation of his being. And what is that? That "One Day" and "Formerly," future and past, *are like* "Today." And the present is like the past and like the future. All three phases of time merge as one, as the selfsame, into a single present, an eternal Now. Metaphysics calls the permanent Now "eternity." Nietzsche, too, conceives the three phases of time from the standpoint of eternity as a permanent Now. But for Nietzsche, the permanence does not consist in something static, but in a recurrence of the same. When Zarathustra teaches his soul to say those words, he is the teacher of the Eternal Recurrence of the same.[26]

This eternal return, as Heidegger suggests in "The Anaximander Fragment," is not very much unlike the translations of Anaximander: the eternal repetition of that which is known as that which is unknown, the familiar as the unfamiliar. The eternal return disconfirms identity and introduces difference which is disruptive to our everyday conceptions of temporal movement. Zarathustra's performance of philosophy—his teaching—deconstructs identity and difference as a principle of noncontradiction. Heidegger situates this destabilizing of identity and difference in terms of a performance of philosophy as temporal event in which a teacher wishes to cross over to another philosophy which can never be thought, merely, from beyond where one begins. Heidegger calls this condition the nearness of what lies afar.

But the nearness of what lies afar brings to our attention also a notion of Aristotelian metaphor as that figure which is near though it refers to something far away, perhaps something so far away that it is not entirely recoverable. "There is metaphor," Derrida writes, "only in the extent to which someone is supposed to make manifest, by means of statement, a given

thought that of itself remains inapparent, hidden, or latent."
Still, as Aristotle's writings disclose, metaphors do not necessarily produce analogical closure. Rather, metaphor "risks dis-
rupting the semantic plenitude to which it should belong. . . .
metaphor also opens the wandering of the semantic." The risk
of metaphor, then, is the chance of missing what is apt or true.
"If metaphor, the chance and risk of *mimesis,* can always miss
the true, it is that metaphor must count with a determined
absence." Referring to Aristotle's example, "sowing around a
god-created flame," wherein something with essentially no
name (the sun's casting forth its flames) is equated with an
action that has a determinate name (sowing), Derrida acknowledges the problem of reference by calling such a figure an
" 'enigma,' a secret narrative, composed of several metaphors, a
powerful asyndeton or dissimulated conjunction" describing
what Aristotle calls "an impossible combination of words."[27]
Perhaps Derrida should have called this metaphor a "disseminative conjunction" wherein the action of bringing together what is near (the act of sowing) and far (the sun's
scattering of rays) can no longer be reduced to self-identity and
therefore to the representation of an agency's thought that is
self-contained or "proper to man." Disseminative conjunctions, in other words, exceed the mimetic recovery of the subject. They exceed the determinable action of analogizing,
which is recoverable as a self-identical act through interpreting
the metaphor back to its performative source. Such a reduction
to the act of metaphorization is, of course, a reduction to a
temporal present, or now, in which the metaphor eternally
presents itself. However, a disseminative conjunction would be
symptomatic of a differentiation of the act of analogizing and
the disruption of a temporal reduction to a moment which can
always be retrieved as something eternally there. In short, the
disseminative conjunction divides the temporal performance
that is metaphor or analogy, the bringing together what is near
with what is far.

In Heidegger's "Who Is Nietzsche's Zarathustra?" philosophy is being read from the standpoint of performative analogies that break the metaphysical horizon of temporality as that
which is self-identical and determined within the moment of
the now. As Fredrick A. Olafson clarifies in *Heidegger and the*

Philosophy of Mind, Heidegger's philosophy works against the classical view that time as events and processes belong to a totalized world wherein all entities are occupying the same temporality. "This is because *Dasein* is the entity that *has* a world, as trees and rivers do not." [28] Olafson's remarks point out that Heidegger dismisses the classical objectification of the subject whose temporal subjectivity has to be subordinated to the objectivity of a world-time wherein all moments are fixed according to an overall schema that is identical to itself. Such a schema, as Olafson notes, can be conceptualized only from a transcendental and eternal point outside of itself.

> What is never explained, however, is how the referential power of this transcendental position and of its tenseless present is established in such a way as to make it invulnerable to the skeptical doubts that stem from the presentness of all the representations of those who are placed *within* world-time. To all appearances, this [transcendental] standpoint is simply assumed to be available so as to make up for the limitations that the theory of world-time imposes on the representational activity of those who occupy positions in it and thus secure against skeptical doubts the referential capacity that we are nevertheless so sure we possess."[29]

Heidegger's "Who Is Nietzsche's Zarathustra?" interrogates Nietzsche's analogies of the near and the far in order to investigate an alternative notion of temporality wherein a representational activity or performance breaks with the classical assumption of a transcendental present, or now, through which self-identity (presence itself) is metaphysically conceived. Nietzsche himself, Heidegger argues, had already begun dismantling this classical conception of time through his interrogation of both "the will to power" and "the eternal return." Not surprisingly, Heidegger views these phrases as a questioning of the relation of beings to Being, a point clearly made in "The Anaximander Fragment."[30] In fact, "the eternal recurrence" is the name, according to Heidegger, of the Being of beings (in Derrida's terms the difference of difference), and "the will to power" is the persistence of that eternal recurrence. At the end of "Who Is Nietzsche's Zarathustra?" Heidegger notices an analogy. The snake and the eagle which enigmatically soar in the air above Zarathustra respectively represent the eternal recurrence and the will to power. This analogy stands for "the belonging-together of Being and human being" to which the *Übermensch* is in horizonal relation. The *Übermensch* breaks with the classical manifold of world-time, since it is not simply a name for someone who is to arrive at some moment, like a metaphysical notion of the Messiah, or the name for some deliverer who is already here, like a Siegfried. Rather the *Übermensch* is a subject constituted as the relation which is "the belonging together of Being," as eternal recurrence or return wherein metaphysical ontology is dismantled and the "event" of the *Übermensch*'s coming is disengaged from a classical notion of world-time. We must emphasize that if the *Übermensch* is to be considered a subject, it is one whose action or performance as a subject never comes into being as anything other than a metaphor or disseminative conjunction which brings together what is near and what is far in such a way that a metaphysics of self-identity and world-time is eluded. This accords well with Gilles Deleuze's perception that for Nietzsche the eternal recurrence is the "repetition of difference." And one might say, considering Heidegger, that Zarathustra marks the relation between the persistence of repetition and the difference of difference.

In moving to such a position, Heidegger notices that Nietzsche has written, "This, yet this alone, is *revenge* itself: the will's aversion to time and its 'It was.'" Whereas pre-Socratic philosophers like Anaximander view temporality as a parceling out of things due, the classical tradition which came afterward was oriented to time much more in terms of a confrontation: the subject judges the moments of time rather than submitting to time's law. Nietzsche calls this revenge, according to Heidegger. "Revenge is aversion to the 'it was' within time." And the aim of revenge is to make the past present so that we can adjudicate events that are no more, or hold on to time, merely, as something which abides. Metaphysics is revenge on time in that it "posits eternal Ideals as the absolute, compared with which the temporal must degrade itself to actual non-being."[31] We can now see why the texts by Aristotle that were considered by Derrida reject metaphors which are disseminative conjunctions: they do not hold on to the eternal present of a past moment and therefore time cannot abide in them. In short, in performing such metaphors the action of revenge against transience and nonbeing fails. In Nietzsche's texts, Heidegger notices, there is a "yes" to time that would "have transience abide" in its always coming to be as something other, which is to say, as eternal return. This return, in the context of Nietzsche, is the return of metaphor, the translation of translation, as the performance of a disseminative conjunction wherein the "subject" crosses over to the *Übermensch,* and the near is bridged with the far.

In "The White Mythology" such a view of metaphor is reflected in the following passages.

> Presence disappearing in its own radiance, the hidden source of light, of truth, and of meaning, the erasure of the visage of Being—such must be the insistent return of that which subjects metaphysics to metaphor.
>
> To metaphors. The word is written only in the plural. If there were only one possible metaphor, the dream at the heart of philosophy, if one could reduce their play to the circle of a family or a group of metaphors, that is, to one "central," "fundamental," "principal" metaphor, there would be no more true metaphor, but only, through the one true metaphor, the assured legibility of the proper. Now, it is because the metaphoric is plural from the outset that it does not escape syntax; and that it gives rise, in philosophy too, to a *text* which is not exhausted in the history of its meaning (signified concept or metaphoric tenor: *thesis*), in the visible or invisible presence of its theme (meaning and truth of Being).[32]

The notion that tropes do not escape syntax is fundamental to Nietzsche's remarks on rhetoric, collected by Philippe Lacoue-Labarthe and Jean-Luc Nancy, and suggests that philosophy itself could be considered to be metaphor.[33] This approximates Jean-Michel Rey's thesis in *L'enjeu des signes: Lecture de Nietzsche,* in which Rey argues that philosophy for Nietzsche is explicitly a metaphorical detour in whose syntax the subject is deconstructed.[34] A similar reading of metaphor is already suggested in "The White Mythology" when Derrida writes:

Metaphor, then, always carries its death within itself. And this death, surely, is also the death *of* philosophy. But the genitive is double. It is sometimes the death of philosophy, death of a genre belonging to philosophy which is thought and summarized within it, recognizing and fulfilling itself within philosophy; and sometimes the death of a philosophy which does not see itself die and is no longer to be refound within philosophy. [. . .] This supplement of a code which traverses its own field, endlessly displaces its closure, breaks its line, opens its circle, and no ontology will have been able to reduce it.[35]

Heidegger calls this supplement of a code which traverses its own field the teaching of Zarathustra, the yes to time which carries its death within itself. "The White Mythology," of course, sights this death not in Nietzsche but in Aristotle; yet, in so doing it functions as an analogy or metaphor for other philosophies, since it is itself a disseminative conjunction that breaks the metaphysical horizons of an academically inspired intellectual history. By recollecting Aristotle, Derrida asks us to remember Nietzsche and Heidegger, both together, and apart—both (together and apart): at once/separately.

Reading To Apeiron *under Erasure*

In the previous sections we noticed that Heidegger and Derrida are not so far apart in their performance of the philosophical tradition as a wearing and tearing of metaphors or the *phthora* of translations significant for the dismantling of a classical conception of temporality and the subject. But we must recognize, too, that even if such an agreement of views and approaches can be located, we can also find close approximations that reveal a fundamental distance. A very good example is the way in which both Heidegger and Derrida share a sophisticated mode of reading that tactically disregards or fails to recognize what in terms of the Anaximander fragment is a crucial word that points to a consideration of temporality that implicitly rejects a classical concept of world-time: Anaximander's *to apeiron* (the undetermined). Although Heidegger's

"The Anaximander Fragment" is explicitly a commentary on Anaximander's phrase wherein the *apeiron* is being investigated, Heidegger dismisses the term en passant. To some extent this is in keeping with the fragment which itself does not say the word *apeiron,* though it has generally been agreed upon ever since antiquity that Anaximander's fragment is explicitly about this term. Heidegger's essay, of course, indirectly acknowledges the fact and does not disregard the term *apeiron* because of skepticism over its relevance to Anaximander's fragment. Rather, Heidegger's essay reperforms this lacuna as if the *apeiron* could be adequately talked about only "under erasure" or in eclipse. This is an "erasure" Derrida will respect, too, in his remarks on Heidegger's "Anaximander Fragment," though the erasure becomes acutely troublesome, because Derrida does not make the effort to let a reader unfamiliar with Anaximander know that Heidegger is addressing a text explicitly addressing a term wherein the *différance* between Being and beings is openly acknowledged in ways that are not taking place wholly within the Western metaphysical tradition. Here we begin to notice that a reading of terms under erasure may well reflect what Nietzsche called the "will to deception," wherein knowledge comes about not through *a-letheia* (unforgetting) but by *letheia,* or forgetting itself. Indeed, Heidegger underscores this attitude when he writes in "The Anaximander Fragment" that "error is the space in which history unfolds."[36] Both Heidegger and Derrida "err" in remembering or recollecting the *apeiron* by disregarding or forgetting it. Both, therefore, are writing about that which remains "under erasure" even if its traces can still be recognized in "other" words, which is to say, in that process of trans-lation which is metaphor.

But if Heidegger and Derrida share in interpreting that which is under erasure, it is precisely here that Heidegger takes his distance from the more deconstructive possibilities which he could not have easily missed, whereas Derrida takes the occasion to inaugurate a philosophical vocabulary that we call deconstruction. That this divergence or difference between Heideggerian and Derridean philosophies may be a matter of the "difference" of metaphors, or the wear and tear of translations, I will leave aside, bearing in mind the previous discussions of metaphor as "disseminative conjunction" and of Heidegger's sensitivity to translation as metalepsis. However, what is clear from the perspective of an interpretation of Heidegger is that the effacement of the *apeiron* is not accidental, since "The Anaximander Fragment" from *Holzwege* is not the only text by Heidegger that we have on the fragment of Anaximander. It is, rather, a very canny reperformance of an earlier text written in the summer of 1941, namely the seminar entitled "Das anfängliche Sagen des Seins im Spruch des Anaximander."[37] And interestingly enough, in this text the *apeiron* is discussed at length in the context of a translation by Heidegger of Simplicius's rendering of the Anaximander fragment, a translation almost completely effaced in the rendition Heidegger gives in "The Anaximander Fragment" from *Holzwege*. That this earlier translation engages the *apeiron,* whereas the later one omits it, reflects the "erasure" noted above.

Since *to apeiron* is a complex term with a substantial history among scholars of pre-Socratic texts, we ought to review some background in order to demonstrate Anaximander's formulation of a term which not only anticipates Heidegger's radical critique of metaphysics but also announces the advent of what Derrida will call *la différance.* Of most concern, naturally, is not that Anaximander can be seen as the genuine precursor or "original" that stands behind these contemporary philosophers, for this would simply reenact a "white mythology." Rather, we should appreciate how the *apeiron* marks a phantomized locus wherein Derrida's reperformance of Heidegger's performance of Anaximander is established as an interplay of imitations which turn away from their original and its valorization as origin in order to disclose its truth.

In discussing what Heidegger in *Holzwege* and Derrida in "Ousia et grammè" have left "under erasure" we need to consider the translation of Simplicius rendered by C. S. Kirk and J. E. Raven: ". . . some other *apeiron* nature, from which come into being all the heavens and the worlds in them. And the source of coming-to-be for existing things is that into which destruction, too, happens, 'according to necessity; for they pay penalty and retribution to each other for their injustice according to the assessment of Time,' as he (Anaximander) describes it in these rather poetical terms."[38] Simplicius's reference to the *apeiron* is mediated by Theophrastus and, of course, Aristotle, and it refers to the primary or originary substance on which the cosmos is based: the "indefinite," or as that which is the "between" of elements. Kirk and Raven write: "Aristotle, when listing various monistic theories of the *physiké* on a number of occasions speaks of a substance *between* the elements—normally between fire and air or between air and water. In three or four of these passages it looks as though Anaximander is meant as the proponent of an intermediate substance, not because he is directly named but because the substance is implied to have been called simply *to apeiron*."[39] Aristotle's interpretation of *apeiron* as an intermediate substance either alongside or mixed in with the elements is, Kirk and Raven point out, false with respect to being a position of Anaximander, since Anaximander himself had a much more abstract notion in mind. That is, for Anaximander *to apeiron* signified something "indefinite in kind" or "spatially indefinite."

Abstracting from Aristotle's position, Werner Jaeger in *The Theology of the Early Greek Philosophers* preserved the commonsense reading of *to apeiron* as that which was borrowed from familiar sources. However, his definition also transcends such historical reductionism, for he defines *to apeiron* as the boundless "from which all Becoming draws its nourishment, not that which is qualitatively undetermined."[40] This view marks an adherence to an essentially Aristotelian definition of *to apeiron* in *The Physics,* where it stands for the notion of the indefinite. However, George Burch, in the 1940s, stressed the idea that *to apeiron* probably meant something more like "the indefinite," which is a meaning Kirk and Raven accept as much more accurate. Burch argued that *to apeiron* signified a notion of Godhead with no definable attribute, and he notes that the indefinite is tracked precisely in terms of the oppositions of the elements in whose ontological difference, as Heidegger might have called it, this indefiniteness and boundlessness are disclosed as manifesting limits. Here the *undecidability* of boundlessness/boundedness is clearly brought to the forefront of considering Anaximander's *to apeiron.* Furthermore, Burch argued that, in the fragment, existence as a definite thing is considered unjust, for "we are encroaching on each other by our existence."[41] And the only way to atone is by passing into oblivion.

Such a view complements, quite obviously, the views Heidegger maintains about nihilism in the texts of Nietzsche written at about the time of "The Anaximander Fragment," and it also has parallels in Heidegger's translation of the fragment.

Another scholar of classical texts, Harold Cherniss, challenges this theological reading of *to apeiron* and argues that neither consciousness nor volition are related to the *apeiron*. Anaximander's "unlimited" or "boundless" is composed of "ingredients so thoroughly mixed together as to be severally indiscernible in the mixture but which when segregated from the mixture are recognizable as all the differences of the articulated world."[42] *To apeiron* refers not to a primordial chaos but transcends such marking off, since it is an unlimited and unbounded multitude which is in everything yet distinct, being in matter but neither as matter nor as pure spirit. *To apeiron* is, to use Derrida's idea once more, an undecidable with respect to its manifestation in nature, and one cannot therefore define it within the metaphysical or philosophical categories familiar to Western thought. This, of course, is why for Heidegger the Anaximander fragment is so appealing and why he chose to retranslate it.

Paul Seligman, in *The Apeiron of Anaximander: A Study in the Origin and Function of Metaphysical Ideas,* argues that *apeiron* in Anaximander is both monistic and dualistic, hence breaking with noncontradiction, and he takes seriously the metaphorical presentation of the term *to apeiron,* for the term circumscribes as metaphor even as it evades or fractures boundedness, just as it does by hovering between the monistic and the dualistic, participating undecidably in both and neither. This view suggests that *to apeiron* can only be grasped as itself a translation or displacement, as a term that evades the kind of categorical appropriation typical in Aristotle's *Physics. To apeiron* at best is an analogy whose signified is undetermined, a metaphor that as in Heidegger's account of analogy in "Who Is Nietzsche's Zarathustra?" breaks the metaphysical horizons of closure. According to Seligman, Anaximander was deeply aware that the notion of origin was not reducible to anything, that origin is, to borrow Derrida's vocabulary, inherently differed and deferred from itself.

In the 1941 seminar on the Anaximander fragment, Heideg-

ger takes his distance as a translator from philology, something
that reappears in the Anaximander essay collected in *Holzwege*.
"We cannot demonstrate the adequacy of the translation by
scholarly means," we read in "The Anaximander Fragment."[43]
And in the seminar, "The translation will draw the fragment
away from us and leave us in an astonishing and disturbing
place."[44] The translation distances or, as Heidegger puts it,
"ent-fernt." The seminar clarifies that the purpose of translating
the fragment is to dismantle the philological (i.e., metaphysical) apparatus of philosophy and what we would today call its
nineteenth-century humanist underpinnings. The seminar
maintains that the notion of world or cosmos which translators
have assumed in rendering the fragment is an inappropriate
conception for pre-Socratic thought, as is the focus on ethics.
In fact, what Heidegger has set out to dismiss is the received
idea that the fragment has to be interpreted in terms of "the
unity of a grand religious, ethical, rational, and physical mode
of thinking."[45] Once there was no physics and no physical
mode of thinking, no ethics and therefore no ethical mode of
thinking, because these categories had not yet been articulated
or constructed. As in "The Anaximander Fragment," Heidegger is most concerned with analyzing those precategorical aspects of reflection in which the question of Being is raised, as if
Anaximander's fragment were key to grasping what in section
32 of *Being and Time* was called a "forestructure of understanding," in this case a forestructure that anticipates the history of
metaphysics even as it presupposes its main concerns. The
seminar touches on the *apeiron* in this context by interpreting it
in relationship to the terms *genesis* and *arché* in order to establish that whatever we call the origin is inherently divided, or, as
Derrida might put it, differed and, with respect to "prior"
terms, deferred, meaning that the relation between what comes
earlier and later is disarticulated. There is also an attempt to
structure the *apeiron* metaleptically in terms of an iteration of
words beginning with the letter "a": *a-letheia, a-rché,* and
a-peiron. In examining these terms, Heidegger takes a radical
step: he articulates the terms as what Derrida in *Of Grammatology* will call a trace structure, meaning that each of these "ar-
chaic" terms comes before and after one another, that they are
all traces of prior traces and as such "belong" together or

"bear" on one another insofar as in their coming to presence they are said or decreed in a temporality wherein chronological retrogression to the origin is affirmed even as it is effaced. In coming to presence, then, these terms are disclosed or unconcealed as not present in themselves but only in relation to being affirmed or decreed in the context of other terms. This may occur, Heidegger argues, because the prefix, "a," drifts over the boundaries of words and is itself what might be called "boundary drift." The "a," in Greek, marks a lack or privation similar to our prefix "un," and Heidegger argues that the prefix does not stand for something negative but simply resists boundedness. "Das a bezieht sich auf Grenze, Begrenzung und Entgrenzung" ("The a concerns itself with limits, limiting, and de-limiting"). The Anaximander fragment, then, is the decree that announces the being of Being as boundaries of language which are proximate entities wherein notions of limit, limiting, and delimiting bear on one another. Hence terms like *a-letheia, a-rché,* and *a-peiron,* although they can be defined singularly, are, in fact, identical. "Sie selbst ist das Selbe. Dieses Selbe, die Verfügung (*arché*), dieses Selbe, das *apeiron,* ist *to chreon* . . ." ("It itself is the same. This itself, the decree [*arché*], this itself, the *apeiron,* is *to chreon* . . .").[46] Heidegger, in his concluding section to this seminar goes so far as to suggest that in the Anaximander fragment is disclosed the relation of Being to time which occurs not in our saying "Time is . . ." but in saying "It is time." For Heidegger, the "saying" that "it is time" means that time is recognized as arriving, as going, as occurring. Time is the coming to pass of the saying as the delimitation of Being's coming to presence in language, and as such time transpires in the relatedness of words that cross their own zones of specificity. The truth of time, then, is the truth of the relatedness of *a-letheia* to *arché* and *apeiron*: the unconcealment of their identity in difference and their difference in identity. Time, in short, is to be detected in the spacing of metalepsis, or the *espacement* of the "a," wherein presence comes forth as that which abides in the saying of philosophy.

Heidegger's seminar of 1941 on the Anaximander fragment corresponds to the classical scholarship on the *apeiron* to the extent that the term has gained recognition as an "undecidable" radical. Moreover, Heidegger has gone beyond much of the scholarship by suggesting that the *apeiron* cannot be localized and examined as a single term or entity. Rather, the *apeiron* appears and disappears in the drifting and clinging of the prefix "a" that gives rise to determinate terms even as it effaces or places them under erasure. Even more crucial, perhaps, is that already in this analysis a linguistic turn has been made. The relation of Being and time is suddenly examined in the context of linguistic drift, in the metalepsis or translation of words that disclose how time abides as Being and Being abides as time. However, in "The Anaximander Fragment" from *Holzwege* this intensive examination of the metalepsis of language is downplayed, even as it remains active in the contexts of translation and history. Indeed, one must wonder why Heidegger's "Anaximander Fragment" conceals the analysis of *to apeiron* in the 1941 seminar as well as its implications for a theory of time which will emerge prominently much later in the essay "Zeit und Sein" (1969).

Heidegger's Metaphysical Resistances

Given the examination of what lies "under erasure" in "The Anaximander Fragment," to say nothing of the scholarship on the *apeiron,* it is curious that Heidegger's meditations on the undecidable drifting of the Greek prefix "a," (and, later, Derrida's perceptions concerning *la différance*) are already inscribed in the *arché* of the oldest philosophical text vouchsafed to us by Occidental thought. As if at the beginning there was undecidability, difference with an "a", an "A" which signs for *apeiron, aletheia,* and *arché* (not to mention, in Derrida's contexts, *différAnce*). This return to Anaximander is, without doubt, what Heidegger and Derrida would view as a necessary eternal return, one affirming that the ground of thought locates itself in the eclipse or "forgetting" of the *to apeiron.* That the function of translation or transposition as I have outlined it may contribute to a philosophy of forgetting in which the *to apeiron* is obliquely coming forth as trace should be borne in mind.

Still, such an orientation, however consistent with much of Heidegger, cannot be said to accord fully with his thinking overall. This is reflected in studies like David Halliburton's *Poetic Thinking* when in his interpretation of "The Anaximander Fragment" he develops another Heideggerian view of history.

> Over the centuries—in Heidegger's account of history—the sense of the presently present gradually becomes dominant, bespeaking as it does its nearer relation to unconcealment, so that *eonta* comes to stand for what is present here and now in the same way that the present-at-hand (as depicted in *Being and Time*) comes to stand for beings in general. The irony is that in the process we have forgotten the relation that inspired the dominance in the first place: and to say that we have forgotten the relation between presence and unconcealment is to say that we have forgotten to think about the nature of presence, this being tantamount to saying, again, that we have forgotten Being.[47]

Phrases like the "presently present gradually becomes dominant" indicate that we are being asked to consider Heidegger from the perspective of eschatology. If Being is becoming unconcealed, we, at the same time, have forgotten to think the nature of presence. This, too, is eschatological if one recalls the apparent Christian parallels. The parousia of Christ is being fulfilled through history even if as time elapses we are more apt to forget his second coming. This is the irony upon which every Christian sermon is founded: we have forgotten Christ who has come for our redemption and who is at hand, who "comes to stand for beings in general." Such an interpretive context for Heidegger represents a pietistic and theological view of Being in a metaphysical context of the unforgetting (*a-letheia*) and revelation of God's presence. And it is an interpretation relying on the classical notion of a "world-time" diverging strongly from a view of the *apeiron* which discloses temporality as an inherently divided or deconstructed manifold of moments, a manifold in which the metaphysical notion of "origin" is obliterated.

Not surprisingly, Derrida's deconstruction is committed to a reading of Heideggerian texts challenging the views of interpreters like Halliburton whose writings could be said to recover metaphysics and ignore the occasions in Heidegger's work for dismantling the metaphysical tradition. Yet, we should acknowledge that Heidegger's dismissing the *to apeiron* in "The Anaximander Fragment" can be interpreted as marking not merely a radical departure from the metaphysics of intellectual history but also a pietistic resistance to the more metaphysically challenging seminar of 1941. And this, certainly, might justify interpretations of readers like Halliburton. Without doubt, Heidegger's dismissing and ignoring of the *apeiron* functions as a double gesture which, in disclosing the "undecidable" in its very "forgetting," also discloses outright rejection and resistance to an "undecidability" perceived to be a threat to Heidegger's meditations on the nature of Being.

Naturally Derrida is very much aware of this "conservative" Heideggerian position which maintains rather than breaks the metaphysical tradition, and Derrida's rhetorical posture is explicitly directed against this conservative dimension in Heidegger's thought, while the performative identifications with Heideggerian strategies function to disclose how at the same time a conservative maintenance of the metaphysical tradition contains within it those elements which are capable of deconstituting the grounds upon which that maintenance is predicated. The performative in Heidegger, too, assesses time as *to apeiron* whose indeterminacy implies a nihilistic wear and tear on that which is given by Being. The *apeiron* is not simply a genesis in which Being is gathered, or a forgotten origin, but a temporal *retrait* in which Being is at once revealed and concealed, given and obliterated. *To apeiron* is neither the beginning nor something which comes after; rather, it transpires in a manifold of temporality whose moments are constituted in "boundary drift." In such time Being is at once appropriated and disappropriated, as Heidegger will notice of time in "Zeit und Sein." Thus *to apeiron* is that moment in which time as something linear (time as *grammè*) and ontologically determinate (*ousia*) is violated or negated. Yet if Heidegger invokes such a notion of time, and especially in the seminar of 1941, his reading of ontology also views such a radical concept of time as threatening to the notion of Being whose proper understanding requires metaphysics.

A key passage in Heidegger which Derrida expects us to

keep in mind occurs in "Over 'The Line'" wherein one again explicitly recognizes how strongly Derridean deconstruction is resisted by Heidegger. This is a particularly important passage because it is a crucial context for the coining of the neologism deconstruction (it is a metaphor), as well as a context disclosing an incipient orientation of Heidegger to this term.

> The restoration of metaphysics is the restoration of the oblivion of Being. This restoration turns towards the essence of Metaphysics. It entwines itself around it through that towards which this essence itself yearns, insofar as it summons that zone which lifts it into the freedom of its truth. . . . It is hardly possible to surpass the grotesqueness (*das Groteske*) of proclaiming my attempts at thinking as smashing metaphysics (*Zertrümmerung der Metaphysik*) to bits and of sojourning at the same time, with the help of those attempts, on paths of thinking and in conceptions which have been derived—I do not say, to which one is indebted (*zu verdanken*)—from that alleged demolition (*Zertrümmerung*). There is no gratitude needed here, but some reflection. However, the lack of reflection (*Besinnungslosigkeit*) already began with the superficial misinterpretation (*oberflächlichen Missdeutung*) of the "destruction" ("*Destruktion*") which was discussed in *Being and Time* (1927) and which has no other desire than to win back the original experiences of metaphysics as conceptions having become current and empty in the process of abandonment (*Abbau*).[48]

Heidegger's resistance to the *to apeiron,* or his "forgetting" of the term in "The Anaximander Fragment," may be motivated by the strong antipathy above to the notion of "smashing metaphysics." For in his "obliteration" or "forgetting" of the term *to apeiron,* Heidegger allows for that absent signifier or proper name to return *as metaphysics,* wherein the "original experiences of metaphysics" are "won back." In not talking about Anaximander's term in its own terms, Heidegger resists its conceptual power to threaten metaphysics, and this resistance is precisely what Derrida wants to overcome. Indeed, the passage above is one of the sources for Derrida's repeated insistences that one cannot simply step outside of or beyond metaphysics, that the resistance to overcoming metaphysics is itself part of Western thought and not so simply dismissed. This, Heidegger is already saying, was one of the major weaknesses of the thesis of *Being and Time*, that it did not respect the resistance from within metaphysics to its own overcoming. Curiously enough, the passage from "Over 'The Line'" suggests that it is itself a moment when Heidegger had felt his project was too bold in its intent to surpass or go beyond an intellectual history which is the metaphysical tradition. In his earlier essays, Derrida highlights Heidegger's resistances in contrast to his own much less nostalgic approach to philosophy.

As the scholarship on the *to apeiron* shows, Anaximander's formulation of the term is by no means a settled matter among students of the pre-Socratics. But Heidegger's consideration of the *apeiron* in the seminar acknowledges the term as extremely disruptive from the perspective of traditional ways of considering questions of ontology and temporality. In "The Anaximander Fragment" Heidegger, in acknowledging this disruption, substituted a far less troublesome word in the *apeiron*'s place: *genesis*. Still, even that aspect of "The Anaximander Fragment" which performatively recognizes the *apeiron* from the seminar in its more destabilized senses comprises one of Heidegger's more important attempts to reformulate what in *Being and Time* had been called the radical temporal clue, and Derrida's "Ousia et grammè" is extremely significant for Heidegger studies in that it recognizes this possibility (again, before Heidegger's seminar on Anaximander was published in 1981) and points the way for us to begin comprehending how the abandoned project on time in *Being and Time* was by no means given up but reworked later in contexts that appear to be fairly remote from those in the earlier work.

Derrida's earlier essays suggest that in order to grasp Heidegger's philosophy one must engage in an assessment of his attempts to settle the question of temporality with regard to Being. Moreover, Derrida suggests that Heidegger was, in the earlier work, looking for a radical temporal clue by means of which to destroy metaphysics but was either not able to come up with such a radical temporal formulation or, for pietistic reasons, resisted doing so. In reperforming the *to apeiron* Heidegger does, according to Derrida's analysis, formulate the radical temporal clue discussed in *Being and Time,* but in formulating it, Heidegger carefully conceals or "erases" its most radical and destructive consequences for philosophy. To overcome this resistance, however, Derrida must himself reperform the Heideggerian project so that its radical temporal clue will come forth.

From Apeiron *to* Différance

If we noted Derrida's reperformance of Heidegger's "Anaximander Fragment" in "The White Mythology," it is also important to recognize how Derrida reperforms the *to apeiron* which he, too, has "forgotten" in order to better disclose it. Indeed, this reformulation could be seen as the *raison d'être* for the key article to deconstruction, "La différance." Quite evident is that the essays, "La différance," "Ousia et grammè," and "Les fins de l'homme," collected in *Writing and Difference* belong to a suite of articles in which essentially the same questions are interrogated from very different perspectives. "La différance" might best be considered a fragment or missing portion of "Ousia et grammè" in which a reading of "The Anaximander Fragment" addresses the *to apeiron* in order to disclose deconstruction's indebtedness not only to Anaximander but to Heidegger's reading of the Anaximander fragment. For "La différance" develops passages in "Ousia et grammè" by positing the term *différance* as it concerns the difference between Being and beings. One suspects, in fact, that had Derrida merged these two essays our understanding of *la différance* might have been much altered through contextualization.

In "La différance" Derrida writes, "In this text ["The Anaximander Fragment"] Heidegger recalls that the forgetting of Being forgets the difference between Being and beings."[49] And quoting Heidegger, Derrida notes, *"The oblivion of Being is oblivion of the distinction between Being and beings."*[50] This leads to a consideration of the trace: "What Heidegger wants to mark is this: the difference between Being and beings, the forgotten of metaphysics, has disappeared without leaving a trace. The very trace of difference has been submerged. If we maintain that *différance* (is) (itself) other than absence and presence, if it *traces*, then when it is a matter of the forgetting of the difference (between Being and beings), we would have to speak of a disappearance of the trace of the trace."[51] These words address Heidegger's implicit remarks on the *to apeiron* and more or less repeat quite literally what Derrida has written in "Ousia et grammè," though in "La différance" the commentary is extended a bit further. Notable is the fact that whereas Heidegger talks about reinscription of the fragment—its translation—Derrida talks about erasures and trace effects.

> Since the trace is not a presence but the simulacrum of a presence that dislocates itself, displaces itself, refers itself, it properly has no site—erasure belongs to its structure. And not only the erasure which must always be able to overtake it (without which it would not be a trace but an indestructible and monumental substance), but also the erasure which constitutes it from the outset as a trace, which situates it as the change of site, and makes it disappear in its appearance, makes it emerge from itself in its production. The erasure of the early trace (*die frühe Spur*) of difference is therefore the "same" as its tracing in the text of metaphysics. This latter must have maintained the mark of what it has lost, reserved, put aside. The paradox of such a structure, in the language of metaphysics, is an inversion of metaphysical concepts.[52]

Derrida's conclusion is that the present becomes "the sign of the sign, the trace of the trace . . . it is a trace, and a trace of the erasure of the trace."[53]

Such a reading of Heidegger is extremely remote from an eschatological interpretation that looks forward to the fulfillment of Being. Indeed, Derrida's interpretation insists that the *mise en abyme* of traces and erasures takes us "beyond the history of Being, and also beyond our language, and everything that can be named in it."[54] We now see another reason why Derrida has refused to engage explicitly Heidegger's discourse on trans-lation as historical reinscription: Derrida, unlike Heidegger, sees the history of Being as a trace structure of erasures and effacements. The history of ontology is not a translation of marks or the handing down of textual residues but an un-writing, a whiting out. From this perspective connections with "The White Mythology" become somewhat more evident, for in "La différance" one notices the white mythology recognizes a presence at the core of Western thinking that is discursively presenting itself to us only under erasure. Also, in "La différance," Derrida notices Heidegger's translation of the ancient Greek term *to khreon* (usage),[55] which, quite possibly, suggested *usure* in the senses it takes on in "The White Mythology."[56] Lastly, Derrida acknowledges in "La différance" that *to khreon* is associated in Heidegger with *Über-setzen* (trans-lation) and that the trace of *to khreon* is part of the destiny of the history of Western metaphysics.

In case we had any doubts that Derrida had not seen the subtlety of Heidegger's argument in "The Anaximander Fragment" concerning the relationships of metaphysics to reinscription, or in case we might have had any doubts as to the intimate relationship between an essay like "The White Mythology" and Heideggerian thought, the pages in "La différance" on "The Anaximander Fragment" put all that to rest. Derrida not only is sensitive to the issues I have put forward earlier in this chapter, but he wants to go beyond them in "La différance" by means of analyzing the oblivion of Being, which is the oblivion of textual erasure, the *Destruktion* or deconstruction of discourse. In the destruction of the difference between Being and beings there is revealed not just trace structures but what Derrida is calling *la différance*. This, he says, has no essence and therefore cannot appear: "There is no essence of *différance;* it (is) that which not only could never be appropriated in the *as such* of its name or its appearing, but also that which threatens the authority of the *as such* in genera, of the presence of the thing itself in its essence. That there is not a proper essence of *différance* at this point, implies that there is neither a Being nor truth of the play of writing such as it engages *différance*."[57] But having said that, Derrida also says, "For us, *différance* remains a metaphysical name, and all the names that it receives in our language are still, as names, metaphysical. And this is particularly the case when these names state the determination of *différance* as the difference between presence and the present (*Anwesen/Anwesend*), but already, and above all, when they state the determination of *différance* as the difference of Being and beings."⁵⁸ Derrida's wish, here, is to go beyond the name, *différance,* itself that "pure nominal unity" as he calls it, in order to posit *différance* as something unnameable, "the play which makes possible nominal effects." In itself this involves usage and translation, performance and transference. "The nominal effect *différance* is itself enmeshed, carried off, reinscribed, just as a false entry or a false exit is still part of the game, a function of the system."⁵⁹ To put into question the name of the name is for Derrida the understanding of the trace of the trace as the double gesture of inscription and erasure. This would be to engage that white mythology which is its own demystification, or more aptly, its own demythification.

Heidegger, Derrida says at the conclusion of "La différance," turned back from this going beyond names, for Heidegger seeks the unique word, the "finally proper name," *Sein.* This is where Halliburton's reading of Heidegger's Anaximander essay is so correct, where the eschatology situates itself. But the role of *différance,* Derrida suggests, is never to affirm the properness of a final term. More accurately, *la différance* in breaking with Occidental categories as determined in Platonic and Aristotelian thought is part of a Nietzschean eternal return to a notion whose unnameability is cited in the commentary on Anaximander by Simplicius: *to apeiron.*

Of course *to apeiron* is a temporal marker, and this is most relevant to "La différance." In fact *différance* poses itself as the disclosure of the radical temporal clue Heidegger had only broached without allowing to carry out its mission: the destruction of metaphysics. *Différance,* then, is the formulation of the radical temporal clue toward which the entire Heideggerian philosophical apparatus inclines. That Derrida perceives this, entitles him, according to the argument of "La différance," to claim a success where Heidegger has evidently failed, even if it is a success which could never have taken place without Heidegger's having preceded Derrida.

In the following quotation the radical temporality of *différance* is set forth.

> It is because of *différance* that the movement of signification is possible only if each so-called "present" element, each element appearing on the scene of presence, is re-

lated to something other than itself, thereby keeping
within itself the mark of the past element, and already
letting itself be vitiated by the mark of its relation to the
future element, this trace being related no less to what is
called the future than to what is called the past, and constituting what is called the present by means of this very
relation to what it is not: what it absolutely is not, not
even a past or a future as a modified present.[60]

Already at the outset of this passage, which I am temporarily
breaking at this point, one sees the tacit influence of Heidegger's "The Anaximander Fragment," for it is in talking about
the "mark" that Derrida is repeating Heidegger's argument
about trans-lation or trans-scription. Moreover, Derrida, in
considering the mark as that which is trans-scribed through the
auspices of difference, begins to notice that from within the act
of trans-scription the question of temporality is directly engaged. Trans-scription suggests relations not only of presence
but of the present. Derrida continues:

An interval must separate the present from what it is not
in order for the present to be itself, but this interval that
constitutes it as present must, by the same token, divide
the present in and of itself, thereby also dividing, along
with the present, everything that is thought on the basis
of the present, that is, in our metaphysical language,
every being, and singularly substance or the subject. In
constituting itself, in dividing itself dynamically, this interval is what might be called *spacing*, the becoming-
space of time or the becoming-time of space (*temporization*).[61]

The interval is not merely a cut or rupture but a punctuation
which allows us to see time and being as a manifold of relations
which is as much held together as it is pushed apart by the
division. Constituting means dynamic dividing. The space is
essential in order that relations of being, time, and language
can be articulated, disclosed. Lastly, the interval must be
thought of at once as the becoming space of time and the
becoming time of space. "And it is this constitution of the
present, as an 'originary' and irreducibly nonsimple (and there-

fore, *stricto sensu* nonoriginary) synthesis of marks, or traces of retentions and protentions (to reproduce analogically and provisionally a phenomenological and transcendental language that soon will reveal itself to be inadequate), that I propose to call archi-writing, archi-trace, or *différance*. Which (is) (simultaneously) spacing (and) temporization."[62] Toward the end of the passage Derrida's reading of Heidegger has led him to view "writing" as the proper context in which to pursue a philosophy seeking to deconstruct the metaphysical bases of Western thought. Time does not exist alone but always already concerns a synthesis of marks disclosing relations of Being (presencing), spacing (intervals, divisions, differences), and signification (translation, meaning, truth).

Much of "La différance" generalizes the homage and critique of Heidegger by means of contextualizing *différance* in various systems of thought. Quite important is Derrida's challenge to a Saussurean view of language that the notion of the phonemic opposition must give way to a more sophisticated philosophy of differentiation. Here the familiar binaryism characterizing much structuralist thought is under attack from a post-Heideggerian perspective, and this attack is most visible in *Of Grammatology*, where both de Saussure and Claude Lévi-Strauss come under heavy fire. The strategic gain in mounting such a critique of the distinctive feature of binary opposition is that Derrida can make credible the transposition of ontological questions into a linguistic context in which the trace becomes the track of a mark in differential transit where undecidability transpires.

Heidegger, it is charged, never really attempted to transpose his ontological arguments into a thoroughly linguistic context, though in "The Anaximander Fragment" Heidegger appears to be moving in that direction. Derrida is very keen on making the linguistic transposition because it appears that once a linguistic or literary critical discourse is taken up there is much less metaphysical contamination likely by way of a rhetoric of being. Indeed, consideration of the trace in a linguistic context makes irrelevant Heidegger's concern with Being as that to which, in Derrida's reading of Heidegger, all else must be subordinated. By transferring Heideggerian philosophy into a post-Saussurean context, Derrida moves his base of operations from "voice" to "writing," from "presence" to "trace." And yet, in doing so, he has risked a new binaryism, that is to say, a new table of terms which can be divided along an axis of inclusion/exclusion.

In *Of Grammatology* the juxtaposition of phenomenological trace structures and Saussurean linguistics is also significant, since it is here that the question of time in its relation to language and spacing is addressed in terms of Heideggerian method. At issue is the revision of Heideggerian *Sprache* such that it conforms to a philosophy of the trace within which spacing can be viewed as part of an undecidable temporal/spatial relation. *Sprache* itself has the potential for recovering Derrida's project within a metaphysical framework, and in moving away from the possibility of such a recovery Derrida writes:

> It is thus that, after evoking the "voice of being," Heidegger recalls that it is silent, mute, insonorous, wordless, originarily *a-phonic* [*die Gewähr der lautlosen Stimme verborgener Quellen* . . .]. The voice of the sources is not heard. A rupture between the originary meaning of being and the word, between meaning and the voice, between "the voice of being" and the "phoné," between the "call of being," and articulated sound; such a rupture, which at once confirms a fundamental metaphor, and renders it suspect by accentuating its metaphoric discrepancy, translates the ambiguity of the Heideggerian situation with respect to the metaphysics of presence and logo-centrism. It is at once contained within it and transgresses it. But it is impossible to separate the two. The very movement of transgression sometimes holds it back short of the limit.[63]

Producing this fault or division with regard to the voice of being is the repetition of the question: "Because it is indeed the *question* of being that Heidegger asks metaphysics. And with it the question of truth, of sense, of the *logos*. The incessant meditation upon that question does not restore confidence. On the contrary, it dislodges the confidence."[64] That Heidegger finds it necessary to interrogate Being, that this interrogation is itself the structure of an iteration whose obsessiveness verifies the gaps, lacks, or traces in the object of inquiry, dislodges our confidence in the notion of piety as an attempt to preserve or respect the integrity of its object. Rather, piety resembles skepticism. By way of the repetition of the question of Being, through the iteration of the language of being, the history of ontology is always already deconstituted by way of a temporal clue which is hidden in the folds or creases of the questions, in those repetitions or numerous false starts. The repeated question is the structure of Being's history, the textuality of Being, the written of Being; the trace structure of Being as being has disclosed itself to us through the lived record of time. By asking the question of Being, Heidegger discloses "that 'being,' as it is fixed in its general syntactic and lexicological forms within linguistics and Western philosophy, is not a primary and absolutely irreducible signified, that it is still rooted in a system of languages and an historically determined 'significance,' although strangely privileged as the virtue of disclosure and dissimulation."[65] Derrida's argument is that Heidegger's entire philosophical project is a reading of Being whose destiny is to discover that Being appears only in the track of its own being-written, and that "nothing escapes the movement of the signifier" which is, as we noticed in "La différance," a temporal/ spatial movement.

Everything is to be read within the horizon of the temporal, a horizon that is disclosed to us within the history of the meaning of Being, or, to put it another way, within the history of a certain discursive practice. And yet, what does time mean in this context? Whenever Derrida touches on this kind of problem it is the "signifying trace" which comes under close scrutiny.

> To come to recognize, not within but on the horizon of the Heideggerian paths, and yet in them, that the sense of being is not a transcendental or trans-epochal signified (even if it was already dissimulated within the epoch) but already, in the truly *unheard of* sense, a determined signifying trace, is to affirm that within the decisive concept of ontico-ontological difference, *all is not to be thought at one go;* entity and being, ontic and ontologi-

cal, "ontico-ontological" are, in an original style, *deriva-tive* with regard to difference, and with respect to what I shall later call *différance,* an economic concept designat-ing the production of differing/deferring. The ontico-on-tological difference and its ground (*Grund*) in the "trans-cendence of *Dasein*" . . . are not absolutely originary. Différance by itself would be more "originary," but one would no longer be able to call it "origin" or "ground," those notions belonging essentially to the history of onto-theology, to the system functioning as the effacing of difference.[66]

This passage from *Of Grammatology* does not emphatically dis-cuss temporal significance of the ontico-ontological difference, and yet the phrase "all is not to be thought at one go" is extremely important, because Derrida is arguing that the tem-poral clue which is elicited by the ontico-ontological difference is itself a manifold of relations that are not presented all at once in a now but are also not all concealed in an *arché* or *eschaton* either. The difference, or *différance,* breaks radically with a Kantian teleology, which views time as linear, progressive, con-tinuous. Time, from a post-Heideggerian perspective, is any-thing but such a linear movement of the history of being or meaning; rather, time is a manifold of relations in which the difference between moments is itself undecidably given in a trace structure in whose indeterminacy the various modalities of time (arche, moment, lapse, eschaton, duration, present, past, future, suspension) are given not simultaneously but also not unsimultaneously.

In uncovering this interpretation of time within the inter-pretation of text as the "movement of the signifier," Derrida benefits from the rhetoric of ontology without becoming dis-tracted by the question of Being as nostalgically seeking a plenitude within parousia—the revelation of Being. *Différance* becomes the complex marker by means of which a temporal consideration of the question of Being allows us to read the history of ontology in a way that does not simply dismiss teleology as has often been done within various religions. Rather, in recognizing the continuum of temporality *la dif-*

férance has the effect of deconstituting from within a continuous teleological structure, a path of thought moving from origin to end.

Throughout this chapter we have been considering those points at which deconstruction is positioned close to the work of Martin Heidegger. Although Derrida's stance(s) with respect to Heidegger has never been anything else than highly ambivalent, we do notice in Derrida's earlier essays the extent to which Derrida's philosophy identifies itself with Heidegger and where it explicitly distances itself. Indeed, Derrida, who probably did not, in the 1960s, have access to Heidegger's 1941 seminar on Anaximander, suggests both indirectly and unmistakably that during the late 1940s Heidegger did see his way to a radical temporal clue but that he resisted bringing it to philosophical fruition because of a resistance (perhaps pietistic) to destroying the metaphysical tradition. Deconstruction, in contrast, formulates that radical temporal clue and repositions it within a linguistic critique which allows the clue to open onto a reflexive demolition that Heidegger wanted to forestall.

Yet, there is another indirect and unmistakable thesis that Derrida appears to be advancing as well. This suggests that Heidegger was not capable of seeing his way to a radical temporal clue at all and that deconstruction has to invent one for him within the loose-ended infrastructures of Heidegger's miscellaneous articles that come after *Being and Time*. This is the thesis to which I turn in the next chapter, wherein we engage those major arguments that are highlighted in "Ousia et grammè" on the philosophical handling of time by Aristotle, Hegel, and Heidegger.

Before I turn to this, there are two last points I want to make about the interrelations between Derrida and Heidegger as I have just left them. First, one can only suppose that the reason both Heidegger and Derrida "forget" to mention the *to apeiron* is, among those already given, that for Heidegger this notion is too strong, in many respects, and that for Derrida it is too weak and therefore needs reformulation. Yet, it is curious, and perhaps ironic, that in their failure to mention the *to apeiron,* Derrida stands in a metaphoric or analogous relation to Heidegger that confirms the Heideggerian thesis of trans-lation, as if this metaphorical relation were, in fact, but part of a much larger metaleptic chain of substitutive texts that reperform by way of a Nietzschean eternal return the *apeiron* of Anaximander which, as fragment or as trace under erasure, has been given over to oblivion. Second, the materials we have studied disclose points where Heideggerian thought comes into close proximity to deconstruction. However, when Derrida discusses the implicit affinities between himself and Heidegger it is the *to apeiron* of Anaximander that is indirectly involved, and this *to apeiron* is an example of a destructive, disjunct, or disappropriating notion of time. But when Derrida explicitly discusses his distance from Heidegger it will be Aristotle's temporal notion of the *hama* that is raised, that is to say, in terms of a constitutive concept in which moments of time are appropriated. The chiasmus is odd. When Derrida discloses affinities or identities to Heidegger it is in terms of a temporality that forecloses identification. And when he shows his differences with Heidegger he does so in terms of a temporality that forces identification to come about.

Given the philosophy of *différance,* we know that these "different" positions are not simply contradictory but that they are positioned deconstructively, or undecidably. These temporal relationships—*la différance*—are themselves what deconstruct intellectual history as the narrative of conceptual filiation which takes place in what Olafson calls "world-time." But how can an intellectual history of Derrida's relation to Heidegger be written if intellectual history has itself been deconstructed? My sense is that this can be done only as the performance of the deconstruction of intellectual history, a performance which occurs not in a sentence or paragraph or chapter but in the relations between them, relations that form correspondences wherein the bringing near of that which is far transpires as the persistence of an eternal recurrence: the repetition of difference.

T W O

T H E   E A R L Y

H E I D E G G E R

In the previous discussion of "Ousia et grammè" I have not mentioned the essay's central
or major claims about a lengthy note on
temporality in Heidegger's *Being and Time*
(2.6.82). But in eliding the major occasion for Derrida's remarks, I am recognizing that his astonishing revaluation of
Heidegger occurs mainly in the materials surrounding the interpretation of the note (*Being and Time*, 2.6.82), and that it is in
these supplementary remarks that Derrida acknowledges a continuity between Heidegger's formulations and those of deconstruction as Derrida develops them in the late 1960s. In this
chapter, however, I wish to discuss Derrida's reading of Heidegger's note as part of an interpretation that counters the
philosophical sympathies between Derrida and Heidegger. For
in this chapter we will encounter an attitude in Derrida's work
that assumes Heidegger never developed a very radical temporal
clue, that, in fact, Heidegger resisted the destination he announces in the beginning of *Being and Time*: the undoing of the
history of ontology. Naturally, we are limiting ourselves to the
early Heidegger. But Derrida's reading of the note suggests that
early and late Heidegger are not so easily differentiated and that
discussing them in terms of identity and difference poses enormous problems.

In this chapter I must reconstruct the main outlines of Derrida's remarks on Heidegger's note and the tutor texts that
Heidegger is discussing before proceeding to discussions of the
unwritten parts of *Being and Time* as well as of the lectures
written during the late 1920s. I will turn to *Basic Problems of
Phenomenology* in order to demonstrate within a text not available to Derrida at the time of writing his essays on Heidegger

during the late 1960s that Derrida's intuitions about the note to *Being and Time* are borne out by evidence that has subsequently been edited and published. In addition, I wish to discuss *The Metaphysical Foundations of Logic* in order to show that evidence has also emerged that demonstrates Heidegger's capacity to mount parallel arguments to those advanced in *Being and Time* and *Basic Problems in Phenomenology,* which do, in fact, more than anticipate a deconstructive moment, even if it occurs in the working through of a largely existential approach. Lastly, I will discuss Derrida's essay, "The Ends of Man," which, once more, makes the claim that Heidegger resists the radical project he has himself undertaken not only in his earlier but even in his later periods. It is here, once more, that Derrida will distinguish deconstruction from Heideggerian philosophizing, though, as my study will bear out in later chapters, Derrida will retreat somewhat in the mid-1970s from the stringency of these positions, for example, in "Pas" and "The Retrait of Metaphor."

It is well known that in the note to *Being and Time* (2.6.82) Heidegger acknowledges Hegel's conception of time in the *Encyclopedia,* and also the *Jena Logic,* as vulgar, since it establishes the essence of time in a metaphysical now. Heidegger's projected and unwritten sections on time were, in part, meant to provide a long critique of Hegel's formulations in order to uncover from within metaphysical speculations a temporal clue breaking with the history of ontology. Derrida argues that Heidegger was correct in noting that time cannot, as Hegel thought, be considered as some "other thing" or thought of as "otherwise," in Hegel's sense, because in such an estrangement of time one would invent a dialectics resulting in a conception of the "other" of time as merely a replication of a "now" that is presenced.

Derrida reads the notes' remarks on Hegel, as well as its comments on Aristotle, in order to orient the analyses of time as ones that raise the question of difference and identity, being and nonbeing. And, as readers familiar with the overall project of deconstruction can surmise, Derrida wants to show that Heidegger's analyses routinely manage to raise the issues while failing to take a deconstructive turn through which difference would be viewed as something analogous to *différance.* But

Derrida, in making this point, will also attempt to suggest that Hegel and Aristotle were not so crude or vulgar as Heidegger supposes. For in them we can see the repetition of a problem which resurfaces in Heidegger's discourse: the engaging in a discussion of time that the philosopher knows may potentially destroy the very categories of metaphysical thinking by means of which the problematic of time itself was raised. Moreover, the invoking of the problematic of time necessarily brings about numerous aporias or double binds which are so destructive that in addressing the radical aspects of time there must be a gesture or tactics by means of which this appeal can resist the violence it risks. In short, the philosopher wants to release the genie in the bottle but also wants to capture it once again, having seen the damage it is capable of producing. Philosophically, time is easily underestimated as a problematic, and Derrida suggests that even minds like those of Aristotle, Hegel, and Heidegger were not properly oriented in such a way that they could master the philosophical effects of raising the question of time. From the broadest of perspectives, Derrida is also suggesting that perhaps temporality inheres in philosophy as precisely that which cannot be thought and that philosophy poses itself historically as a resistance to the thinking through of time, despite time's attractiveness as a "radical" in metaphysical discourse. Given this view, the relevance of Derrida's interrogation of Heidegger's note becomes quite obvious, since deconstruction is itself inscribed into the Western problematic of thinking about time.

In considering Hegel, Derrida appreciates, above all, the risk involved for the Hegelian system when it attempts to think through the question of time in a way that threatens the coherence of the dialectic. "There is produced in the thought of the impossibility of the otherwise, in this *not otherwise,* a certain difference, a certain trembling, a certain decentering that is not the position of an other center. An other center would be an other now."[1] Hegel, especially, is not afraid to "negate" the now, to introduce "differences" into his dialectics which debilitate closure and presencings of stable nows. And Hegel risks such debilitating and perhaps chaotic effects because he recognizes *difference* itself to be very problematic. "How do space, how do nature, in their undifferentiated immediacy, receive difference, determination, quality? Differentiation, determination, qualification can only overtake pure space as the negation of this original purity and of this initial state of abstract indifferentiation which is properly the spatiality of space."[2] Heidegger must have learned from Hegel, Derrida implies, that the history of ontology is largely the history of the problematic of difference. It must have been obvious to Heidegger that if one is going to deconstitute the history of ontology by means of a temporal clue, that from Hegel one learns precisely what that clue or key to time must be: differentiation/identification. However, Heidegger never grasps this key very firmly in *Being and Time,* even though he has its elements under scrutiny. And, curiously enough, it is not until one reads "The Anaximander Fragment" that it becomes clear Heidegger uses the temporal clue, manifest in Hegel's text, in a very displaced context in which the difference of being is under discussion within a text about the assessment of time. The function of Derrida's reading of the note by Heidegger, then, is to reperform the whole argument in order to see and develop a clue in Hegel which Heidegger discusses but does not fully grasp in its overall significance for philosophy. This will be repeated, once more, when Derrida rereads Aristotle along with Heidegger and shows where in *The Physics* the temporal clue suggests itself. But, after these analyses are made, Derrida will reinscribe them in terms of Heidegger's reading of Anaximander, a reading we have considered in chapter 1. And, through all of these analyses, Derrida will be asking, from a polemical perspective, whether Heidegger fully grasped the significance of difference and, if so, why he resisted taking the question to its most destructive consequences. Derrida's interpretation of Heidegger is "layered," then, because his analyses of texts and contexts are meant to be overlaid much in the manner of an "allegory of reading," as Paul de Man has developed the notion.

That Hegel is stressed more in *Being and Time* than is Aristotle and consequently addressed first by Derrida is due to the fact that Hegel's texts on time are much less cryptic and fragmentary than Aristotle's in *The Physics.* In part, this means that one is reading largely from Hegel *into* Aristotle, and especially in Derrida's comments it is evident that Aristotle is mediated by Hegelian thought. In *The Encyclopedia,* Hegel relates space, time, and the mark through the figure of the point. (As we will see, the figures of point, line, and space are central in Aristotle's remarks in *The Physics*.) Hegel argues that the point both replaces and conserves the undifferentiatedness of space. It delimits (negates) but also articulates (posits) space as undifferentiated. "As the first determination and first negation of space, the point spatializes or *spaces* itself."3 The point negates and retains, but it also extends into line. This *Aufhebung* of the point is the linear truth of the point, its destiny. But the line is itself spatial. Hence, in the negation of space by the point, the stretching of the point into the line only reaffirms, once more, space in terms of the spatiality of line. The negation of space by the point is *aufgehoben* into the affirmation of space as line. It follows in Hegel that time is the negative moment through which undifferentiated space *becomes* differentiated space. "Time is *spacing*," or, "[Time] is the relation of space to itself, its for-itself." Heidegger writes, "According to Hegel, this negation of the negation as punctuality is time."4 In terms of ontology this is significant in that the relation of Being to nature is precisely that of space to the point. Nature, in other words, is in a negative, because temporal, relation to Being. Derrida proposes that we reread section 258 of the *Encyclopedia*, since it is this text that will become quite problematic from the point of view of *Being and Time*. It is, as Derrida says, a truly extraordinary passage.

> Time, as the negative unity of self-externality, is
> similarly an out-and-out abstract, ideal being. It is that
> being which, inasmuch as it *is*, is *not*, and inasmuch as it
> *is not*, *is*: it is Becoming *directly intuited* (*das angeschaute
> Werden*); this means that differences, which admittedly
> are purely momentary, i.e. directly self-sublating (*unmit-
> telbar sich aufhebenden Unterschiede*) are determined as *ex-
> ternal*, i.e. as external to themselves.5

Derrida draws three main conclusions from this passage: (1) that a Kantian conception of time is reproduced in it—time as pure form of intuition; (2) that Heidegger similarly accepts that "Time and the 'I think' are no longer opposed . . . they are the same" but that "it is not in time (*der Zeit*) that everything comes to be and passes away; rather, time itself is becoming, this coming-to-be and passing away"; and (3) the Hegelian determination of temporality allows us to consider the present—"the very form of time"—as eternity. This eternity is like the absolute, neither inside nor outside of time. "Eternity as presence is neither temporal nor intemporal." For Derrida this means that "presence is intemporality in time or time in intemporality: this, perhaps, is what makes anything like an originary temporality impossible."[6] However, it is also true that "eternity is another name of the presence of the present." And yet this presence is not naively metaphysical but marked by difference of the finite and the infinite. The question Derrida is asking in "Ousia et grammè" concerns how we are to assess *Being and Time,* given that the "application" of Hegel is precisely the context wherein a deconstruction of Western ontology could be carried out by Heidegger, though it is most evidently being resisted, either because Heidegger does not clearly see his way to the deconstruction of ontology by means of the clue to time Hegel offers, or because he sees it but suspects that it might be too disruptive in terms of the philosophical contexts already established in *Being and Time.* Certainly, as we will notice much later in the notes and lectures, which are, to a large degree, parts of *Being and Time* either not included in the volume or treated as ancillary textual materials, Heidegger may have been most interested in working toward a radical temporal clue not by means of interrupting or punctuating a philosophical text—this, indeed, is Derrida's overriding tendency— but by working through the categories of phenomenology (for example, in *History of the Concept of Time,* which is an early draft of *Being and Time*) and existentialism (*Being and Time, Basic Problems in Phenomenology,* and *The Metaphysical Foundations of Logic*) to the point where a movement from the emphasis upon Dasein gives way to an emphasis on what lies in the "being beyond" of Dasein: that is, time and Being. However, this is an approach that Derrida implicitly views as a liability, since it suggests a forestalling, or resistance, to that philosophical horizon called deconstruction.

Leaving the question concerning Heidegger's missed opportunity for deconstruction by way of Hegel in suspension, Derrida's reperformance of Heidegger's note turns to Aristotle. For it is in terms of *The Physics* that the entire problematic of time, as Hegel inherits it, is oriented with respect to the metaphysical method of inquiry. Without doubt, Hegel not only draws his examples through parallels with *The Physics* but his conception of negativity is strongly indebted as well to Aristotelian conceptions. In *The Physics,* Aristotle writes: "That time is either altogether nonexistent, or that it exists but hardly or obscurely, might be suspected from the following: One part of it has come to be but no longer exists; the other part will be but does not yet exist; and it is of these two parts that infinite time, or any time one might take, is composed. But it is thought that what is composed of nonbeings cannot participate in *substance.*"[7]

It is crucial to acknowledge that *The Physics* is enormously obscure and very difficult to paraphrase, since its remarks are fragmentary, its references largely lost to us, and much of its sense dependent, for us, upon passages elsewhere in Aristotle. Derrida's reading of *The Physics* does not problematize this aspect of the text but assumes we are aware of the traps of interpretation. And, since the stress is upon Heidegger, Derrida chooses to interpret *The Physics* from a distinctly Heideggerian perspective: the idea that Aristotle is most fundamentally concerned with the contradiction that time (nonbeing) can be said to manifest presence (being). In its simplest form the question is, how can nothing (be) something? Aristotle's project, from this point of view, is to justify the paradox, and this is done by thinking of time as presence insofar as in the determination of beings there is the determination of time. In noting the entelechy of time, Aristotle resolves the contradiction of how time as nonbeing is also being.

The last sentence of *Being and Time* asks a similar question raising Aristotle's paradox when it remarks, "Does time itself manifest itself as the horizon of *Being?*" And Derrida's analysis in recognizing such a compatibility between Heidegger and Aristotle will develop two points about Heidegger. First, Heidegger's philosophy recognizes that time is not to be considered identical to Being, but second, Heidegger's *Being and Time* does not, in itself, ever go outside an Aristotelian consideration of temporality such as outlined in *The Physics.* Rather, Heidegger's analysis of time at the end of *Being and Time* merely discusses how Dasein is situated in ordinary time, how

Dasein in turning away from its own finitude (death) grasps time as an infinitude in whose presence Dasein feels at ease with itself. More generally, Heidegger argues that the "primordial structure of *Dasein's* totality of Being" is temporality, and in this sense Heidegger, too, attempts a demonstration of how something secondary to being like time can be shown to be little else than the structure or determination of the totality of Being. In this Heidegger largely repeats *The Physics*.

The significance of this Heideggerian dependence upon Aristotelian thinking is that whereas Hegel offers the opportunity for a highly radical and deconstructive theory of time, Heidegger's engagement with Aristotle, even through Hegel as mediator, provides a means whereby to retreat into the safety of metaphysics. Derrida, at this juncture, reads once again the theory about the point and the line. In *The Physics*, Aristotle's reference to time by way of the analogy of the point and the line is a celebrated passage, and Derrida notes that it represents the condition of time from the standpoint of metaphysics. For just as the point is a spatial marker which is essentially nonspatial, the now is a moment in time which is not temporal. The now, in fact, breaks with the continuity of moments in asserting itself as not past and not future. But if the now is not these other moments, is "other" than them, this now cannot be understood except in terms of them, though it is clear that as yet these moments do not exist. When something is said to exist, Aristotle says, then all its parts exist. But with time this is not the case. The now is defined precisely by that which does not exist (it is meta-physical), of that of which it is and is not a part. The now, because it is distinct from the past and the future, is not part of time as a continuum, but then, it would be unthinkable to consider the now to exist as simultaneous with another now. Therefore, while the now in relation to its nonexisting moments (past, future) appears in itself to be defined according to that which has no being, the now, insofar as it may not be simultaneous with any other moment, achieves a certain presence as it appears to consciousness. And this, Aristotle knows, is a contradiction. But in having outlined these problems, Aristotle's text breaks off. "Let this, then, be the discussion of *difficulties* faced in connection with what belongs to time."[8] Acknowledging these, the discussion then turns to the essence or nature of time. Aristotle's consideration of the analogy of the point and the line stresses the metaphysical problematic of the relation of time to being and nonbeing. Yet the analogy is closed off quite abruptly with the flippant statement that such examples are only part of the "discussion of *difficulties* faced in connection with what belongs to time." Why is Aristotle being so casual? Derrida's reading makes such questions more urgent because he notices that at such junctures in Aristotle the history of ontology and metaphysics is being determined, that had Aristotle not closed off the discussion so abruptly, Western philosophy might have taken a different direction. This is not to say that the history of metaphysics hangs in the balance because of one passage or statement, but that in the abrupt cutting off of an argument Aristotle displays an attitude or orientation with respect to questions of being and time which is itself ingrained in him and becomes habitual within the history of philosophy. It is these habits of thinking, of course, that we unconsciously pick up, and, as someone intensely interested in psychology, Derrida is quite concerned with this metaphysical unconscious, the transmission or transference of these habits of thought.

It is, perhaps, impossible to ever know for sure why Aristotle breaks off his analogy of the point and the line so abruptly. Perhaps he thought time was an unknowable concept, perhaps even a pseudo-concept, and that it was better left to thinkers like Anaximander or Heraclitus. But if one reads Aristotle's *Metaphysics* another answer is suggested. We recall that in the *Metaphysics* the analogy of points and lines is raised once more, but in this case the analogy is meant to answer the question of what is an *arché*, or beginning: "'Beginning' means: The first point whence a thing's movement proceeds, such as the beginning of a line or of a road which has an opposite end." Aristotle also says, "What all beginnings have in common is that they are points of departure either for being, or becoming, or knowing."[9] In other words, the analogy of the point and the line suggests not time's relation to the problem of being/nonbeing but its determination and direction in the orientation of Being. This means that Aristotle can put aside the paradoxical formulations about how time is both nothing and something with the implicit understanding, among his students, that time is a becoming under the sway of being. And this is precisely how St. Thomas Aquinas in his commentary on *The Physics* will read the analogy of the point and the line: "Aristotle says that that which was said about time and the 'now' agrees in a certain way with what is found in a line and a point. For a point makes a line continuous, and divides it insofar as it is the beginning of one part and end of another."[10] Without doubt, Aquinas is not aware that the analogy of the line and the point refers to the metaphysical question about the contradiction of time's being at once nothing and something. Rather, for him the metaphysics of entelechy is preeminent.

It could be argued that Derrida's reading of Aristotle has to invent a self-critical moment in metaphysics when the question of being is subjected to temporal scrutiny, when, in fact, Aristotle is merely dismissing what to him are endlessly arguable speculations about the paradox of time which are of no practical value for *The Physics*. Derrida argues, of course, that Aristotle is not dealing squarely with the question of time but is merely evading it. And ironically, in evading the issue, Aristotle supposedly also poses it. Yet, readers of *The Physics* might well contend that Aristotle is insisting that the kinds of problems Derrida wants to expose are, for Aristotle, nonproblems and that Aristotle is self-consciously ridiculing these old-fashioned metaphysical speculations which date back to Anaximander and probably before.

But whether *The Physics* is the result of a self-conscious elision of analysis whose purpose is to resolve problems in philosophical methods or the product of a philosopher who felt enormously sure of himself and simply did not see enormous problems where later readers have come to be most perplexed matters less than the fact that the textual effects of whatever Aristotle thought pose themselves at a critical juncture in the history of metaphysics. And it is in this sense that Derrida intuits in *The Physics* that the text acts as if time has to be kept under control, unless the philosopher is willing to let it play havoc with the metaphysical system of terms which cannot handle the dissemination of contradiction. This threat of time can be detected, after all, through close reading, though Aristotle may not have been considering it at all, since what he recognizes in *The Metaphysics* is that time is a direction or orientation of being and that what matters in *The Physics* is the relation of time to number and motion. Certainly, Derrida's analysis of *The Physics* interprets this text as if there, as in Heidegger, the horizons of deconstructing metaphysics or maintaining it for the sake of methodological consistency are always a writerly concern which any philosopher, aware of it or not, will necessarily address as a feature of the ways in which questions like being and time are formulated.

We arrive, in this way, at what for Derrida will be an extremely important juncture in the analysis of Aristotle, the interpretation of the Greek word *hama*. Unlike St. Thomas Aquinas, whose entelechy, itself derived from Aristotle, assumed that *The Physics* demonstrates a unification of moments, or nows, Derrida, who presupposes no such entelechy, demonstrates that the Aristotelian notion of the now is plural and disseminative: "In Greek *hama* means 'together,' 'all at once,' both together, *at the same time*. This locution is first neither spatial nor temporal. The duplicity of the *simul* to which it refers does not yet reassemble, within itself, either points or nows, places or phases. It says the complicity, the common origin of time and space, appearing together [*com-paraître*] as the condition for all appearing of Being."[11] Of course, Aristotle himself tacitly acknowledges this, and Derrida's achievement, if we are convinced by him, is to have found in the metaphysical doctrine of becoming, as outlined in *The Metaphysics,* a logic of the discontinuous, unlinear, or plural. The now belongs to a constellation of temporal features which are not reconcilable within a continuum of becoming into an entelechy.

The Physics, in Derrida's opinion, reveals a structure not dissimilar from that in "The Anaximander Fragment," a structure of undecidability, of *la différance*. And it is this unmetaphysical network of relationships that can be detected from within the armature of Aristotle's metaphysical alibis. Derrida's analysis, of course, is the result of the key given him by Hegel, who points us in the right direction without himself detecting in Aristotle a network of relations deconstituting or deconstructing the metaphysical armature, reflected in its plenitude in St. Thomas Aquinas's commentary on *The Physics*. Heidegger, who notices Hegel's important clue—difference—still fails because he cannot read Aristotle's famous analogy of the point and the line so that *hama* becomes the term for the difference of difference, the mark for that limen which cannot determine even as it determines the fate of philosophy. Yet, Derrida has made this breakthrough having himself intuited the radicality and importance of Heidegger's own analysis of difference in his reading of a fragment by Anaximander. Recall once more the quotations from "Ousia et grammè" cited in chapter 1: "The determinations which name difference always come from the metaphysical order," and "Beyond Being and beings, this difference, ceaselessly differing from and deferring (itself), would trace (itself) (by itself)—this *différance* would be the first or last trace if one still could speak, here, of origin and end."[12] Notice how these conclusions are both supported by the reading of Anaximander, a pre-Socratic, and of Aristotle, a philosopher who comes after Socrates. Derrida suggests that Anaximander and Aristotle are metaleptic variants of one another. And this contradicts Heidegger's thought that Anaximander and Aristotle are thinkers who inhabit radically different philosophical frameworks. In this sense Derrida, in reperforming and transposing Heideggerian thought, reveals blindspots in Heidegger's analyses. However, in the discussion of *hama*, Derrida, in developing the aporias that Aristotle inherits from Anaximander, suggests that such aporias prohibit *The Physics* from establishing satisfying hypotheses on time and being, because such aproias initiate metaphysical concepts of time and being eluding adequate definition. Therefore, even if one can take the metalepsis of intellectual history further than Heidegger did, one will find that even in such instances a metaphysical recovery becomes apparent.

Grundprobleme

Although Derrida has closely examined the implications of a note concerning time in *Being and Time,* he makes no mention of the conditions under which *Being and Time* were written, no attempt to recover that history concerning the abrogation or fragmentation of the treatise. Indeed, an adequate history of this subject has as yet to be outlined, but there is enough published material now to suggest that Heidegger had written extensive materials paralleling those included in *Being and Time* which offer much evidence enabling us either to corroborate or to disconfirm Derrida's intuitions based on his reading of a particular note. Of interest, too, is a recent essay by Thomas Sheehan, a somewhat conservative reader of Heidegger, who has documented the history of the composition of *Being and Time* as well as outlined the background notes on temporality which Heidegger was developing at about the period when he was completing *Being and Time* in 1926. The essay is very informative, given our interests, and it is entitled "'Time and Being,' 1925–1927."

Sheehan explains that one of the determining conditions for the shape of *Being and Time* was Heidegger's attempt to gain academic promotion at Marburg. It is a typical story of someone who has promised much but who had delivered very little in the way of publications, and thus when the question of Heidegger's promotion to Nicolai Hartmann's chair was raised, Professor Rudolf Wedekind wanted to know when Heidegger would publish work demonstrating his capacities as a philosopher. The controversy at Marburg over this issue forced *Being and Time* into print, though, oddly enough, even after the Ministry of Science, Art, and Education at Berlin had reviewed the proof pages submitted for the promotion in 1926, it had declared them "inadequate." As Sheehan says, Heidegger "had published *and* perished." More important, however, are these remarks: "He had rushed his 'long-guarded work' into print and in so doing had 'ventured forth too far too early,' perhaps chiefly in an effort to get a job. That venture was to block the fulfillment of his philosophical program for years to come."[13] Sheehan's hypothesis is that because of academic politics, Heidegger's reflections on being and time were prevented from developing gradually and ineluctably at their most critical and formative stages. Just at that point, then, when the radical temporal clue was to be formulated, the entire work upon which Heidegger had been reflecting was forced into print, hence rupturing the complex network of relationships that were steadily growing and transforming. And, of course, Heidegger was unable to recover what would have been his train of thought given the pressures and anxieties caused by the institution.

Sheehan's theory is very tempting, though it depends entirely upon a presupposition that philosophical thought is organic or developmental and therefore cannot recover when cut in the middle of its period of growth. Moreover, the theory Sheehan develops supposes more or less on faith that if Heidegger had been allowed to develop at his own pace, the project of *Being and Time* would have not resulted in a kind of philosophical blockage. Without doubt, the publication of one's work in book form does produce a sense of closure, even of a death of the text, which means for the author that its ideas become curiously inaccessible or remote. Psychologically, the book's publication may, indeed, have inhibited Heidegger from restoring his train of thought as developed in the parts of *Being and Time* which appeared. Yet, the publication of texts like *Basic Problems of Phenomenology* and *The Metaphysical Foundations of Logic* demonstrate not so much an estrangement from voice by writing—this is, essentially Sheehan's position—but, rather, a lengthy continuation of ideas in *Being and Time* which parallel the remarks Heidegger makes in the footnote studied by Derrida. More significantly, we are indeed able to anticipate analyses in later chapters of this study by saying that Heidegger's texts of the late 1920s disclose a certain "correspondence" of discourses on time in which "corresponding" temporality in its more radical Heideggerian formulations of the 1950s is already brought to pass. This is why Sheehan's very traditional historical approach to understanding the early Heidegger remains so very naive: it completely overlooks the linguistic or discursive relations of Heidegger's various texts on temporality as itself a manifold of temporal relations in which notions like development, chronology, telos, or history (in the familiar humanist sense) are invalidated and surpassed, even as their questioning the validity of Heidegger's own program is posed. The difficulty, of course, is in suspending the absolutism of the "difference" between a chronological or historical evaluation of Heidegger and a deconstructive analysis which, from the hitherside of concepts like history, chronology, and development or telos, would merely reject the historical as such. And this is why in our analyses we must often traffic between these two orientations whose "difference" is itself being put into jeopardy by Heidegger and then, much later, by Derrida.

We recall that *Being and Time* was to have two divisions, each containing three parts. What we have, of course, is only division 1 and parts 1 and 2. The last part of division 1 and all of division 2 were never written. Part 3 of division 1 was to be called "Time and Being," and in the first edition of *Being and Time* there is a cryptic footnote referring to division 1, part 3, chapter 2. Sheehan thinks this suggests Heidegger must have had at least an outline in mind when he wrote the footnote, though the materials for this have not turned up, probably because Heidegger destroyed drafts for the uncompleted work. But Heidegger and Max Müller had an exchange concerning the sketch for the missing part, an exchange which Müller later reconstructed. The new part, he said, was to contain a "turn" from being to time and was to be called "Time and Being," focusing on three kinds of "difference": (1) transcendental difference, the difference of entities and their beingness; (2) transcendence related difference, the difference of entities and their beingness from being; and (3) transcendent difference, the difference of Being and being. The project was to have importance in terms of considering the "horizon" of difference posed by the question of transcendence. In short, the sketch for the third part of division 1 was to have deconstructed ontic-ontological relations in terms of horizons of transcendence as posed by the question of time as the medium through which being is situated as becoming. Sheehan's conclusion is that Heidegger abandoned this project because he had come to a sudden realization that the project was too metaphysical in the classical sense of the term. In short, the sketch as reconstructed by Müller demonstrates the inadequacy as Heidegger himself perceived it of carrying through the itinerary of *Being and Time*. Indeed, this corroborates Derrida's suspicion that Heidegger had failed conceptually in the treatise, that his method at that time was not capable of supporting thinking beyond classical metaphysical limitations.[14]

Yet, from a Derridean perspective it is also (and perhaps simultaneously) likely that Heidegger resisted developing the sketch because of the inevitability of the deconstruction of the question of being through the rigorous deconstitution of metaphysical difference as it is posed in the horizons of temporal transcendence. *Basic Problems (Grundprobleme) of Phenomenology,* certainly, can be read as one exposition of the problematic of temporality which belongs to, even if it is not part of, *Being and Time.* In Heidegger's development of these lectures, the *Grundprobleme* contributes to the analysis of Dasein and time, which is to be found in 2.6 of *Being and Time,* "Temporality and the Within-Time-Ness As the Source of the Ordinary Conception of Time." And in itself *Basic Problems* leaves open the question of what to do with a much more radical theory of temporality as suggested in the sketch reconstructed by Müller. However, there is also *The Metaphysical Foundations of Logic* to be considered, which goes much further than *Being and Time* (2.6.81) in developing the more radical aspects of "ecstatico-horizonal temporality," even to the point, in fact, of making the turn reflected in Müller's reconstruction of the sketch outlined by Heidegger. In other words, whereas *Basic Problems* resists the sketch, *The Metaphysical Foundations of Logic* more or less embraces its impulses. The turn in Heidegger, then, from Dasein to Being simultaneously turns in two directions: toward and away from deconstruction.

Before considering how Heidegger moves toward deconstruction, I wish to discuss briefly *Basic Problems of Phenomenology,* the text which bears out Derrida's view that Heidegger is reluctant to engage the kind of temporal clue which will threaten the history of Western ontology. In *Basic Problems of Phenomenology* there are some obvious opportunities to reveal a destructive temporal clue which are curiously elided, and a reading of *Basic Problems* demonstrates, to a large extent, Derrida's correctness in his assumption in "Ousia et grammè" that, in fact, Heidegger is not only the philosopher who has most genuinely anticipated deconstruction but the philosopher who has also most vigorously resisted it.

We recall that in *Basic Problems* Heidegger elaborates and radicalizes Aristotle's notion of the now but situates it in words like "transition," "continuity," "following," and also "limit/nonlimit," "difference/identity." Heidegger's attempt is to establish the now as a proximity which does not take place between an ordinary notion of before and after but between an earlier and a later, what Heidegger sees as Aristotle's existential interpretation of the before and after. Proximity and distance support the familiar Heideggerian idea of Being as clearing and lighting. Also, this reading of "proximity" allows for a later analysis of time as a horizon for Dasein, a dimension or manifold through which Dasein understands itself as being in the world. Of interest is the way in which Heidegger develops the now as limit/nonlimit so that the now can be interpreted as number. And it is at this point that a crucial opportunity for deconstruction is missed and recovered in terms of an existential dimension of everyday experience, counting.

> The *now*—and that means time—is, says Aristotle, *by its essential nature not a limit,* because as transition and dimension it is open on the sides of the not-yet and the no-longer. The now is a limit, in the sense of a closing, of the finished, of the no-further, *only incidentally* with reference to something that ceases *in* a now and *at* a definite point of time. It is not the now that ceases as now; rather, the now as now is, by its essential nature, already the not-yet, already related as dimension to what is to come, whereas it can well be that a motion determined by the said now can cease in this now. With the aid of the now I can mark a limit, but the now as such does not have the character of a limit so far as it is taken within the continuum of time itself. *The now is not limit, but number,* not peras but arithmos. Aristotle explicitly contrasts time as arithmos with peras. The limits of something, he says, are what they are only in one with the being they limit. The limit of something belongs to the mode of being of the limited. This does not hold true for number. Number is not bound to what it numbers. Number can determine something without itself being dependent, for its part, on the intrinsic content and mode of being of what is counted.[15]

Were Heidegger a deconstructionist he would have pointed out that the now can disarticulate the limit as open/closed, since that now has been replaced by a mark, or number. Heidegger comes extremely close to Derridean analysis when he says above, "With the aid of the now I can mark a limit, but the now as such does not have the character of a limit so far as it is taken within the continuum of time itself." Indeed, the now as transition gives way to the mark that is the number. From Derrida's perspective it could be said that this number marks the undecidability (amply discussed by Heidegger above) between limited/unlimited, before/after, presence/absence. Moreover, the number is disseminating, dispersing into a signifying chain of marks or *traces* that stakes out a proximity to progression, regression, stasis. The number as mark can be interpreted in a Saussurean way, via "La différance," to call attention to the arbitrary as well as the differential. Mark as number thus announces "an irreducible and *generative* multiplicity," or set of positions.[16] The mark or number is *différance,* of course, though not *différance* in the sense of a master word, but as "pulled through" a series of moments, of disseminating traces, of numbers or figures. Since the number does not install itself as a presence in order to reify limits or oppositions, its effect is to deconstruct, or disseminate, the differences closure/openness, limited/unlimited, finitude/infinitude. Aristotle already has some awareness in *The Physics* about number as a mark without being, without enjoying full presence. But Heidegger turns away from that radical glance and recuperates number in terms of mere counting on the part of Dasein's existential projection into the world. Heidegger has merely an epistemological interest in finding out how Dasein comes to understand itself through the horizon of time as count, span, public time, and so on.

A Derridean reading of number as disseminating mark, as trace structure, would recall the analysis of *hama* in "Ousia et grammè," which is a plural and a single at the same time. *Hama* like number can play the signifier as clock time or the signified in terms of event or history, that is, as arithmetic (counting) and as topos (place), the *where* of time. As Derrida says, *hama* is both time and space, and yet it is neither of them. The same is true for Heidegger's mark of the now, termed number. Like *hama,* number does not really install itself as a presence in any signifying chain, does not represent itself, and yet it has an effect, a trace effect. In the following quotations from "Dissemination" Derrida talks about number, about a novel concerning numbers by Sollers entitled, fittingly, *Nombres*. And I cite these quotations as an oblique gloss.

> But these *Numbers* dismantle such a representation; they take it apart as one deconstructs a mechanism or as one disconcerts the self-assured pretensions of a claim. At the same time, in this very gesture, they assign a determinate place to what they take apart, granting it a relative position within the general movement of the apparatus.
> Et *coetera,* for everything in this text is generalized in sum. The *triggering* (which unclenches the teeth of discourse, loosens the teeth of the machine, allows the face to speak, feigns a frontal exposure, a face-to-face view, whereas it simultaneously entrains the face toward enumeration. . . .) You will be expected—let us mark it here in the hollow of a mute, invisible angle (about which more later)—to measure, to sum up, in a statistical accumulation of "quotations," the well-calculated, rhythmically regulated effects of a recurrence. Like the constraints of that angle, this accumulation will be the only means, not of presenting, but of feigning to present the text that, more than any other, writes and reads *itself,* presents its own reading, presents its own self-presentation, and constantly deducts this incessant operation.[17]

Here, too, number is spacing, installed in the relation of signifier/signified though not a part of them, what amounts to an alterity which unclenches the teeth, triggers or releases the clamps which enmesh oppositions and thus deconstructs and disseminates. Number feigns frontal exposure, is accumulation but not presence. Number pretends to present a text, to be a text, to be at all. Numbers present their own self-presentation though they constantly deduct this incessant operation.

Though it may be fantastic to gloss Heidegger's passage above on the now with this "reading" of Sollers's *Nombres,* it would have to be admitted that the kinds of readings which Heidegger would have had to make were he to have followed through with a so-called deconstructive project in *Being and Time* would have triggered or broached a disseminating discourse such as Derrida has written in *Dissemination*. Indeed, a careful reading of the kinds of passages I have excerpted from the essay on Sollers betray an immediate recognition that the kinds of statements Derrida makes are excessively Heideggerian, what Edward Said in "Abecedarium Culturae" identifies as a curious "inflation" or "exaggeration."[18] Indeed, the passages from "Dissemination" appear "surreal" and "grotesque" and yet their hyperbolic dimensions betray "an overaccurate relationship" which overwhelms and mocks their model, in this case, Heideggerian style. Yet, this inflation or dissemination is the consequence of philosophical disarticulation, and we will see it in the later Heidegger in terms of paronomasia.

Still the Heidegger of the *Basic Problems* is pulling back from such dire stylistic and philosophical consequences. In *Basic Problems,* Heidegger says that moments have span or range, and this is accessible to Dasein as a transcendental horizon in which our being comes to be, to stand forth. Time is ecstatic and ek-sistence transpires in that ec-stasis. Moreover, if Dasein is thrown into the ecstasis of time, then Dasein can come to understand itself only in time. Time is the horizon, then, through which understanding is brought about. Since Dasein has to project itself, to apprehend itself in the ecstatic horizon of temporality, and if in only this way understanding can be brought about, then one's understanding of ontology will necessarily be apprehended through the horizon of time; this is one's apprehension of how time conditions or mediates one's apprehension of Being. Time is thus the horizon through which Being is revealed. The effect of this interpretation of Dasein and time is hermeneutical closure. And clearly this construction belongs to the first half of *Being and Time*'s itinerary and not the last, in which Western ontology is destroyed.

At a later point in *Basic Problems* another deconstructive opportunity occurs, or at least an opportunity avails itself for a more radically unmetaphysical temporal theory than Heidegger posits. For even if Heidegger recuperates the possibility of number as dissemination with number as existential counting, as the existential apprehension of a moment for the sake of understanding being, Heidegger notices that with regard to Dasein, self-understanding opens up once more the possibility for a time theory that is not self-enclosed.

In resoluteness, that is, in self-understanding via its own most peculiar can-be—in this coming-toward itself from its own most peculiar possibility, the *Dasein* comes back to that which it is and takes itself over as the being that it is. In coming back to itself, it *brings* itself with everything that it is *back again* into its own most peculiar chosen can-be. The temporal mode to which it is as and what it *was* we call [bringing-back-again, that is] *repetition*.

[In der Entschlossenheit, d.h. im Sichverstehen aus dem eigensten Seinkönnen,—in diesem Zukommen auf sich selbst aus der eigensten Möglichkeit kommt das Dasein auf das, was es ist, zurück und übernimmt sich als das Seiende, das es ist. Im Zurückkommen auf sich selbst *holt* es sich mit all dem, was es ist, *wieder* in sein eigenstes ergriffenes Seinkönnen hinein. Der zeitliche Modus, in dem es, wie und was es *gewesen*, ist, nennen wir die *Wiederholung*.][19]

This repetition could be viewed as spacing, as *différance*, frustrating the decidability between same and different, self and other. This kind of repetition would broach a Nietzschean displacement as figured forth in the dynamics of the eternal return. Had Heidegger deconstructively taken up number at the previous juncture in *Basic Problems* it would be at this current point when repetition is being discussed that a deconstructive critique of time could be advanced by way of considering number and repetition as capable of disarticulating a purely teleological understanding of Dasein. Something similar, in fact, is undertaken by Gilles Deleuze in *Différence et répétition*, wherein both number and time are considered at some length in terms of perceptual or cognitive experiences that are defined through understanding the interrelations between repetitive and differential structures.[20] Deleuze hypothesizes that the "subject" is constituted according to an intratemporal manifold of relations wherein synthesis depends upon repeated identifications which are, in fact, threatened with difference. An organism's habits are largely attempts to codify repetition in order that the organism may achieve stability through repeated identification. Yet, these habits, themselves temporally connected, disclose differences that threaten a single noncontradictory identification. Although Deleuze develops his argument by way of epistemological investigations, he does broach certain ontological questions that parallel Heidegger's considerations in *Basic Problems,* namely, the relation of being to self-understanding. After reading Deleuze, one may well conclude that if Heidegger had bothered to think through the question of repetition more carefully he might have been able to develop much further the second half of the design of *Being and Time.* It is clear, however, that in the passage above on repetition Heidegger is not concerned with displacement but homecoming, the congruence of the "it is" with the "what it was." Again, as Friedrich Wilhelm von Herrmann, German editor of the *Grundprobleme,* points out, Heidegger resists the more radical perspective broached by his phenomenological and existential project, such as it was worked out in advance in *Being and Time*; he resituates or neutralizes what would have been opportunities for destruction in the arms of Western tradition.

If we consider *The Metaphysical Foundations of Logic,* however, the existential recovery of temporality appears less firm than in *Basic Problems,* as if in *The Metaphysical Foundations of Logic* Heidegger were examining the problematic of time from outside of Dasein and in fact turning toward a deconstruction of being by means of an examination of temporality. Indeed, *The Metaphysical Foundations of Logic* could be said merely to elaborate section 81 of *Being and Time* 2.6, yet the seminar on foundations goes much further in terms of the sketch noted by Sheehan which Heidegger had related to Max Müller, since these ancillary remarks by Heidegger demonstrate rather clearly a remarkable turn from the problematic of Dasein seen from the existential perspective of Dasein to that problematic as constituted from the perspective of a Being in the "being beyond" of Dasein's being. Certainly, the materials on time in *The Metaphysical Foundations of Logic* are crucial, if only because they make possible the path from *Being and Time* to the much discussed "ontological difference" which is developed in *The Essence of Reasons,* yet another text composed in the late 1920s. Together, *The Essence of Reasons* and *The Metaphysical Foundations of Logic* make up that more radical horizon from which

Heidegger can be said to have turned toward a deconstructive moment.

In *The Metaphysical Foundations of Logic,* the section entitled "Transcendence and Temporality" is mainly concerned with an interpretation of time from the perspective of Dasein's ek-stasis.

> We must learn to see how *Dasein,* on the basis of its metaphysical constitution, on the basis of being-in-the-world, is always in its very possibility already beyond all beings. And in this being-beyond it does not come up against absolute nothingness. Rather, on the contrary, in this very being-beyond *Dasein* holds before itself the binding commitment as world. [. . .] Now we have the task of understanding temporality with regard to this basic phenomenon of transcendence.[21]

In *The Metaphysical Foundations of Logic* time is interrogated in terms of Dasein's being beyond being, its ek-stasis wherein time is disclosed. Heidegger considers everyday anticipations or expectations as incipient awarenesses that our being is constituted not in a temporality of finite moments but as a temporalization which exceeds our linguistic senses of tense. "This means that time 'is' not, but rather temporalizes itself." And, "thus every attempt to fit time into any sort of being-concept must necessarily falter."[22] With respect to Dasein's consciousness of time, Heidegger writes, "What we called expecting [*Gewärtigen*] is nothing other than that getting-carried-away [*Entrückung*] into the then-quality which lies at the basis of those comportments, which has previously already overleapt all possible beings about which we can and must say, they will be 'then.'"[23]

Such conclusions reflect Heidegger's bringing into proximity Dasein's transcendence or "being beyond" with the temporality of a moment such as the "then." Certainly, as in *Basic Problems,* time is approached from the perspective of Dasein's experience as that which is capable of going beyond itself, the "stepping out of itself." Indeed, Dasein becomes expectant or anticipatory not because it must pass serially through temporal moments but because it "goes gradually through the open path made way by the raptus of temporality itself." Temporality, in this sense, is defined as "the self-unifying ecstatic unity in ecstatic temporalization."[24] That is, temporality is that manifold of moments into which Dasein comes by means of its capacity to be ahead of itself, a manifold of moments through which Dasein is itself declared as existing being. While maintaining an existential perspective Heidegger writes, "Expectance means to understand oneself from out of one's own capacity-for-being: one's own capacity for being is in turn understood in the essential metaphysical breadth to which belong being-with and being-by." An incipient "structuralism" is already under way in Heidegger to the degree that Dasein is defined in terms of how it is constituted within a manifold of relationships: being-with, and being-by. "Expecting one's own capability-for-being as mine, I have also come toward myself already and precisely through expecting. This approaching oneself in advance, from one's own possibility, is the primary ecstatic concept of the *future*."[25] In other words, my capability for being as myself arrives from a moment beyond my finitude as given in a temporal horizon beyond my being. But it is precisely through my capacity to expect or await that such an understanding of human being is possible. Heidegger has outlined only one temporal horizon, in this instance, and he will outline others, moving toward a discussion of the unification of all these ecstatic horizons which is itself ecstatic or transcendent. "The essence of time," according to Heidegger, "lies in the ecstatic unitary oscillation," an oscillation of temporal horizons which "belong" to a peculiar "unity of time." This leads Heidegger to consider that "it is therefore essential, in first defining the unity of temporality, to eliminate the notion of anything thing-like, present on hand, which is between, as it were, having-been-ness and the future. Nor should one smuggle in any sort of personal center, an I-nucleus, but the essence of time lies in the ecstatic unitary oscillation."[26]

If one were looking for an early text concerning what has become well known as "decentering," it might be well to cite this passage from *The Metaphysical Foundations of Logic*. My point, of course, is that in this interpretation of temporality, more or less simultaneous with that of *Basic Problems*, it appears that Heidegger is already abandoning the metaphysical, or humanist, notion of "man." In fact, many of the points made much later in a text such as "Zeit und Sein" can already be glimpsed in this very suggestive section from *The Metaphysical Foundations of Logic,* particularly the "giving" of time within a manifold of moments which cannot be reduced to notions of presence or of the "is." What Heidegger discovers is that Dasein as well as world are constituted in that interpretive unity of temporal horizons as seen from the perspective of an "ecstatic momentum" whose ground is not consciousness, nor being in the Aristotelian sense, nor Dasein as I-nucleus. Rather it is the possibility of a temporalization of temporality in terms of which transcendence comes to play such a fundamental role that to conceive of mere finite selfhood or subjecthood as even a fundamental structure in the investigation of being and time becomes quite absurd. In this sense, Heidegger succeeds in completing, perhaps more satisfactorily than in *Being and Time,* the first moment of that treatise's itinerary: "the interpretation of Dasein in terms of temporality, and the explication of time as the transcendental horizon for the question of Being." That is, *The Metaphysical Foundations of Logic* bears on the turning by means of which Dasein in its going beyond itself allows us to reinterpret its significance, indeed, its beinghood, from the perspective of what lies beyond its finitude, hence utterly evacuating Dasein of those very notions which are needed in order to comprehend the turn from Dasein to time as that transcendental horizon from which Dasein is itself to be redefined. It could be said that whereas *Being and Time* goes beyond the phenomenological vocabulary which is reflected in its draft, published in English as *History of the Concept of Time,* *The Metaphysical Foundations of Logic* goes beyond the existential vocabulary of *Being and Time* as well as of *Basic Problems.* In fact, it is itself superseded by a text written at approximately the same time as the others entitled *The Essence of Reasons,* in which transcendence is recontextualized in terms of "ontological difference," the difference between Being and beings, which, as is well known, Heidegger was thinking about while writing *Being and Time.*

Evidently, not unlike Derrida, Heidegger was a thinker who

produced many texts written more or less simultaneously, writing, as it were, beyond himself and in his wake at the same instant. Indeed, this feature of Heidegger's earlier work deserves lengthier treatment than I can give it here, but I mention it if only to suggest that in *The Metaphysical Foundations of Logic* we glimpse a text that exposes in Heidegger himself a countermovement to what one might expect, that is to say, a text which pursues a reading of being and time that goes against our expectations, a reading which Heidegger may not have been inclined to integrate in *Being and Time* but which, nevertheless, suffices as a fragment indicating the need to read Heidegger as a philosopher who developed his early thought by way of the variation, even to the point of arguing two sides—that of being, that of time—toward the middle. Still, even *The Metaphysical Foundations of Logic* does by no means bring to fruition the second part of *Being and Time*'s itinerary, that moment in which a temporal clue is sighted through which the history of ontology is destroyed. Rather, *The Metaphysical Foundations of Logic* ends with the recognition that the existential problematic that is Dasein must be subjected to a revaluation from the perspective of transcendence that reorients our understanding of time as that oscillation or movement of horizonality without which being-in-the-world cannot be properly thought. In so doing, *The Metaphysical Foundations of Logic* accomplishes that part of the sketch reconstructed by Max Müller which calls for the deconstitution of ontic-ontological relations as posed from within metaphysics by means of interrogating horizons of transcendence where time is revealed as an ecstatic oscillation or temporalization not recoverable under the aegis of an "I-nucleus," "presence," or "Being." This strongly departs from the Aristotelian logic that time must be nothing if it is not something; for, Heidegger is saying that time is neither something nor nothing even if it is the condition without which it would be impossible to talk about that which is and is not.

In *The Essence of Reasons* (*Vom Wesen des Grundes*, 1929), Heidegger develops the analysis of transcendence in the seminar on logic at length, developing the notion of transcendence as a stepping beyond, or *Überstieg*, which Maurice Blanchot later will translate as *le pas au-delà*, the step/not beyond. *Über-*

stiegen is a moment breaking with noncontradiction to the extent that a stepping beyond is both enacted and canceled in its taking place as a condition for Dasein.

> Transcendent *Dasein* (a tautological expression in itself) surpasses neither a "boundary" which stretches out before the subject and forces it to "remain in" (immanence) nor a "gap" which separates it from the object. Moreover, objects—objectified beings—are not that *toward which* surpassing happens. *What* is surpassed is simply *being itself*, i.e., every being which can be or become unconcealed to *Dasein, even and precisely* the very being as which *Dasein* "itself" exists.

> [Dann übersteigt aber das transzendente *Dasein* (ein bereits tautologischer Ausdruck) weder eine dem Subjekt vorgelagerte und es zuvor zum Inbleiben (Immanenz) zwingende "Schranke," noch eine "Kluft," die es vom Objekt trennt. Die Objekte— das vergegenständlichte Seiende—sind aber auch nicht das, *woraufzu* der Überstieg geschieht. *Was* überstiegen wird, ist gerade einzig das *Seiende selbst* und zwar jegliches Seiende, das dem *Dasein* unverborgen sein und werden kann, mithin *auch und gerade* das Seiende, als welches "es selbst" existiert.]

Heidegger continues a bit further:

> Only in and through surpassing can we distinguish and decide, within the realm of being, who and how a "self" is and what it is not.

> [Im Überstieg und durch ihn kann sich erst innerhalb des Seienden unterscheiden und entscheiden, wer und wie ein "Selbst" ist und was nicht.][27]

This statement bears on the notion of being as that which is present-to-itself-as-such-and-such. Certainly, there is more than an implication in these statements that Heidegger considers not only being in general but being as Dasein, that is to say, a Dasein essentially constituted in moments of transcendence, of *Überstieg* or a logic of threshold which, even more than in the lectures on logic, serves to de-center a Cartesian sense of self as well as the Husserlian notion of a "transcendental ego." This working through of transcendence as *Überstieg* or *pas au-delà* not only subverts a Cartesian sense of selfhood whose reductiveness would make the notion of transcendence one of mere difference but radicalizes even further the Husserlian notion of "transcendental ego," which is still confident within the parameters of logic within which difference itself is an essential concept. Heidegger's discussion of transcendence in *The Essence of Reasons* delimits a boundary wherein the difference between difference and identity is thoroughly threatened, and it appears that such an understanding of transcendence as "undecidable" threshold well anticipates Derrida's program of deconstruction, reviewed at the end of this chapter, which considers thought from the perspectives of the undecidable limit: inside/outside. Although Heidegger is still considering Dasein in *The Essence of Reasons,* it is a Dasein which always exceeds itself even as it lags behind; it is a Dasein which always already surpasses a boundary which stretches out in front of itself, accedes to a limit/nonlimit in terms of which the values upon which a classical notion of the subject is disarticulated.

Evidently, in Heidegger this disarticulation of the metaphysical subject concerns nothing less than temporality: "We should note that even the principles of identity and contraction are not merely 'also transcendental' but refer back to something more primordial, something which does not have the character of a principle but belongs to the happening of transcendence as such, namely, temporality."[28] It is, in other words, through the question of time that *übersteigen* has to be thought in its most radical sense as that transcendental moment in which Dasein comes to know itself as groundless, what Heidegger calls the *Ab-grund des Daseins*: "While surpassing being in projecting its world, *Dasein* must surpass itself in order, from this height, to be able to understand *itself* as groundless. [Aber das *Dasein* muss im weltentwerfenden Überstieg des Seienden sich selbst übersteigen, um *sich* aus dieser Erhöhung allererst als Abgrund verstehen zu können."][29] Heidegger will conclude that the essence of reason is manifested in the always already of the *Überstieg,* through which Dasein discloses itself as the freedom through which reasons or grounds are posited. "Das Wesen der Endlichkeit des *Daseins* enthüllt sich aber in der *Transzendenz als der Freiheit zum Grunde.*" The notion of man (*der Mensch*) is nothing less than that of a creature of distance, "ein Wesen [essence] der Ferne." And mankind's relation to being is problematic precisely because this distance cannot be abstracted and determined ahead of our capacity to posit it within our own existence, our existential experience of being. And yet, if Heideggerian transcendence takes from us precisely those metaphysical categories by means of which we are enabled to think our experience as being of such and such, how are we supposed to proceed existentially? It is this question the later papers on aesthetics and literature attempt to answer through the close investigation of how we are constituted with respect to the problematic of language. And it is there, as we will see in the next chapter, that temporality is raised in an extremely radical and deconstructive sense which can only be hardly glimpsed in *Vom Wesen des Grundes.*

The Ends of Man

In "The Letter on Humanism," Heidegger remarked that the section "Time and Being" of *Being and Time* was held back because "thinking failed in the adequate saying of this turning [*Kehre*] and did not succeed with the help of the language of metaphysics."[30] David Krell cites this passage in *Intimations of Mortality: Time, Truth, and Finitude in Heidegger's Thinking of Being* as Heidegger's admission of having failed to develop a language capable to think through the question of time. In fact, what Heidegger is addressing in "The Letter" concerns the "understanding of Being" as " 'the existential analysis' of Being in the world," "as the ecstatic relation to the lighting of Being." It is the understanding of this relation, Heidegger says, which is "made more difficult by the fact that in the publication of *Being and Time* the third division of the first part, 'Time and Being,' was held back."[31] In other words, what concerns Heidegger is the turn from being to time as a turn which would occur in the movement from Dasein to Being. Again, it appears that temporality as such can be discussed only in terms of the ontic-ontological.

Krell's *Intimations of Mortality* advances a rather important though sketchy reading of the early Heidegger with respect to the project on time. Essentially, Krell notices that during the writing of *Being and Time* Heidegger struggled with the question of time as the a priori of Being, which is to say, time as that which comes prior to any thinking about the origination of being, presence, thereness. Before one can begin to consider any ontological category, is there not, a priori, a sense of time without which ontology cannot be thought? And does not the "recollection" of Being require an a priori notion of time without which Being cannot be re-membered? Krell cites the relevant passage from Heidegger's Marburg lectures: "To what extent does temporality make the understanding of Being in general possible? To what extent is Time as temporality the horizon of the explicit understanding of Being as such, insofar as it is to become the theme of the science of ontology, which is to say, of scientific philosophy?"[32] What immediately appeared to Heidegger as devastating for his project was the realization that from this perspective any thinking of time parallels the Augustinian assumption that time is the "source" for our comprehension of Being and that, as such, it is the eternal ground, indeed, eternity itself, upon which ontology must be based. Heidegger's subsequent reworkings of phenomenology, ontology, transcendence, and language become a means by which to subvert the protocols of time as an eternal and a priori concept which determines the categories of ontology. Heidegger's *Essence of Reasons* is particularly important in this respect, because it suggests that Heidegger was able to subvert a theological or metaphysical notion of time by means of thinking through the "difference" between beings and Being. That is, Heidegger's consideration of the question of ontological difference necessarily affects the priority of an Augustinian notion of time which is itself inherited from Plato. Instead of the a priori of time, something which Kant still maintains, Heidegger discusses time in terms of the *immer schon,* or "always already," which reflects priority not as a given that exists ab-originally but as what Derrida in *Of Grammatology* calls a "trace structure," that is to say, a ground without ground, or a priority without determinable priority. It is by way of the ontological difference, then, that Heidegger moves away from the priority of time, subordinates temporality to questions pertaining to being and Being. This subordination could be said to mark a necessary failure in the project that is *Being and Time* crucial for the overcoming of a metaphysics conditioned by theological presuppositions, namely, time as eternity, a priori, or ground. It is interesting that Derrida never entertains this possibility which, as we have implicitly noticed, is quite evident in *The Metaphysical Foundations of Logic.*

In "The Ends of Man," Derrida discusses Heidegger's turn against an anthropological existentialism as outlined in "The Letter on Humanism" and argues that Heidegger actually allows such an anthropology to recover or reclaim Dasein. "Everything transpires as if one had to reduce the ontological distance acknowledged in *Being and Time* and to state the proximity of Being to the essence of man."³³ That is, Derrida suspects that the temptation of an existential anthropology is never eluded by Heidegger's meditations on language, ontological difference, or the "turn." Certainly, such a reading is not meant to disqualify Heidegger's remarks in "The Letter on Humanism" about humanism and French existentialism; rather, such a reading delimits a resistance which turns the Heideggerian enterprise toward existential and anthropological concerns. Yet, in Heidegger's writings of the 1920s, and especially in works such as *Basic Problems,* it is evident that Heidegger's philosophical project is, even in its increasing orientation toward a consideration of the difference between being and Being, recovering itself in terms of an existential anthropology which precludes the uncovering of a radical temporal clue. Derrida suggests this condition of Heideggerian discourse continues throughout Heidegger's career, and in *De l'esprit* he suggests it has unfortunate political consequences.

In a long footnote to "The Ends of Man," Derrida specifically refers to temporality. It is important to keep in mind that not long before the footnote citation, Derrida writes:

> Whence, in Heidegger's discourse, the dominance of an entire metaphorics of proximity, of simple and immediate presence, a metaphorics associating the proximity of Being with the values of neighboring, shelter, house, service, guard, voice, and listening. As goes without saying, this is not an insignificant rhetoric [. . . .] Several exam-

ples of this language, so surely connoted by its inscription in a certain landscape: "But if man is to find his way once again into the nearness of Being (*in die Nähe des Seins*), he must first learn to exist in the nameless." "The statement 'The "substance" of man is eksistence' says nothing else but that the way that man in his proper essence (*in seinem eigenen Wesen*) becomes present to Being (*zum Sein anwest*) is ecstatic inherence in the truth of Being."[34]

Derrida's point in the footnote is that just as the metaphorics of proximity delimits a notion of "man" as the horizon within which Dasein is ultimately to be considered—"we can see then that Dasein, though *not* man, is nevertheless *nothing other* than man"[35]—the metaphorics of temporality even in the later Heidegger will disclose a similar anthropological recovery thanks to a rhetoric of proximity which Derrida excerpts at length from the essay "Zeit und Sein." Terms such as "four-dimensionality," "nearhood," "delivering over," and "appropriation" are all indices for Derrida that Heidegger's attempt to make a turn from being to time through a lengthy interrogation of Dasein cannot succeed, since this notion of Dasein carries along with it an attachment to the "ends of man" whose consequence is a metaphorics of proximity wherein "man" is at once, to recall a later Derridean reading of Freud, *fort!* and *Da!* Again, as in "Ousia et grammè" and "La différance," Derrida sees a missed opportunity for deconstruction, since in "The Ends of Man" it is Heidegger's attachments to an anthropological existentialism which survives the very critique by means of which such an existentialism is surpassed or deconstituted, resulting in a humanism beyond humanism, or man beyond man. Heidegger invokes it when he writes, "Such standing in the lighting of Being I call the ek-sistence of man. This way of Being is proper only to man." Derrida argues that it is the "security of the near" which deconstruction may threaten in its critique of notions like belongingness, co-propriety, or the name of man and the name of Being.[36] Incidentally, this remark about the name could, if we let it, embark us on a lengthy analysis of texts like *Glas* or *Signéponge,* which can be read as glosses on this critique of Heideggerian proximities. For it is under the auspices of such Heideggerian thematics that the "end of man" can be viewed as always having been a key to the rhetoric of metaphysics.

> In the thinking and the language of Being, the end of man has been prescribed since always, and this prescription has never done anything but modulate the equivocality of the *end,* in the play of *telos* and death. In the reading of this play, one may take the following sequence in all its senses: the end of man is the thinking of Being, man is the end of the thinking of Being, the end of man is the end of the thinking of Being. Man, since always, is his proper end, that is, the end of his proper. Being, since always, is its proper end, that is, the end of its proper.[37]

This conclusion leads to one of Derrida's most well known outlines of deconstruction as philosophical method. Unlike Heidegger, whose hermeneutical interrogation of the "truth of Being" is recovered as humanism, even in its surpassing of classical conceptual structures which underwrite humanist metaphysics, Derrida proposes to effect a "radical trembling" from the "outside," from "the violent relationship of the whole of the West to its other," as well as from the inside, "a deconstruction without changing terrain, by repeating what is implicit in the founding concepts and the original problematic, by using against the edifice the instruments or stones available in the house, that is, equally, in language."[38] If the inside easily accommodates itself to what is outside (the different), hence turning deconstruction into a texture of "false exits," a deconstruction by means of staying on the same terrain (the identical) and repeating what is implicit risks recovery or recuperation of that which one deconstructs. Yet, effecting both a deconstruction from inside (homogeneity) and outside (heterogeneity) will serve to destabilize those identifications produced from within the system—recoveries, repetitions, *Aufhebungen*—as well as topple those easily established differences produced by stepping outside the system. That is, inside (the terrain illuminating identities) and outside (the terrain illuminating differences) become metaphors which deconstruct, by means of posing a radically undecidable logic, a landscape of philosophical proximities which Heidegger produced in order to recover the very humanism he had supposedly abandoned.

In a final volley, Derrida invokes Nietzsche's Zarathustra as the "man" who is destroyed as "man" in the overcoming of "man." Zarathustra is the one who can think the end of man from beyond man. Zarathustra is himself at once on the inside and the outside of the "humanist" question regarding man. And Derrida insists that it is "we" in May of 1968 ("but who, we?") who stand between these two men and in whose standing the temporality of the end is deconstructed in the undecidability of what it means to talk about "man" and "ends," given a metaphor or prosopopoeia undecidably inside and outside of that system, always already defaced, wherein the concept of man can be thought at all.[39] Yet, is not this proposition precisely what Heidegger had already posed in *The Essence of Reasons,* that of "man's" *Überstieg,* of a "transcendence" in which the "limits" of "man" are at once established and disestablished in the very step (not) beyond, what Maurice Blanchot calls *le pas au-delà* of *le dernier homme?*

In "The Ends of Man" Derrida completely ignores *The Essence of Reasons,* though perhaps for a good reason, since Derrida was largely interested in demystifying the recovery of humanism in Heidegger by way of advancing what in the late 1960s was a major theoretical position: that of grammatology. Derrida's assumption was that grammatology (the deconstructive study of writing as that which posits itself as *différance* with regard to voice) would serve as a sort of linguistic turn even more radical than Heidegger's own considerations of language in texts like Hölderlin's "Andenken," because the metaphysics of voice, which Heidegger's vocabulary of proximity delimits, inscribes an "attachment" to being that is mediated by residues of thought determined from within the discourse of a phenomenology unable to abandon entirely a Cartesian cogito. It is quite interesting, however, that by the mid-1970s Derrida begins to move away from the strictness of the grammatological departure toward a more accommodating stance mediated, in large part, by Blanchot, who facilitates a way to the existential from the hitherside of deconstruction. Indeed, Derrida's interest in texts like Blanchot's *Le dernier homme, La folie du jour,* and *L'arrêt de mort* brings us back to the Heideggerian "turn" within ontological difference as it is posited from the perspectives of a transcendence or *Überstieg* with decided existential overtones concerning the destiny or "ends" of man.

Together, "Ousia et grammè," "La différance," and "The Ends of Man" make up three very distinct though closely related critiques of Heidegger's failure to develop the radical temporal clue announced at the outset of *Being and Time*. In "Ousia et grammè" Derrida maintains that Heidegger was unable to unearth in Aristotle the more radical aspects of *hama* and, in the margins, critiques Heidegger's "Anaximander Fragment" for not taking further the relation between ontological difference and language. "La différance," more pointedly, "supplies" (with all the senses that "supplementation" has in *Of Grammatology*) the radical temporal clue which Heidegger himself resisted and demonstrates how that clue is given in the question of ontological/temporal differentiation. In "The Ends of Man," Derrida delimits the recovery of humanism at that point when Heidegger meditates on the "end" of man or the "being beyond" of Dasein. Like the early Heideggerian texts which bear on the concerns of Dasein, even the later discourses on temporality remain tied to notions of transcendence whose limit is this "end" as disclosed by Derrida's analysis. Hence, in the essays on Heidegger of the late 1960s, Derrida believes that the much discussed "turn" in Heidegger does not quite take place even as it is announced and that metaphysics superseded it in its very arrival on the Heideggerian landscape of proximate terms.

However, as we will notice in the chapters that follow, Derrida will himself engage the vocabulary of proximities in the "later" Heidegger—for example, in the "Viens" or "E-loignement" developed in "Pas," not to say the *retrait* of metaphor in "The Retrait of Metaphor"—and by the 1980s Derrida will make a decided rapprochement with the very existential horizon in Heidegger that "The Ends of Man" appears to deprecate so strongly. That this rapprochement comes in terms of autobiography, the love letter, or telepathic message is indeed quite surprising when one considers the antipathy to Heidegger's existential recoveries cited in the 1960s. Yet, as I have noted, the change or turning in Derrida's own thought occurs, perhaps, because of Maurice Blanchot, a figure who does not become well known until the 1970s. And it is to Blanchot and his mediations of Heidegger that we ourselves soon turn.

THREE

PARONOMASIA

It is true that the work of Blanchot has been very
decisive for me. At first, by attaching myself especially
to Blanchot's so-called critical or theoretical text, I
thought I had introjected, interiorized, assimilated
Blanchot's contribution and had brought it to bear in
my work, although obviously in another language. In
a certain way, I thought I had read Blanchot. And
then, rather recently, a few years ago, I read what I
had never managed to read in a way which was at
bottom—how shall I say?—an experience.
—J. Derrida, *The Ear of the Other*

*I*n the lectures grouped under the title *Logik,*
Heraklits Lehre vom Logos in the *Gesamtaus-*
gabe, Martin Heidegger takes up the concept
of man as "animal rationale," or *vernünftige*
Lebewesen, arguing that it is the metaphysical essence of man's
destiny. "From within it the man who stands under the mastery
of metaphysics speaks his essence."[1] The notion that man is
determined or singled out because he possesses reason or logic
is one of the chief arguments that these lectures set out to
dismantle during the years 1943–1944. Given the thorough
disarticulation of the metaphysical subject or ego that made up
Being and Time one might wonder why Heidegger would have
interpreted the fragments of Heraclitus in order to demonstrate what had already been brilliantly executed so many years
earlier with respect to the Heideggerian formulation of Dasein.
In *Heraklit* we find that, instead of emphasis on Dasein as an
existential entity for which there is necessarily a world in which
it can come to understand itself as there in relation to Being,
Heidegger turns to a close linguistic analysis of Heraclitus's
Greek in order to drive wedges into what has come down to us
as a unified formulation, the notion of *logos* = logic = reason =

will to power = essence of humankind. As in his seminar on Anaximander of 1941, Heidegger is particularly interested in how pre-Socratic words evade what we normally think of as logical relationships which are part of a cultural formation that we see very clearly at work in the dialogues of Plato and the writings of Aristotle, wherein the principle of contradiction plays such an important role. Heidegger's attempt in the Heraclitus lectures is to demonstrate that, in fact, the *logos* of Heraclitus is not at all logical in the ancient metaphysical contexts of techne, ethics, and physics, which Heidegger views as logocentric. Rather, the *logos* is itself a saying wherein other words can be heard, as if the *logos* were not a term but a sound structure against which other words come out of what Heidegger calls concealment.

Hence, *logos* gives rise to the word *legein*, which means saying aloud. "*Legein,* or in Latin *legere,* is the same as our word '*lesen,*' but not that '*lesen*' which occupies us so often with writing and thus the written word or once again talk and language."[2] Rather, *lesen* is to be understood in the broader and more original sense of *die Ähren auf dem Acker lesen* or *das Holz lesen im Wald,* that is, picking ears up from the fields or taking up wood in the forest. *Logos,* in other words, has to be comprehended in terms of gathering or collecting, and for Heidegger the word *logos* is itself a site where other terms are brought together or gathered even as they fall away as one term comes to stand for another. Unlike the metaphysical notion of logic in which only absolutely necessary entities are all saved and systematized, the *logos* of Heraclitus is a much more open field in which there occurs *Ver-Sammlung* (appropriation and disappropriation). The significance of this view for a conception of humankind is that Heidegger views "man," or *anthropos,* not as a controlling ego whose essence is reason or logic, but as *Ver-Sammlung,* a collection of closely related attributes that in their proximity to one another have achieved both nearness and distance. If these attributes are in close proximity, however, they are not this way because of any essential reason or logic that dictates this to be the case. Rather, these relations have occurred according to the way in which *logos* as gathering or collecting has been enacted over time. Hence the ancient Greeks already noticed attributes such as the following: *zoon* (life), *psyche* (mind), and *physis* (body). The "subject" is, like the term *logos* itself, a space, or openness, where such attributes are gathered or appropriated or brought into "its letting lie together" even as this relation is subjected to disappropriation or destruction (*das Aus-holen*) for the sake of the subject's making itself "deep."

Unlike the later essay "Logos (Heraclitus, Fragment B 50)," from *Vortträge und Aufsätze,* the seminars on Heraclitus from the early 1940s stress much more the disappropriation of the subject as that which resists coming to be as an integral unity whose essence is *logos.* Rather, this subject is viewed more and more in the seminars from the perspective of those words which are appropriated and disappropriated in the field of the *logos,* which is itself linguistic. This suggests that a notion like "man" is constituted in the verbal slippages of *logos, legein, logike, lexos, loxos,* and *alego,* slippages whose logic is not reducible to the ratios of metaphysical speculation whose verbal economy obeys principles of conceptual conservation.

Of special interest in these lectures is that we can begin to see how Heidegger made a turn from the Analytic of Dasein in his earlier writings to that of Being in the later works and how this turn occurs in the analysis of language, wherein there is a metaleptic movement from one term to another. In the Heraclitus seminars particularly, although Heidegger considers the metaphysical notion of man, he quickly shifts emphasis onto the gathering of words within fundamental pre-Socratic terms and thus reconceptualizes the notion of man as a set of proximate relations that under the aegis of words like *logos* discloses particular orientations to Being. Whereas in studies like *Being and Time* Dasein comes to understand itself in relation to Being through the thereness of other entities and its own Being-in-the-world, in *Heraklit* the saying of *logos,* wherein human being is articulated, comes from the side of Being as it is given in the metaleptic language of the pre-Socratics.

In "The Letter on Humanism" (1947) Heidegger formulates this turn in the following well-known passage:

> Thinking accomplishes the relation of Being to the essence of man. It does not make or cause the relation. Thinking brings this relation to Being solely as something

handed over to it from Being. Such offering consists in the fact that in thinking Being comes to language. Language is the house of Being. In its home man dwells. Those who think and those who create with words are the guardians of this home. Their guardianship accomplishes the manifestation of Being insofar as they bring the manifestation to language and maintain it in language through their speech.

[Das Denken vollbringt den Bezug des Seins zum Wesen des Menschen. Es macht und bewirkt diesen Bezug nicht. Das Denken bringt ihn nur als das, was ihm selbst vom Sein übergeben ist, dem Sein dar. Dieses Darbieten besteht darin, dass im Denken das Sein zur Sprache kommt. Die Sprache ist das Haus des Seins. In ihrer Behausung wohnt der Mensch. Die Denkenden und Dichtenden sind die Wächter dieser Behausung. Ihr Wachen ist das Vollbringen der Offenbarkeit des Seins, insofern sie diese durch ihr Sagen zur Sprache bringen und in der Sprache aufbewahren.]³

Certainly this turn from the perspective of Dasein to that of Being transpires, as Paul Ricoeur has said, "on the level of the philosophy of language and no longer on the level of an analytic of *Dasein*."⁴ The English translation cannot easily show that *Sprache* functions in the German like *logos* does in the Greek of Heraclitus: for *Sprache* is a manifold or field wherein we are to pick up or glean proximate entities that are not bound by any essential logic. *Sprache* itself houses the following terms: speech, language, style, expression, idiom, voice, and, more rarely, what has been written. In "The Letter on Humanism," *Sprache,* not unlike *logos,* is the place where guardians of thought gather what lies-together-before. As gatherers of what lies-together-before the guardians will emerge as sages. This is not because the sages gather ready-made concepts but because they see into the relations of words to one another. Anticipating the structuralists, Heidegger maintains that "man" is preceded by language and that concepts like "man" or "cogito" impede philosophical reflection, because they stress an internalization of thought wherein subtle linguistic differences are compressed into general concepts or denotations convenient for a world in which action takes precedence over reflection, and particularly reflection on the question of Being. In "The Letter on Humanism" philosophy is the intensive study of how these terms are gathered by the listener for whom *Sprache* is a network of "correspondences" by means of which terms are let-to-lie-together-before. As in "The Anaximander Fragment," Heidegger stresses the transference or metalepsis between texts—in this instance, those terms gathered under the term *Sprache*. As such, *Sprache* is the medium wherein our relation to Being can be heard, though not simply as speech or voice, nor merely as writing or grammar, but as tuned correspondence. To gather what is laid down in the letting-lie-together of words is to enact the guardianship of language, to recognize language as a dwelling of Being.

An important feature of "The Letter on Humanism," *Heraklit,* and the essay "Logos" is the decided turn to the rhetorical figure of paronomasia (i.e., *logos, legein, logike, lexis*). Specialists in Heidegger's philosophy have not overlooked this feature in Heidegger's work. Erasmus Schöfer, in "Heidegger's Language: Metalogical Forms of Thought and Grammatical Specialties," discusses its significance in the context of the following definition in which he says paronomasia is "a stringing of words of different word types which, however, belong to the same word stem." Schöfer argues that Heidegger used paronomasia in order to give "intellectual objects" variation and hence to shift their aspects or appearances. Thanks to paronomasia, language is capable of turning an object around and around. "In view of this, Heidegger is able specifically to illuminate the structures found within the phenomenon in question—for example, the question (*die Frage*), the questioning (*das Fragen*), what is asked in a question (*das Gefragte*), the putting a question to (*das Anfragen*), that which is questioned about what is asked in the question (*das Befragte*), the questioner (*der Frager*)."[5] Schöfer fails to recognize, however, that paronomasia is especially significant in terms of how Heidegger realizes a radical temporal clue from within language itself, that is, from the perspective of the signifier rather than the signified. Schöfer does so because he has overlooked the possibility of a linguistic turn which goes beyond mere rhetorical troping. Schöfer therefore ignores the Heideggerian dissolution of the subject in the advent of *Sprache* or *logos,* wherein thought occurs as the "espacement" of paronomasic slippages. Given this "espacement," questions of identity and difference bearing on both space and time are drastically resituated and bring about the turn in the itinerary of *Being and Time* where the dismantling of Western ontology becomes thinkable.[6]

We should recall that in *Being and Time* Heidegger wrote:

> The Being of *Dasein,* upon which the structural whole as such is ontologically supported, becomes accessible to us when we look all the way *through* this whole *to a single* primordially unitary phenomenon which is already in this whole in such a way that it provides the ontological foundation for each structural item in its structural possibility. Thus we cannot Interpret this "comprehensively" by a process of gathering up what we have hitherto gained and taking it all together.[7]

Such statements, quite clearly, conflict with the later positions in *Heraklit,* wherein the "primordially unitary phenomenon" which comprises the Being of Dasein is considered as a gathering up or *lesen* (*die einholend-ausholende Sammlung*) which Heidegger views as a relation to what stands open before the one who gathers. This openness, or *Offenheit des Offenen,* is not a closed or unified field wherein relations are inherently gathered but an expanse wherein relations are both disclosed and concealed, gathered and lost. The words *einholend* and *ausholend* are synonyms, meaning "to obtain." But Heidegger often separates the prefixes and juxtaposes *ein* to *aus,* suggesting that even if these terms paronomasically repeat one another, they also bear within their prefixes a resistance to gathering, unifying, bringing together. The *logos* characterizing man is therefore inherently undecidable (metaphysically illogical) with respect to its primordial unity/disunity, an undecidability disclosed not in Dasein's understanding or interpretation of itself as disclosed as Being-in-the-world but by how Being speaks through the paronomasia of *lesen* as appropriation/disappropriation. In this manifold of undecidable proximities, then, "The question of Being itself is at once the question of Non-Being and of Nothingness" that cannot be recovered dialectically in a humanist context, for example, that of Hamlet's "To be or not to be" speech.[8] Therefore Heidegger's earlier idea of the Being of Dasein conforming to a primordial structural whole is explicitly dismantled, turned against.

Not until the mid-1970s do the essays of Derrida begin to appreciate the more radical consequences for the thinking through of Being and time from such a perspective. Indeed, the essays suggest that after the late 1960s Derrida began reading Heidegger in a manner emphasizing not his conceptual distance from Heideggerian thinking but his stylistic and intuitive affinities with it. No doubt, already during the 1960s Derrida had recognized the linguistic turn in Heidegger's "The Letter on Humanism" if for no other reason than such a turn had been crucial for the French structuralist overturning of Sartrean existentialism. Historically, the Heideggerian "turn" clearly transpired not merely in Heidegger alone but in the French appropriation or interpretation of Heidegger by revisionary readers such as Jean Wahl, Emmanuel Levinas, Maurice Blanchot, Jacques Lacan, Jean Beaufret, Michel Foucault, and René Char. No reading of Derrida should therefore overlook this dimension of the necessary indebtedness to a much larger and prior cultural revaluation. Indeed, the "French" Heidegger is even the consequence of an interpretation in which Martin Heidegger, personally, played an active and willing role in conferences held at Cerisy-La-Salle and in various stays with thinkers like Beaufret, Lacan, and Char.

In her lively *Histoire de la psychanalyse en France,* Elizabeth Roudinesco, for example, notes that Jacques Lacan was introduced to Heidegger through his analysand Jean Beaufret, who, in being irritated at the analyst's silence, mentioned to Lacan during a session that he had been well acquainted with Heidegger and that Heidegger had mentioned Lacan's work. "Que vous a-t-il-dit?" Lacan immediately snapped back. Beaufret's comments, it turns out, were merely a ruse. But Lacan did go to Freiburg to meet Heidegger and again met with him when Heidegger came to France in 1955. Although Roudinesco believes Lacan and Heidegger probably had little to say to one another (Heidegger was not interested in psychoanalysis), clearly Heidegger's work had an influence on Lacan's decentered psychological theories.[9] Lacan translated, with the help of an expert in German, the "Logos" essay of Heidegger from

Vorträge und Aufsätze and probably drew from Heidegger's perspective of analyzing the subject through a parceling out of terms drawn from a word matrix. Moreover, Lacan's way of "collecting" a series of mental formations (i.e., the Other, the small *objet-a,* the *moi,* etc.) accords well with a Heideggerian notion of the subject as Heraclitean *logos* wherein an essentialism is replaced by an interrogation of proximities pulled out through discourse.

Although it is not likely that Derrida came to Heidegger by way of Lacan's writings, one should note that Lacan was part of a widespread intellectual rereading of Heidegger in France within which Derridean thinking is very much situated. One French intellectual influenced by Heidegger who is very crucial to an understanding of Derrida's Heidegger readings, particularly those of the 1970s, is the essayist and novelist Maurice Blanchot, who demonstrated already in the mid-1940s a sensitivity to the linguistic turn in Heidegger even before it was explicitly announced by Heidegger himself. Moreover, by the late 1950s Blanchot had advanced a vocabulary derived from Heidegger (i.e., dissemination, decentering, the end of the book, the *en retrait, écriture*) which many critics might ordinarily think of as more or less original with Derrida.[10] Therefore when one reads a text such as *Of Grammatology,* wherein Heideggerian thought is situated in the linguistic contexts of Saussurean theory in order to question both the timidity of Heidegger's linguistic turn and the limitations of Saussure's understanding of linguistic difference, it is already within an established French context of reading Heidegger's linguistic turn—that of Blanchot—wherein Derrida's work takes place. This is not to say that Derrida's Heidegger interpretations are by any means merely derivative but to suggest that there are important figures who mediate deconstruction.

In this chapter, therefore, I turn to a reading of Blanchot, an especially important and overlooked early French reader of Heidegger, not only because he spiritually accompanies Heidegger in making the linguistic turn but because an understanding of Blanchot is necessary for studying Derrida's renewed interest in Heidegger during the mid-1970s. Judging from Derrida's publications of that time, evidently by way of Blanchot, Derrida came to an understanding of Heidegger's work in ways that strongly depart from the positions of the early essays on Heidegger written during the 1960s. For example, in "The Ends of Man" Derrida severely criticizes Heidegger's vocabulary of proximity as a backsliding into humanist assumptions about the priority of an idealist subject. Moreover, in works like *Of Grammatology* there seems to be little sympathy for a Heideggerian emphasis on the vocative. But by the mid-1970s, in essays like "Pas," nothing less than the vocative is being stylistically invoked by Derrida when he recalls the *à venir* and the reinvigoration of a vocabulary of proximity brought about when the term *pas* is used to develop Blanchot's translation of Heidegger's *Überstieg* as *le pas au-delà* (the step [not] beyond). In itself this phrase is not only metaleptic as a translation, "Überstieg . . . pas au-delà," but also paronomasic, since in the unfolding or dividing of *pas* we are required to gather what lies before us: the "pas . . . pas" signifying the "no . . . step," the "step . . . step," the "not . . . no," the "no . . . no."

In considering Blanchot's important role as a mediator of Heidegger, it will be essential to recognize a most seminal essay on Heidegger published in *Critique* in 1946, somewhat before Heidegger's "Letter on Humanism" appeared. And most astonishing is the fact that Blanchot's essay more than anticipates the major thinking of Heidegger in the "Letter" and, too, in the work to come written in the late 1940s and throughout the 1950s. Blanchot's essay is entitled, "La parole 'sacrée' de Hölderlin," and was later included in the collection *La part du feu* (1949). In the discussion of this essay by Blanchot, I wish to make the point that not only is deconstruction already very much under way in its most disruptive senses in Blanchot's writings of the 1940s but that Blanchot's work, at a time before Heidegger himself was well known, implicitly cites a linguistic turning in Heidegger that reflects a temporal clue through which the history of ontology is threatened and wherein the itinerary affirmed at the beginning of *Being and Time* is carried out.

After discussing "La parole 'sacrée' de Hölderlin," I turn to a section of Blanchot's *Le livre à venir* (1959) to discuss Blanchot's reinterpretation of Heidegger in terms of what is viewed as the end of the logocentric text or "book"—here the turn

from voice to writing is announced in the Heideggerian linguistic turn—as well as in terms of the temporality of a writing
which transpires as what Blanchot calls the "espacement"
(spacing) of "espace" (space). In moving to the writings of the
1950s, it should become evident not only how Blanchot clears
a path for Derridean deconstruction but to what degree that
path is directly connected to a profound interpretation of Heidegger's 1930s writings on language.

Furthermore, one must discuss Blanchot's *Le pas au-delà*
(1973), since it has been very influential for Derrida. This text
is particularly incisive on the topic of time and language in
relation to an overall reinterpretation or appropriation of Heidegger. Whereas previous critical texts by Blanchot are analytical and essayistic, *Le pas au-delà* is much more resonant and
consists of a correspondence of fragments both analytical and
fictional. In the correspondence of these fragments, Blanchot
inherently demonstrates a mode of philosophical writing that
performs Heidegger's descriptions of *Ereignis* as an appropriation and expropriation of moments. And in them the givenness
of time is disclosed as what Blanchot calls an "hors temps dans
le temps." Derrida's "Pas," recently republished in *Parages*
(1986), meditates on such *Ereignis* mediated by the *à venir* of
Blanchot, in which time is disclosed as the beyond-time-in-
time, the time not-(yet)-beyond. Derrida himself, in turning
away from his earlier critical stands on Heidegger, reorients
himself, then, with respect to the general problematic of
whether Heidegger did, in fact, achieve the radical temporal
clue announced in *Being and Time*. My argument is that the
essays "Pas," "The Retrait of Metaphor," and "Restitutions"
reflect a major reconsideration of Derrida's earlier work on
Heidegger and that a rapprochement with his writings comes
about because Blanchot has clarified in ways Derrida may not
have noticed before the more radical bearings of Heideggerian
thought upon deconstruction, and particularly that which is
disclosed in the paronomasia of Heideggerian language.

But if there is a gathering, or *Lesen,* of Heidegger that
stresses *Einholen,* or bringing in toward one's own readings,
there is also that aspect which Heidegger calls *Ausholen,* which
we might call dis-appropriation. In this chapter I also wish to
consider how Derrida in the mid-1980s considers paronomasia

as a temporality, a consideration through which Derrida takes
distance from Heideggerian theory. My example is the recent
book on Heidegger by Derrida entitled *De l'esprit*. This study
develops what had already been a turning away from Heidegger in essays published in the 1980s such as "Of an Apocalyptic
Tone Recently Adopted in Philosophy," "Geschlecht I,"
"Geschlecht II," "Feu la cendre," and the lecture on negative
theology delivered in Jerusalem under the title "How to Avoid
Speaking: Denials." That the temporal question will engage
Jewish history will also become pertinent to how Derrida considers the darker resonances in Heidegger's writings, resonances implicit in a Heideggerian linguistic turn emphasizing
the expropriation of the notions "man" and humanity. In *De
l'esprit* Derrida develops a Heideggerian parallel to the remarks
on *logos* in studies such as *Heraklit*. The parallel encompasses
instances in which Heidegger revokes or invokes the word
Geist and its various modalizations. Just as the term *logos* marks
an open field of *Ver-Sammlung*, the term *Geist* similarly brings a
field of terms into such proximity. However, what comes into
proximity by way of *Geist* is a manifold of philosophical orientations whose politics is particularly unsettling. Not only that,
but Derrida suspects that in Heidegger's uses of the word *Geist*
we can detect spirits of a ghostly sort who could tell a story of
ashes and flame. It is this story which Derrida tells in the
collocation of a four-sided figure whose angles delimit the
following topics: the animal, the question, technology, and
spirit. That this figure which is brought into relation by *Geist*
could be deciphered as a cryptophor of the dead is one of *De
l'esprit*'s hectoring suggestions.

Consideration of *De l'esprit* is particularly relevant at this
juncture in this study, because it could be said to form metaleptically a de Manian allegory of reading that is counterpointed
to Heidegger's remarks on *logos*. In other words, *Geist* and *logos*
are in metaleptic proximity and as such allow us to comprehend
to what degree the translation of ancient Greek philosophy
into a German context both enables Heidegger further to demolish or (as Derrida says) deconstruct metaphysics, even as it
reconstitutes what had been supposedly passed beyond. Although Derrida does not develop the point, it is particularly
curious that if the *logos* in Heidegger can be said to break

ostensibly with a humanist philosophy, it seems to be much less politically distressing than the consideration of *Geist,* which at one point in Heidegger's career is meant to reinvoke humanism or spirituality. In part, the significance of Derrida's study is that if *Geist* is inextricably related to that which is metaleptically gathered together as *logos, logike,* and *legein,* the relation between Greek and German terminologies discloses that in the *Ver-Sammlung* of these Heideggerian guide words the ends of man are thought through from a particularly catastrophic vantage point, one in which the "difference" of *Geist* and *logos* discloses itself with respect to the fate of those consumed in the ashes and flame of the Nazi debacle.

Reading Hölderlin

In "La parole 'sacrée' de Hölderlin" Blanchot considers Heidegger's writings on Hölderlin's hymn "Wie wenn am Feiertage" at length. Blanchot's immediate question is whether Heidegger's analysis of Hölderlin's poetry is "legitimate," since unlike the critic Friedrich Gundolf, Heidegger does not appear to interrogate the poem as a "whole." Rather, Heidegger questions each word in turn and offers a complete yet wholly disarticulated interpretation. This makes for an impression that is very strange, Blanchot says, yet justifiable when one considers that the analysis "ends finally, not in reconstructing a general meaning beginning with all the particular meanings which it specifies, but in recovering at each moment the passage of the totality of the poem beneath the form where it is momentarily laid aside and stopped."[11] Blanchot more than anticipates remarks Heidegger will make in the 1950s in texts such as *What Is Called Thinking?* for Blanchot says of Hölderlin's hymn that it is "a poem . . . not without date, but despite its date it is always arriving (*à venir*); it speaks itself in a 'present' which does not respond to historical references."[12] The poem is sent, dispatched, and is always *à venir,* in the process of coming to us from the past, but, too, announcing itself from ahead of us, from the future (*avenir*). "It is a foreboding or portending [*pressentiment*] requiring of the reader the same foreboding which will make him part of an existence which has not yet occurred [*non encore advenue*]."[13] Blanchot's understanding of Heidegger focuses on a temporality which exceeds presence and requires of the reader an anticipatory consciousness "en avant de soi." Heidegger, as Blanchot recognized in the 1940s, was appropriating a poetic vocabulary from Hölderlin which allowed for philosophy a clearing or opening by means of which interpretation could go beyond the temporal restrictions of historical reference, formal analysis, and critical appraisal, all of which presuppose that one's reading of a work transpires in a now wherein everything can be actualized by the strong reader. Blanchot is particularly struck by the fact that in reading Hölderlin, Heidegger will appropriate a term such as *offenen,* which in its poetic context forestalls the possibility of making the poetic work present and available to consciousness even as it announces the coming, arrival, or destiny of the work as a horizon of Being in which the reader is himself "to arrive" at what is "open" to the "opened." In glossing the line "Und dem offenen Blick offen der Leuchtende sei" ("Et qu'à la vue qui s'ouvre s'ouvre ce qui est rayonnement de lumière" [Blanchot's translation]), Blanchot is particularly interested in the repetition of the word *offen,* because he believes it responds to a "double movement" of an opening upon that which opens, as well as the illumination of that which illuminates. ("S'ouvrir à ce qui s'ouvre, et *der Leuchtende,* le pouvoir d'éclairement de ce qui éclaire. . . .")[14]

Already during the 1940s, then, Blanchot is exploring the extent to which in the appropriation of poetic language the philosophy of Heidegger disinvests itself of an interpretive strategy which would attempt to talk about literature as an object available or present to philosophical analysis; rather, Heidegger in appropriating poetic terms allows for a transference between philosophy and literature, the effect of which is to decenter the priority of the reader's existence as that which is self-consciously assumed to be present-to-itself and thereby forming the basis or ground for hermeneutical understanding. Heidegger's reading of Hölderlin in considering the repetition or iteration of the open allows for an understanding of the relationship between reader and work as that which is not constituted a priori in the temporal present of the act of reading or analysis, an idea fundamental to any formalist or new critical approach, but that is itself in the process of coming or arriving from a poetic and hermeneutical horizon for whom the self-presence of the reader or the work is displaced by the destining of thought, the *à venir* of language as openness, wherein the proximities of our nearness and distance to thought is mediated.

In "La parole 'sacrée' de Hölderlin," Blanchot not only considers the openings announced in the iterations of *dem offenen* but also raises the point that Hölderlin and Hegel are haunted by "the idea of the whole." Blanchot writes that for Hölderlin, "nature is all presencing, the present as totality." Yet, it is a "totalité sans bornes," a totality without limits.[15] Heidegger's commentary respects the delimitations of this totality, because it intuits from within the poetic vocabulary an incessant interrogation of hermeneutical limits. This is crucial, in fact, with respect to temporality, because time is commonly taken for granted by traditional critics in terms of a uniform present within which the critical reading takes place, an idea which supports the assumption that literary works can be made totally available to analysis. Heidegger, to the contrary, uncovers from within the language of poetry those temporal moments in which the horizons of a poetic presencing (or presenting) of meaning are held back, concealed, or, as Blanchot will say a decade later in *Le livre à venir*, held *en retrait*.

Throughout "La parole 'sacrée' de Hölderlin," Blanchot pays specific attention to a linguistic feature of Heidegger's writing which might easily escape one's attention, though it is perhaps one of the most crucial features of Heidegger's "linguistic turn." This feature is paronomasia and occurs, in Blanchot, in examples such as "et qu'a la vue qui s'ouvre s'ouvre," "la poésie est chargée de l'accomplir, et, en l'accomplissant, s'accomplit," "cette rencontre est le fond et la vérité de ce qui se rencontre," and the slippage between words like *à venir, avenir,* and *advenir*.[16] Although Blanchot's essay precedes Heidegger's publications of the 1950s, the essay is remarkably astute in focusing on the paronomasic significance of both Heidegger's own writing and that of the poems he considers, presupposing that just as Heidegger appropriated a poetic vocabulary from writers like Hölderlin, he also appropriated tropological features disclosed in the work of such poets as well. But more important, Blanchot's essay reflects an awareness that for Heidegger paronomasia may well be a key to an understanding of temporality. In short, we can credit Blanchot with the understanding, long before even the earlier work of Heidegger had, in fact, become well known, that Heidegger had made an important linguistic turn in his philosophy by way of an unusual appropriation of poetic discourse whose tropes revealed important hermeneutical consequences for an understanding of a poetic work with respect to questions of time and being. Therefore, Blanchot, even without the kind of historical distance from which to pose a reading of a Heideggerian turn concerning language as the medium wherein a radical temporal clue is to be disclosed, comes very close, in the mid-1940s, to articulating precisely such a turn as well as its significance for readers of poetry.

The poet's existence, Blanchot says, is given in the adumbration of time by the poem, in the poem's forecastings of time. "Why does the poet forecast, how can the poet exist given this mode of forecasting?"[17] This is, Blanchot says, because the poet exists in the future anterior. In other words, the poem precedes, in its arrival or coming, the existence of the poet and anticipates this poet as the one who will be credited with creating the poem which has, in fact, created him or her. This idea of the text arriving ahead of its author has become somewhat commonplace in the structuralist writings of the 1960s— one thinks of Barthes' "Death of the Author"—but Blanchot had already derived the notion from Heidegger's reading of Hölderlin. "The whole oeuvre of Hölderlin discloses the consciousness of an anterior power exceeding men as well as gods, even those who prepare the cosmos to be 'at one.'"[18] This power is called the "sacred," though Blanchot will not define it in familiar terms, because for him the sacred is disclosed by Heidegger as an uncommunicated immediacy, an unspeakable proximity on which the possibility of communication depends even as it is made to founder in incommunicability. Readers of Blanchot's narratives will be familiar with the thematization of this proximity as the condition for not only dialogue but the deconstruction of the subject that occurs the moment dialogue attempts to think "l'immédiat qui n'est jamais communiqué."[19]

For example, in *Au moment voulu* (1951), we are told in a characteristically deconstructed narration

> how terrible things are, when they come out of them-
> selves, into a resemblance in which they have neither the
> time to corrupt themselves nor the origin to find them-
> selves and where, eternally their own likenesses, they do
> not affirm themselves but rather, beyond the dark flux
> and reflux of repetition, affirm the absolute power of this
> resemblance, which is no one's and which has no name
> and no face. That is why it is terrible to love and we can
> love only what is most terrible.[20]

In the essay on Hölderlin, Blanchot protracts his reading of such an incommunicable immediacy as the precondition for understanding the notion of an openness or availability where-in poetry manifests itself as resemblance and hence appearance which is illuminated in what the narrative *Au moment voulu* will call "the dark flux and reflux of repetition," the openness of opening, of the opened in openhood. In this repetition or paronomasic interplay of language, Hölderlin achieves a closer proximity to what is *à venir* even as this is obscured in the flux and reflux of repetition or language. In calling on metaphors that are again familiar in Blanchot's fiction, such a linguistic intuition of what is *à venir* realizes itself in the coming of day (insight) and its concomitant falling into night (blindness). In *La folie du jour* the wish to see full daylight culminates in the exclamation that "and if seeing was fire, I required the pleni-tude of fire, and if seeing would infect me with madness, I madly wanted that madness."[21] Such moments in Blanchot's fiction are themselves destined to come. That is, the fictional narratives are themselves temporal horizons *à venir*, the *avenir* of a certain influence that comes by way of Heidegger's reading of Hölderlin.

In "La parole 'sacrée' de Hölderlin," for example, the fire and madness of day are already associated with illumination in the work of a poet who foundered in madness, whose clarity is itself unreason, the radiance of dark sayings. This is, according to Blanchot, already foreshadowed or foretold in the great hymns when the notion of the sacred is raised.

If the sacred is a radiant power whose law is a scattering burst, the principle of the appearing of that which appears, one understands that in foretelling the poet is already placed in the heart of a complete presence and that the approach of the sacred would be for it the approach of existence. But, for the present, the enigma takes another form. For at the beginning, the poet is not yet, for he himself depends on Totality in order to exist and the Totality depends on his mediation in order to be a Totality. Now, existing as "not yet," he has seized, forecasted the coming of the sacred, which is the principle of this coming itself, which is the anterior coming to every "something which comes" and by which "everything" comes, the Totality comes.[22]

This "coming" or "approach"—this *moment voulu*, if you will—of the sacred is nothing less than the approach of a limit wherein at its greatest intensity and clarification literature is overwhelmed in what is, finally, a "madness of day" that is itself incommunicative however close or immediate to the poet and those in communication with him. Indeed, the poetry of Hölderlin speaks most clearly to us in the shadowy anticipations of sacrality, for here poetry must "make time" for the appearing of the sacred. This "making time" occurs by delaying the coming of that which one foretells, by a slowing down of its approach, a holding back the dawn of thought. In Heidegger, too, poetic diction is used as a means of slowing down the tempo of the approach of both the question concerning being and of the question concerning time, and as in Hölderlin, by way of paronomasia such a slowing down is brought about. Indeed, this slowing down or gearing down of language must occur, since Heidegger wishes to achieve an analytical discourse that will never pose itself at that point when the questioning about being and time will call for either an essentialist answer or a mystical response, both of which would reduce Heidegger's "guide words" to a disclosure or definition that must necessarily take place in the now or presence of a positing that would merely lead to unreflective reason or outright delirium. Heidegger, therefore, perpetuates discourse in a *pas encore*, or "not yet," wherein the approach or coming of the sacred becomes the precondition for the appearance of the writer as mediator of the sacred. Especially important in Blanchot's passage above is the idea that the writer does not constitute the Totality by means of making language present to itself and declaring the definitions of being and time—this is, we recall, precisely what Aristotle is doing in *The Metaphysics*—but that the writer is himself an articulation of the Totality that comes into being or arrives ahead of itself in the approach of a Totality which always already subsumes it, and which the writer is called upon to announce or portend in order that Totality as infinitude will become mediated as Totality as finitude. Here, of course, we can already glimpse the main outline of a treatise liike Emmanuel Levinas's *Totality and Infinity*, which may owe some debt to Blanchot's rereading of Heidegger.

For Blanchot, "mortal language is persistence, affirmation of a duration which endures, the unity of a scattered temporality."[23] Hölderlin is credited as comprehending the poet as one who in announcing his arrival in the wake of his being-there (or Dasein) brings into proximity a sacred disseminating temporality by means of reflectively holding time together in an *á venir, avenir,* or *advenir* that is literature. The paradox is, of course, that only by passing into an appearance held together by a finite being can the infinity of an immortal time be brought to pass as being. And this bringing to pass is nothing less than that holding together of moments which language enables, which the closure of poetic form facilitates. "The poem is indeed that which holds together, that which gathers in its unanchored unity an open unification of principle, which in the fissure of illumination discovers a foundation firm enough in order that some thing comes to appearance and in order that what appears maintains itself in agreement or in tune (*un accord*), vacillating but stable."[24] By means of language the poet comes to be as the horizon of a gathering together of moments in whose vacillating but stable attunement the poem arrives in an articulation of that which speaks from beyond, which is to say, from a time that is not, properly speaking, our lived or worldly sense of time. Anticipating somewhat the critical readings of Paul de Man, Blanchot demonstrates that in poetic language's articulating and clarifying the arrival of what Hölderlin calls the sacred, the sacred begins to move away and retreat, leaving behind a poetic language which is merely obscure, mad. At the moment of poetic insight, then, there is a concomitant blindness. Heidegger himself noticed this not only in Hölderlin but in Heraclitus, upon whom Heidegger was lecturing during the time he considered Hölderlin's oeuvre.

Blanchot, who may not have had the opportunity to read Heidegger extensively by the 1940s, intuitively recognized that what was particularly interesting about Heidegger's analysis of Hölderlin was the perception that at the moment of the poet's arrival from within the call of his own poetry, the poet as such begins to recede and disappear. That is, the poet vanishes (goes mad) at the moment of his arrival. Certainly, the poet is someone whose being is affirmed in language through the gathering of time even as time is affirmed in the poet's being, and this is what Hölderlin's poetry, not unlike Heraclitus's fragments, often reflects. However, the poet is one whose time and being are threatened, perhaps negated, by the very fulfillment of the wished-for moment in which the sacred falls due to the poet. In this sense, the establishment of the poet's being and time is itself disestablished in its very fulfillment and, correlatively, the capacity of the poet to communicate at his most elevated and illuminated moment is disclosed in the fall of the poet into madness and incommunicability. In fact, this incommunicability greatly interests Blanchot, who in the latter part of his essay on Hölderlin stresses "silence" as the cancellation, or *retrait,* of being. Blanchot says this is "a means for approaching the inapproachable," and, as such, it belongs to the "not said" as that which is itself what makes possible "la communication de l'incommunicable et aboutit au langage" (this locution does not transfer into English, but one might proceed with the idiomatic: "the communication of the incommunicable 'makes it' to language").[25] In a paronomasic turn of phrase, Blanchot says of the poet, "he speaks but doesn't speak," and in the wearing and tearing of this speaking/not speaking in the same place, this turn to and away from speech, the poet elevates himself in the ruin that he is, wherein the speaking speaks from within the silence that refuses speech. In this abrasion the concept of being is disarticulated in an undecidable interplay between existence and nonexistence brought to pass in the coming of

Being. And, lastly, this is an abrasion coming about in the poet's ability to foretell his own arrival, to announce his coming, from the hitherside of his being, an announcing, forecasting, or portending that comes about through the capacity of poetic diction to make possible the arrival of a moment through the delays of a paronomasic interplay of terms.

Indeed, anyone who comes to Blanchot's "La parole 'sacrée' de Hölderlin" cannot fail to see what are by now becoming the more familiar "moves" of deconstruction, and particularly as it has been worked out by Paul de Man, who, curiously enough, in an essay during the 1950s on precisely Blanchot's topic, Heidegger's "Wie wenn am Feiertag," entirely overlooks Blanchot's essay. The result is that de Man will see in Heidegger but a limited turn that is but "a singular ontological reversal" and that has reconciliation within Being, whereas in Hölderlin de Man notices that the "movement of Kehre is transformed into an absolute phenomenon" that knows no reconciliation."[26] But a decade before de Man wrote "Heidegger's Exegesis of Hölderlin," Blanchot had already suggested that Heidegger himself had stepped beyond such ontological recovery and that Heidegger's readings of Hölderlin themselves reflect an irreconcilability within which is expressed a much more radical philosophy than that with which de Man credits him. Surely, this point by Blanchot constitutes what I would call one of the inceptions for the appropriation (perhaps one should say "invention") of a French Heidegger in whose orbit de Man will himself move by the time he writes *Blindness and Insight,* where many thematics are well anticipated in Blanchot's much earlier work.

Literature in Arrival

By 1959, in *Le livre à venir,* Blanchot carries forward many of the thoughts reflected upon in the essay on Hölderlin from *La part du feu* and in so doing not only considers Heidegger's writings of the 1950s but more or less explicitly begins developing a vocabulary that American critics today would ordinarily associate as original with Derrida. Of particular interest in this volume is the section, "Où va la littérature?," which includes a meditation on the end of the book as logocentric text, a meditation that Derrida will himself take up in *Of Grammatology* almost ten years later as a point of departure for deconstruction. Blanchot's concern with the end of the book relates most strongly to Mallarmé's work in which that end is already announced, though not without Mallarmé's occult lapses into metaphysics, magic, and symbolism. Just as Derrida will later read Heidegger as a philosopher at once ahead of and behind himself with respect to a particular project aimed at moving beyond metaphysics, Blanchot in *Le livre à venir* finds in Mallarmé a similar figure, whose writings announce a new epoch of literature even while, at certain junctures, retreating from its possibility. Yet, what makes Mallarmé important as a writer who foresees the end of the book is the fact that for Blanchot such a foreseeing has to be understood in the parallelism that can be made in retrospect by Blanchot between Mallarmé and Heidegger.

The parallel between them is made with respect to Mallarmé's consideration of chance, which is very reminiscent, in Blanchot's handling, of some features developed in the Hölderlin essay from *La part du feu,* since chance, once more, marks both the arrival and dissolution of the writer in the advent of the work's approach, or *la littérature à venir*. Without chance, writing would be seamless, monotonous, anonymous. Therefore in rupturing the writer's studious process of composition, chance gives or donates a particular style to the work. In this sense, chance announces itself as that rupture by means of which the literary work to come is anticipated or foretold. Moreover, chance ensures that the name of the writer will be remembered, because the text affected by chance will be like no other text, no other style. Therefore by giving up one's desire for absolute control over a text in turning the composition over to chance, the author undergoes dissolution as a figure whose voice, always present to itself, masters the work while acceding, as signature of a particular text, to a coming into one's own. As in the essay on Hölderlin discussed above, Blanchot focuses on the chiastic paradox of the writers' dissolution in arrival and arrival in dissolution. However, in "Où va la littérature?" this chiasmus concerns the crossing or turning from voice to writing and writing to voice. That is, just as the voice of the writer must give way to the writing of the text, the writing of the text will give way to the voice of the writer. Yet, this final voice is but an effect or trick of the writing itself, or, to put it another way, a chance occurrence.

In "Où va la littérature?" Blanchot notes that chance ruptures the even transcription of voice into writing and that in doing so it interrupts the self-presentation of the author's being as that which is always present to itself or, in temporal terms, posited in an eternal now. Chance breaks the temporal horizon of authorial unification, if for no other reason than that chance cannot be predicted: we do not know how or when something will happen by chance. For Blanchot the notion that chance makes possible a text's announcing or foretelling of a work that is in the process of arriving is already evidence that such a self-present temporal horizon has been broken or ruptured. The "presence" and the "present" of the author, therefore, is subjected to a certain demolition by *écriture*. This is quite close in spirit to Heidegger's meditations on the pre-Socratics, too, wherein the gathering and scattering which characterize *logos* are themselves not alien to chance, or, as Heidegger says, "lightning." For "lightning abruptly lays before us in an instant everything present in the light of its presencing."[27] Yet, in making oneself open to the demolition of temporal horizons by sudden chance interruptions, which may maintain, nevertheless, the illusion of an eternal presence, one is restored as a writer whose signature marks a correspondence of vocative effects elicited by the writing. Blanchot, then, argues not that a voice is restored in a unified temporal horizon of self-presence but that vocative correspondences are established in an attunement that comes about by chance.

Notions such as correspondence, releasement, and demolition, which underscore the reading of Mallarmé, are keyed to Heidegger's later work of the 1950s. Moreover, the "turning" from voice to writing in Blanchot explicitly imitates the Heideggerian "turn" from Dasein to Being. It is well known that in *Of Grammatology* Derrida initiates grammatology with an analysis in which the turn from voice to writing is strongly emphasized; less well known is that in more recent work Derrida has developed an aspect of the turn in which writing as a correspondence of signifying effects gives voice to the writer's signa-

ture, a voice or, more precisely, tone, that is comprised of the
rhythm or attunement of the vocative correspondences set up
by chance in the writing. Although a lengthier discussion of
"correspondence" has to wait until the following chapter, one
should note that in texts like *The Post Card*, Derrida very much
relies on "chance" (i.e., the fortune-telling book, the technology of the postal system, the chance reception of various phone
calls, etc.) as that precondition for the establishing of correspondences that break with the classical authorial notion of a
writerly temporality in which a text is made present to itself in
the self-presencing of the author in a moment of textual conception.

Blanchot, in specifically addressing temporality at some
length, writes:

> The work is sometimes caught in white virtuality—im-
> mobile; sometimes, and this is more significant, it is ani-
> mated by extreme temporal discontinuity, delivered up
> to temporal shifts: accelerations, slow downs, "fragmen-
> tary arrests"—the sign of a wholly new essence of move-
> ment in which it is as if an other time announces itself, as
> alien to eternal permanence as quotidian time itself: here
> coming before, there coming after, the future, the past,
> underneath a false appearance of the present.[28]

Blanchot recognizes, then, in the linguistic turn from voice to
writing—recall that it correlates with the Heideggerian turn
from Dasein to Being—a demolition of temporality which
opens onto temporal modalities within which signification as
writing takes place. In these various horizons of time there is
announced an "other" time at once coming before (anticipating) and after (reflecting back on), suggesting itself beneath a
false appearance of the present. Such a temporality is "held" by
the work which is de-presented in its re-presentationality. For
Blanchot this extends to an understanding of the "space" or
espacement, and this "spacing" constitutes a text's meaning as a
movement or tracking across language which, nevertheless,
stays in place. What makes Mallarmé's poetry profound, in
Blanchot's view, is not that it reflects language as something
deep wherein one can find semantic levels compressed or piled
upon one another but, rather, that it reflects an expansive and

surfacy space which is itself the infinite "opening" and "unfolding" of language. Especially relevant is Blanchot's idea that *espacement* does not mean the movement of signification in a linear manner as a continuous spreading of semantic densities but reflects a track of signification *en retrait,* in retraction.[29] This idea is a reformulation of paronomasia, which is a figure of the *en retrait,* a movement beyond that which stays where it is. Most striking in "Où va la littérature?" is the fact that this paronomasic movement, or *espacement,* determines a temporality of language, being the linguistic precondition of that temporality itself. Paronomasia is, therefore, a crucial temporal clue for an understanding of language as that which radically breaks with our everyday sense of experienced time.

A somewhat complex passage in Derrida's later work of the 1980s which could serve as an interesting gloss on Blanchot's essay on Mallarmé occurs in "Mes chances" (1984), which by way of the concept of "chance" or "luck" develops a paronomasic understanding of time as genealogy. Although reference to this essay must remain somewhat restricted, this is one of those most peculiar sites in Derrida where it appears the correspondences to a text such as that of "Où va la littérature?" are so strong that what we are reading must certainly be considered a gloss. At one point, Derrida writes: "By chance, I fall initially upon an example. By definition, there are nothing but examples in this domain. Freud tries to *understand* the forgetting of a proper name. He wants, therefore, in understanding, to efface the appearance of chance in the relation between a certain proper name and its having been forgotten."[30] Derrida is referring to Freud's having been spoken to by a man who cannot remember the name of a disciple of Epicurus, a man for whom this slip of memory takes him back to the days when he was himself a disciple. This citation approaches the notion of chance which Blanchot has invoked via Mallarmé, because as in the Blanchot essay, Derrida acknowledges that the status of the proper name depends upon the eradication of chance, which is to say, the maintaining of a certain presence of self, uninterrupted by the "chance" of forgetting, a moment in which what is held present-to-itself suddenly passes into oblivion. Mallarmé is quoted by Blanchot as having maintained that chance interrupts the continuity and homogeneity of writing and has the effect of distinguishing one's text as different from other texts. Chance, then, is a stroke of good fortune to the extent that it brings the text out of the realm of anonymity and thereby turns to the personhood or style of a particular writer. But chance, as Blanchot maintains, also sees to it that the text obeys laws of its own and turns away from the control and personhood of the author. This signifies a turning toward and away from the signature of the text's producer(s). Hence, "that which [the writer] writes, even if it be under his name, remains essentially without name."[31]

Perhaps by "chance" writers have the good fortune to be remembered rather than forgotten, "chance" referring, in this case, to all those contingent factors that make a writer's name popular, important, essential, and so on. Often by "chance" a name survives, stands the test of time due to laws over which the writer himself or herself may have had little control. In short, the inscription of the name in a canon occurs or does not occur by "chances" of various and complex sorts. In "Mes chances" Derrida points out that Freud's worrying about the forgetting of another person's name by chance is in actuality a displacement that repeats something much nearer to Freud: the fact that it may be his name that will be forgotten by "chance." "Freud has only to cite, to reproduce the interpretation of this disciple forgetting the name of a disciple, in identifying himself purely and simply, without taking the slightest initiative in interpretation, with this disciple who explains why he does not by chance forget the name of a disciple of Epicurus."[32] Crucial is the rhythm or correspondence which these chance interruptions establish, a rhythm which is, as one may have already surmised, paronomasic. Someone has forgotten the name of the disciple of Epicurus, a someone who is, in fact, referring to a time when he himself was a disciple, which reminds Freud, in turn, of the time he was a disciple. In the forgetting of a name inscribed in tradition, the one who forgets is, in fact, anticipating the forgetting of his own name, which in turn suggests to others that they, too, are no less vulnerable, that the forgetting of the name comes not only by "chance"— in this case, *méchance* and *malchance*—but is enacted by precisely that person who does not want his own name forgotten even as he contemplates, by means of a slip of memory, his own occlusion. Derrida couches this example within the slippage of paronomasic terms: *malchance, méschéance, pas de chance, mes chances, la chance, échéance, mé-chance,* and so on. These "strokes of luck," as Derrida says, open up a mise-en-scène, or space, of writings and erasures, rememberings and forgettings. This space concerns, therefore, a thinking on the part of Freud and his interlocutor about their time of arrival in a history of teachers and disciples, a time concerning themselves as beings who wish to remain present in time, who wish to survive even their own incapacity to remember who the disciples are. Chance (*hasard*) or luck (*chance*) may be the deciding stroke which preserves the name, but only by giving oneself up to the chancy determinations of fortune may the recollection of a signature come about. Only by embracing the horizon of forgetting and obliteration will one come to risk one's being remembered and instated. For Derrida, the "divisibility" of one's taking place in a heteronomous temporality inherently constituted in the paronomasic slippages of chance can be located in the space (the *espacement* or paronomasia) of writing, in this case, of the signature in its relation to other signatures which we might call the canon. Hence in the workings of this writerly canon which is both determined/undetermined by chance, an "other" time is reflected, a late Heideggerian notion of time, as mediated by Blanchot.

(Not) Stepping Beyond

By the 1970s both Blanchot and Derrida enter into a transferential relationship with respect to one another's writings, for in essays like "L'absence de livre" (*L'entretien infini,* 1969) Blanchot in developing ideas from the 1950s reappropriates thoughts from Derrida's writings, hence borrowing back ideas Derrida had to some degree borrowed from Blanchot. In *Le pas au-delà* (1973) the reappropriation by Blanchot of earlier ideas mediated by Derrida is quite pronounced, and one suspects that the emphasis on the word *revenir,* or "returning," is an oblique reference to this mode of coming back to oneself by way of an other. In *Le pas au-delà,* there are sections which discuss the trace, *écriture,* presence, and difference at length, and they are the means by which Blanchot returns to his earlier writings by way of an other writing at once the same and different from his own. Indeed, the entire problematic of intellectual filiation which Derrida will later appropriate in *The Post Card* is already sketched out by Blanchot rather explicitly in *Le pas au-delà* when he writes:

> Not to write a line (like Socrates) is perhaps not to privilege speech, but to write by default and by anticipation, for in this abstention the space of writing is prepared and decided where Plato is exerting himself already.

> [Ne pas écrire une ligne (comme Socrate), ce n'est peut être pas privilégier la parole, mais écrire par défaut et par avance, puisque, en cette abstention, se prépare et se décide l'espace d'écriture où déjà Platon s'exerce.][33]

As in Heidegger's *Heraklit,* writing in Blanchot performs a metaleptic movement of appropriation at once lagging behind and anticipating. Hence *Le pas au-delà* accedes to a fragmentation wherein writing marks "a dissociation of limit and limitation."[34] The fragment oversteps its place and deconstructs the difference between itself and an other text.

Le pas au-delà inscribes this "difference" in the meeting of two typefaces, the one italicized, the other not. In the italicized sections of the text we hear voices that are in the first person which suggest fragments of a literary undertaking. There are addresses to a you, self-reflexive questions, and flat statements, all of which appear to be obliquely relating to the third-person critical discourse which appears in the unitalicized sections, a critical discourse itself made of a multiplicity of critical saturations in which the voice of Derrida can also be heard. What makes *Le pas au-delà* such an extremely interesting work is the fact that Blanchot allows for a dissemination or dispersal of what Jean-Luc Nancy has, in a reading of Heidegger, called "le partage des voix," the division of voices.[35] Yet, for Blanchot this division is to be discussed in terms of the absence of the subject and the default of meaning in the context of *écriture.*

As in the essay on Hölderlin from *La part du feu, Le pas au-delà* will engage questions of totality and infinity, interiority and exteriority, emergence and dissolution. Also, Blanchot is still very much interested in the idea that a text speaks in its present, even though it cannot be made present within a historical moment that is fully present-to-itself. That is, the presence of the text transpires in its *à venir*, which in *Le pas au-delà* is thematized as *revenir*, or return. Whereas in the Hölderlin essay Blanchot discussed the "open," in *Le pas au-delà* he is concerned with the margins between the fragments and to what extent they are openings for an *Überstieg* in which transcendent being, to recall Heidegger, "surpasses neither a 'boundary' which stretches out before the subject and forces it to 'remain in' (immanence) nor a 'gap' which separates it from the object."[36] However, whereas the essay on Hölderlin remains an analytical discussion of a poem wherein the voice of the critic is unified, in *Le pas au-delà* the voice of Blanchot is gone beyond yet held back. This is a voice both *à venir*, a voice to come which will gather what lies before us and which will affirm itself in the *revenir*.

> The constraint to write does not wrestle *against* presence in behalf of absence, not *for* presence by claiming to preserve it or to communicate. Writing is not fulfilled in a present, nor does it present anything, nor does it present itself: even less does it represent, except in order to play with the repetitive which brings into the game the temporally ungraspable and anterior play of the new beginning with reference to all ability to make a beginning as if it was representing it without pondering a presence still to come or even assigning it to the past in the exceeding multiplicity which the word indicates, as if playing with a plurality always assumed in a return. Writing, in this sense, is first and foremost rewriting and rewriting never forwards itself to any anterior writing anymore than does speech, presence, or signification. Rewriting, redoubling what always precedes unity or suspends it in demarking it, rewriting holds itself apart of all productive initiative and does not claim to produce anything, not even the past or the future or the present of writing. Rewriting in repeating that which has not taken place, will not take place, has not taken place, inscribes itself in a non-unifiable system of relations which cross each

other in a way such that no crossing affirms coincidence, inscribing itself thus under the exigency of a return through which we are trapped by temporal modalities which are always measured by the unity of presence.[37]

Whereas Heidegger discussed transcendence in *The Essence of Reasons* by way of considering Dasein, Blanchot has rewritten or returned to this discussion through the consideration of rewriting wherein temporality is paronomasically disclosed in that coincidence of writing wherein coincidence undecidably takes place. Time is commonly measured by the assumption that writing is unified and always already present to itself, that the text's time is disclosed in the presence of the writer whose expression the text is. However, in the transcendental conditions of being, as outlined by Heidegger in *The Essence of Reasons,* the text could never be reconciled by such a coincidence; rather, textuality must be considered in its going-(not)-beyond which is the condition of what Blanchot calls "re-writing," what is, after all, a paronomasic or metaleptic movement of the signifier that returns to itself in its not returning there. Hence, a voice will say in *Le pas au-delà,* "Toujours, je reviens," though it is understood that such a returning or coming back never takes place except as dis-placement.[38] This "homelessness" of the subject, as inscribed in the text, becomes of much concern not only in Blanchot's fiction but in the writing of Edmond Jabès and, too, of Derrida in *The Post Card.* That is, it concerns the question of transcendence as a distance whose divisions are not capable of being recovered or unified even in the utopian space of a text.

Blanchot notices, in fact, that writing is a defense mechanism whose intent is to "forget" this unappeasable distance and the inevitable inappropriability of a present moment. Hence, he writes, again, in a very attenuated passage with a paronomasic notion of temporal divisibility in mind: "Time, time: the step beyond which is not achieved in time would lead beyond time, without this beyond being atemporal, but there, where time would fall due, a fragile fall, according to that 'outside of time in time' to which writing would attract us, if it were permitted, though invisible to us, to write under the secret of an ancient fear."[39] Writing, in other words, in unifying the paronomasic

slippage of the "time . . . time" suggests the figure of the subject whose purpose is to defend against "an ancient fear." In *Le
pas au-delà* this fear is repeated in many of the italicized por-
tions of the text. "Entre eux, la *peur,* la *peur* partagée en com-
mun et, par la *peur,* l'abîme de la *peur* par-dessus lequel ils se
rejoignent sans le pouvoir, mourant, chacun, seul, de *peur*"
("Between them, fear, a fear shared in common and, by means
of fear, the abyss of fear in terms of which they rejoin without
fear, each alone, dying of fear").[40] Against the paronomasia of
the *récit* of fear the closure of the text strains to expunge the
knowledge that the subject is always already absent, to expunge
the secret of an ancient time wherein closure is not affirmed and
time times as the "out of time in time."

Es gibt Zeit

Anyone who reads Heidegger's seminars on the pre-Socratics during the Second World War and compares them to
the short essays written on the same figures in *Vorträge und
Aufsätze* will notice some striking dissimilarities other than
length. *Heraklit,* for example, is much more aggressive in its
eagerness to dismantle the metaphysical notion of "man," a
dismantling that affects what we have come to depend on as an
ethical armature upon which the concept of "man" depends.
Very acute in these seminars, as I have noted, is the way in
which pre-Socratic words are seen not as separate entities but
as trace structures in terms of which the determinability of
difference and identity of words loses definition as a metaphysical logic wherein the law of contradiction holds true. In the
Anaximander seminar, particularly, Heidegger began rethink-
ing the question of temporality disclosed in the slippage of the
prefix "a" in *a-letheia, a-rché,* and *apeiron.* And he notes that we
should not think of our "having time" but as time being
"given." In the Heraclitus seminars one gleans that if "man" is
also a manifold of words whose difference and identity are not
determinable metaphysically and hence loses its essential qual-
ities so dear to the metaphysical tradition, this rereading of
"man" must also, in terms of its paronomasic slippages, suggest
that such a notion, too, is a temporality "given" in the proxi-

mate relations of what is appropriated and what is disappropriated.

These seminars, of course, have only come to light in the *Gesamtausgabe* fairly recently. Hence their thoughts on temporality have been relatively concealed, whereas the short pieces on Anaximander and *logos* in *Vorträge* have been known much longer and reflect what at least to me is a far less radical set of perspectives on time. But in the essay "Zeit und Sein" of 1962 Heidegger returned to thoughts in the earlier seminars on the pre-Socratics and particularly to the notion of time as that which is given. Although I will postpone a fuller exposition of this so-called later Heidegger until the next chapter, I must explain some of Heidegger's thoughts in "Zeit und Sein," because Blanchot in the 1970s draws heavily from later Heideggerian texts even as he continues working through Heidegger's linguistic turn made earlier.

It should be said at this point that Blanchot has linguistically exacerbated Heideggerian paronomasia and that he has actually dwelled much more than Heidegger upon the *narrative* possibilities of disclosing temporality in metalepsis not only in his philosophical writings but in his fiction, a point that Derrida explicitly works through in "Pas" and, later, "Living On: Border Lines." In the fiction, of course, Blanchot had to consider what one would do given the dismantling of the metaphysical notion of "man" by Heidegger. To put it bluntly, Blanchot sets out to solve the deconstruction of character or subjecthood without reducing literature to a matter of language as language. That is, Blanchot's fiction does not turn into concrete poetry but still represents or narrates aspects of a consciousness divested of metaphysical preconceptions and orientations. Since narrative depends upon an understanding of temporality, Blanchot has naturally inclined to the philosophy of Heidegger and has oriented his narratives and philosophical papers with respect to Heidegger's thoughts on temporality.

In the later Heidegger, temporality again comes to consciousness through paronomasia or the iteration of the indeterminability of identity and difference. This, in turn, comprises an interplay of temporal horizons which Heidegger in "Zeit und Sein" calls the "fourth dimension" of temporality, itself

termed "interplay." Of this interplay—this is a direct conceptual reflection of the manifold of terms disclosed through a
word like *logos* in the seminars of the 1940s—Heidegger will
not disclose a formal logic, for he writes, "logical classifications
mean nothing here." Speaking of the "fourth dimension" Heidegger writes: "But the dimension which we call the fourth in
our count is, in the nature of the matter, the first, that is, the
giving that determines all. In future, in past, in the present, that
giving brings about to each its own presencing, holds them
apart thus opened and so holds them toward one another in the
nearness by which the three dimensions remain near one another."[41] The "giving" refers to "appropriation," and this "appropriation" cannot be thought or claimed by any word, for
"appropriation" is quite obviously a metaleptic movement in
which relations are made and withdrawn. We see this metaleptic or paronomasic movement, this linguistic spacing, in the
following quotation, which we will notice is exemplary of paronomasia and also is a gloss on the previous excerpt from "Zeit
und Sein."

> For as we think Being itself and follow what is its own,
> Being proves to be destiny's gift of presence, the gift
> granted by the giving of time. The gift of presence is the
> property of Appropriating. Being vanishes in Appropria-
> tion. In the phrase "Being as Appropriation," the word
> "as" now means: Being, letting-presence sent in Appro-
> priating, time extended in Appropriating. Time and
> Being appropriated in Appropriation. [Sein, Anwesen-
> lassen geschickt im Ereignen, Zeit gereicht im Ereignen.
> Zeit und Sein ereignet im Ereignis.] And Appropriation
> itself? Can we say anything more about it?[42]

Paronomasia is strongly reflected in the terms *Ereignen, Ereignis, ereignet, Ereignens*. In such instances time is performed as a
transferential eventhood suggesting that temporality is disclosed in language as the persistence of what is. Past, present,
and future belong to this appropriation or persistence, and the
nearness of these temporal moments occurs as the metalepsis of
saying in which repetition and displacement, identity and difference, redundancy and unrecuperability, occur.

In "Zeit und Sein" Heidegger develops a pleonastic notion

of a repeated or metaleptic "it." In the phrase "es gibt Sein" or "es gibt Zeit," Heidegger elicits the meaning of *es*, or "it," as a "limit" wherein an unappropriable *apeiron* is given. Recalling our previous discussion of the *apeiron* in chapter 1 as constituted in a slippage of its prefix "a," one could say that the "it" is merely a marker standing in the origination of the saying of origin by means of enabling a rift in words through which temporality comes about by way of the interrelations of difference and identity. Heidegger prefers to think of the "it" which gives being or time as *unbestimmt*, or undecided, and describes the origination of being and time as a giving, sending, or destining in whose correspondences the interplay of horizonal ontological relations is activated as language. In the "it gives being" or "it gives time" there is an "appropriation" that "brings each in a different way into its own."

This bringing is what Blanchot calls the *à venir*. "It" is the coming about of a coming into an own, wherein own-ness is dispossessed of the "own." Heidegger explicitly mentions this demolition of the own in its own arrival when responding to Joan Stambaugh's English translation of excerpts from *Nietzsche*. Heidegger says, "[Appropriation] is neither 'in time' nor is it the 'temporality' of human being, but rather brings each in a different way into its own. In 'Zeit und Sein,' however, the relation of the Appropriation and the human being of mortals is consciously excluded."[43] In short, the appropriation and interplay which is the fourth dimension of time cannot be situated as existential experience, cannot be thought from the perspective of Dasein. And yet, this is Blanchot's project, to disclose in the exteriority of written space that arrival of the destiny of the "it gives" wherein human being is constituted even as it is excluded.

In *Le pas au-delà* Blanchot acknowledges the Heideggerian *es*, which he describes as the limit/nonlimit of the coming to be of the addresser in the withdrawal of its being as something proper to itself:

> "it": does it not indicate "it" better in the doubled use which this phrase allows, might it be a repetition which is not singular (the second "it," if it restores the first gives something back to it in order to restore the verb in an un-

stable position—will it fall to one side or another?—that is, the interrogative position), that is to say an enunciation that may be called "pleonastic," not because it would be pure redundancy, but because it is there as without usefulness or purpose, effacing itself and effacing itself once more, until confounding itself with the inarticulation of the phrase.

["il" s'indique-t-"il" mieux dans le double emploi qu'en vient de faire cette phrase, soit une répétition qui n'en est pas une (le second "il," s'il restitue le premier, le redonne pour redresser le verbe en position instable—tombera-t-il d'un côté ou de l'autre?—qui est position interrogative), c'est-à-dire une énonciation qu'on peut appeler "pléonastique," non parce qu'il serait de pure redondance, mais parce qu'il est là comme sans emploi, s'effaçant et s'effaçant encore, jusqu'à se confondre avec l'inarticulation de la phrase?][44]

The pronoun *il* is repeated pleonastically and is spaced, divided, yet kept identical. In this temporality, this iteration of the pronoun, one instant comes to replace another and in doing so an obliterating and restituting of the *il* takes place. Hence a trace structure is established as the *il* deconstitutes the "difference" between that "outside" of existential experience and what is "inside" it. This pleonastic *il*, in other words, goes beyond Heidegger's thought that an appropriation can be spoken of in "Zeit und Sein" which is completely outside of human experience, that the "it" marks an exteriority wholly exterior. Much more remote, from Blanchot's perspective, is an "it" that is intimate with consciousness, with what is interior. Without embarking on a lengthy analysis, one should briefly mention a passage in *Au moment voulu* wherein such an "it" is anticipated by Blanchot. A man has lived through a terrible event, though "it" cannot be disclosed. Yet this "it" repeats without declaring itself. "Had it happened once? A first time and yet not the first. It had the strangest relations with time, and this was uplifting too: it did not belong to the past, a face and the promise of a face." The "it" which stands for the horrifying event is no longer so much an ordeal passed through as something that "spaces" out time for the narrator, something quite external to him and unassimilable, and yet something upon which the moments in the novel bear. In other words, in this novel the "it" of the horror "gives time" to the narrator not as a subject but as a relatedness to an interplaying of moments which, as he says, "fall into time." Yet, "that fall had also crossed time and carved out an immense emptiness [*une immensité vide*], and this pit [*fosse*] appeared to be the jubilant celebration of the future."[45] The "it" in *Au moment voulu* is both that which broaches an *einholen* and an *aus-holen* of time, and this, as Heidegger says in *Heraklit,* is what makes man deep.

Pas

Derrida's "Pas" was originally published during 1975 in the journal *Gramma,* which devoted two issues to the work of Maurice Blanchot. "Pas," of course, intentionally refers to *Le pas au-delà,* though it also alludes less conspicuously to texts like Heidegger's *Identity and Difference* wherein the notion of the step or path is thematized as "dem Weg des Schrittes zurück," or the path of the step back. We recall that for Heidegger philosophy steps back in order to move forward and that this stepping back, as we saw in relation to Anaximander, is a means of letting one's philosophy take place in another's language even as that language is being dismantled or overcome. However, in *Identity and Difference* Heidegger wonders whether such a retrogression does not accomplish metaphysics even in its surpassing of that tradition? "Everything that results by way of the step back may merely be exploited and absorbed by metaphysics in its own way, as the result of representational thinking [*eines vorstellenden Denkens*]."[46] The problem, Heidegger suggests, is not so much in the turning back or retrogression than in the language by means of which one steps back in order to go forward, since this language is itself metaphysical. "It must remain an open question whether the nature of Western languages is in itself marked with the exclusive brand of metaphysics, and thus marked permanently by onto-theologic, or whether these languages offer other possibilities of utterance—and that means at the same time of a telling silence."[47]

In "Pas," as in many of Derrida's writings of the mid-1970s (for example, *Glas*), there is an even more aggressive attempt than in the past to perform language so that the "step" of philosophy is no longer dissociable from the step or not of language resisting metaphysical, mimetic recovery, or *vorstellendem Denken*. And this deconstructive performance of language follows from Heidegger's own attempts to write philosophy otherwise. Indeed, the figure who mediates Heidegger in this way to Derrida is Blanchot, in whose writings, as we have seen, the resistance to what Heidegger calls the metaphysical nature of language is itself taken by means of a step back into the writings of Heidegger in order, of course, to move forward.

Derrida's "Pas" presupposes that such a step back may include intermediaries, that any step back is inherently metaleptic. Hence the step back to Heidegger for Derrida occurs only through stepping back to Blanchot. Yet in the step back to Blanchot the work of Heidegger may also not be reached, since it undergoes a certain erasure or abrasion in Blanchot's appropriation of it. In the "step back," therefore, we immediately notice the problematic of identity and difference wherein retrogression is fulfilled as that going back in which what lies prior is never arrived at or recovered as such. Gianni Vattimo in *Les aventures de la différence* notes that such retrogression is called *An-denken* in Heidegger and is intimately associated with the notion of *Verabschieden*: "taking leave of that which has constituted its temporality, of that which has come about according to its measure, of that which has been fulfilled."[48] In "Pas" this taking leave is ironically posed in terms of an unpacking of the word *viens* in the writings of Blanchot. Throughout "Pas" the question is one of how Derrida is to arrive or come to Heidegger in his coming to Blanchot's work. In other words, Derrida's project in "Pas" is to ask how he is to take a step back to these precursors in order to step ahead of them. This, in "Pas," is how Blanchot's phrase *le pas au-delà*, becomes relevant as the Heideggerian *Schritt zurück*.

In meditating on the step taken in order to arrive at a reading of Blanchot, or, better yet, a homage to Blanchot, Derrida cautions, "Oseriez-vous tutoyer Blanchot? [Would you dare to be fresh with Blanchot?]"[49] That is to say, he questions the distances involved in arriving at such a homage, the approach that one has to take in approaching from the standpoint of already having approached Blanchot. What is the appropriate distance of *An-denken*? How can one even dare to speak of Blanchot as if this name gave one access to a proximity from which homage could be paid, a proximity to which Derrida could arrive as a writer who was at home in the language of Blanchot? Some of these concerns are reflected in the following from "Pas."

> Come—
> Come: how do you name that which I am coming from?—that from which I have come? that which I come (am about) to say?
>
> [Viens—
> Viens: comment appeler ce que je viens de—ce que je viens de quoi? ce que je viens de dire?][50]

Derrida wonders whether coming from, arriving at, or paying homage to is ever a return to the same place, the same person, or the same work. "Eternally I say 'Come,'" a voice says in Blanchot's narrative, *L'arrêt de mort,* as if to insist that in repeating the word the coming or arrival of an other is always differed and deferred even in its coming or taking place. Derrida recognizes this division or divisibility of an arrival or coming—in the 1980s Derrida will consider this coming in terms of the Second Coming of Christ—and stresses its (dis)appropriability as follows, "Il dit *maintenant* qu'il le dit, mais qu'il le dit, donc l'a dit et le dira, éternellement [He says now that he says it, but that he says it, and has therefore said it and will say it, eternally]."[51] This divisibility of saying is the divisibility of the arrival of that which is announced, a divisibility said in the paronomasia or *différance* in the approach of the word "Viens," an approach of something that never really comes, of that which is eternally held in abeyance even as it approaches or nears. And this is the *pas,* or step, taken in Blanchot that is the *pas* as not.

In Derrida's "Pas" not only the word *pas* but *viens* functions as a word matrix, like Heidegger's use of the Greek term *logos*. *Venir,* of course, has the advantage of being conjugatable, and Derrida is quite aggressive in working through certain metaleptic conjugations, since they facilitate a deconstructive orientation to language and temporality which Heidegger and, much more boldly, Blanchot have developed. The verb *venir* is, like the Heideggerian words taken from the pre-Socratics, a word that suggests the arrival, coming, or sending of something into Being. That is, like *aletheia* or *logos,* the word *venir* is an originary manifold of proximate terms in whose relationships are disclosed the question of an approach of Being as well as a giving of time, the "Es gibt Zeit." This is not to say that the *viens* is, in fact, a metaphysical groundwork, but rather that it is analogous to a structure of relations like *a-letheia,* which suggest that the ground for the coming of Being is a priori deconstructed and that, moreover, this "approach" of or toward Being is reflected not merely in the ancient Greeks but, as Blanchot demonstrates, in what Heidegger in his early works might have called everyday consciousness. This domestication of Heidegger, if one can call it that, becomes much more pronounced in *The Post Card* with its focus on everyday occurrences which are more often than not trivial except to the person who experiences them. For Blanchot the everyday is perforated with expectation and lassitude wherein the moment of arrival in which experience might be integratable as a teleological history is always promised even though eternally deferred. In this coming, arrival, or promise of a metaphysical event, time is promised to us as a present in which all moments can be rationally synchronized; however, in the promise's unfulfillment, consciousness is denied such a recoverability of a historical time wherein the subject can be present to itself as itself in its past and future moments. Derrida underscores this approach to time by arguing that even in the conjugations of *venir* the terms no longer "belong" or are able to take a step back to their verbal origin: the infinitive. "'Viens' is not a modification of *venir.* To the contrary. And surely this contrary is no more simply contrary, rather it is an wholly different relation. Consequently my 'hypothesis' doesn't delimit a logical or scientific operation, in the usual sense of these words, that one might be able to verify or enfeeble. Rather, it describes the approach of *viens* upon *venir*."[52]

Especially interesting in "Pas" is that Derrida considers Heidegger's thought at length with respect to the notion of distance which in English I hyphenate as dis-stance. We noticed earlier in Heidegger's seminar of 1941 on Anaximander that he himself hyphenated the word *ent-fernen,* and Derrida develops this notion of distance as crucial to an understanding not only of Blanchot's use of the word *viens* but of Derrida's taking it up as a means of approaching his precursors.

> By way of another step, all Heideggerian thought proceeds in terms of its decisive "turnings," by way of the "same" bringing closer the dis-stancing of the near and the far. *Distanciation* dis-stances the far which it constitutes; the approach then brings it closer by keeping it at a distance. The eventual propriation (etymologically forced or risked for the word *Ereignis*) is itself made dis-stant. The proximity of the near is not near, nor proper to itself, then, and you see the annunciation, coming closer and closer, of all the ruptures in secureness. When I will say *distancing,* however, when I will read it in one of its texts, always understand the invisible trace which holds this word open to itself, of itself, dis-stancing itself: of a *step* (a not) which distances the distant from itself. Pas (no/step) is the Thing. "Distancing is here at the heart of the thing." ("The Two Versions of the Imaginary" in *L'espace litteraire*)

> [D'un autre pas, toute le pensée 'heideggerienne' procède, en ses "tournants" de décision, par le "même" rapproachement é-loignant du proche et du lointain. *L-Entfernung* é-loigne le lointain qu'elle constitue, le rapproche donc en le tenant au loin. La propriation éventuelle (étymologie forcée ou hasardé pour l'*Ereignis*) en est d'elle-même é-loignée. La proximité du proche n'est pas proche, ni propre donc, et tu vois s'annoncer de proche en proche toutes les ruptures de barrage. Quand je dirai *éloignement,* désormais, quand je le lirai dans l'un de ses textes, entends toujours le trait invisible qui tient ce mot ouvert sur lui-même, de lui-même é-loigné: d'un *pas* qui

éloigne le lointain de lui-même. Pas est la Chose. "L'éloignement est ici au coeur de la chose." ("Les deux versions de l'imaginaire," in *L'espace littéraire*)][53]

The *éloignement* is the condition of proximity in which the temporality of an event transpires. But this proximity is not so much a place as arrival itself, the coming to "him" or "her" which takes place in its not ever properly taking place. The *é-loigné*, therefore, is the *re-trait* of time, the necessary condition of a difference that withdraws in its coming forth or arrival. *Viens,* then, is the *é-loigné,* the arrival of dis-stance as the dis-stance of arrival. This trait, moreover, appears to us in the segmentation of language as metalepsis or paronomasia. "D'un pas qui éloigné le lointain de lui-même," after all, is a par-onomasic stepping or slippage of sound, *éloigne- -lointain—lui-même,* in which a correspondence between entities occurs even as these entities do not entirely correspond or arrive at each other. Hence the distancing distances, *Entfernung é-loigne* holding the word of its arrival or coming (*viens*) open to itself: proximate, unclosed, at the very same time that it persists about a point. This voicing of distance is what Derrida will later discuss as "tone" or the "tonality" of that anticipatory con-sciousness which considers the ends of man or apocalypse. In *Identity and Difference,* Heidegger calls this the *Zusammenge-hören,* which is a pun on belonging together as hearing to-gether.[54]

However much one can anticipate or talk about an arrival of the end—for example, the end of philosophy—this end is held back, an end that in its coming does not come. To arrive at Blanchot, Heidegger, or Derrida, for that matter, is not to arrive at the end of metaphysics, therefore, unless one takes all three of these figures together for the sake of examining the notion of dis-stance, wherein the economy of metaphysical concepts is very much threatened and capable of being dis-mantled or deconstructed. This arrival/nonarrival at the end of metaphysics concerns the Heideggerian "event" or appropriat-ing moment of the tradition which in Heidegger, Blanchot, and Derrida is articulated as a paronomasic dis-stance disclosed by language. Such distance is not merely collapsed into an aporia, such as the aporia of the *pas,* but itself "gives time" as a philosophical mode of thinking that "makes time" for itself in time thanks to a slowness of semantic approach.

Derrida notices such slowness in *Memoires* when he says that too many people would like him to say what he has to say so that they can "turn the page" and get on with whatever might come after deconstruction is over, after its arrival. But, as he says, such a turning of the page is not in his interests and certainly not an "event" that, given Derrida's thinking in essays like "Pas," could ever arrive or make itself present in the way that the detractors of deconstruction, such as Walter Jackson Bate or René Wellek, would like.[55] Rather, such a mode of reflection "makes time" with words.

> (The slowness) accomplishes (accelerating and retarding infinitely at the same time) a curious displacement of time, of times, of continuous steps (nots) and of move-ments twisted about an invisible axis without presence, passing from one to the other without break, of one time in the other, in preserving the infinite distance of mo-ments. This displacement in all the complexity of its net-work displaces itself, across *l'attente l'oubli*. Initially the narrative always narrates this displacement of these dis-placements. It distances them from themselves.[56]

The *pas* that joins and separates Heidegger, Blanchot, and Derrida is the *pas au-delà* of the philosophical tradition, the *pas* which "gives time." In this *pas* they belong or cohere without either belonging or cohering in the usual historical sense, and through this *pas* they maintain a continuity of thought in a slowness of arrival that, as Heidegger says, "persists." *Viens*: this could mean the persistence of arriving, a persistence of coming that persists as displacement, fracture, fragment, corre-spondence, and dis-stance. "Le pas qui rapproche é-loigne," Derrida writes with Blanchot in mind.

Certainly, anyone who reads Heidegger, Blanchot, and Der-rida should acknowledge the extent, then, that these writers and others closely affiliated to them (one thinks of Samuel Beckett and Marguerite Duras) have a commitment to a lin-guistic turning that occurs in the translation and transference of their writings, a commitment that recognizes the relays of meaning through the *pas* of arriving at the words of another.

These writings disclose a disruptive temporality by means of semantic displacement and replacement, by means of a paronomasic stepping which goes beyond even as it is kept back in an interplay of tenses wherein the self-presentation of the text is determined as an appropriation of moments which never arrives in its coming to pass. Hence what comes to pass in its not passing is, according to Derrida, the philosophical "law" which Blanchot invokes in his fiction, what in another essay on Blanchot has been called "the Law of Genre."

> This law without law of dis-stance isn't essence, but the impossible topic of essentialism. Let's take the most economic route for comprehending this. It crosses into a discursive schema of Heidegger and prepares us to think at once of proximity and, this will not appear until much later, the chiasm forcefully distancing two thoughts from one another: *l'Entfernung*, which I have proposed to translate by dis-stancing, and *l'Ereignis* (the event, a word in which one has arrived, abusively without doubt, to read the "proper" [*eigen*]. . .).[57]

The "event" or *Ereignis* is not a moment present to itself but that of a correspondence of thoughts which in their arrival together are divided or dis-stanced. As such, these thoughts have nothing completely "proper" to themselves, since they depend proximately on other terms and since their fulfillment as thoughts which are entirely self-present is inherently delayed or kept in abeyance.

> (. . . that is the process of the near or of appropriation, and towards which I would like—here—to have you understand the souvenir [*sous-venir*] without the memory of a *viens*) in this collusion without identity of the near and of the far which we broach at this step (*pas*). Hence: something (what? something else) is approaching. We believe we understand what this would mean, most clearly above all: the thing tends to become close. But close to what, of what other thing? Let us leave this question on one side for the moment. Close to an other thing or itself as an other thing, the thing cannot appear close but as that which anticipates what is close and

proximate. Not as a general concept of proximity but as
the essence of the near "beginning with" which such a
concept can be formed. What is then the "near" or the
relation "near-far?" What is the proximity of nearness?
The thing, certainly, can be near, but the near or the
proximate is not near. The proximity of the near is not
an *other thing* but the near thing, yet it isn't near.[58]

The question of proximity or nearness of thought is in this
passage being metaleptically segmented and resegmented, and
in this way Derrida goes even further than Blanchot in the
divisibility of the "approach" to the thoughts of an other. One
should bear in mind that the main issue is no longer the aporia
of the *pas,* wherein arrival/nonarrival is made so indeterminate
as to become undecidable, but rather the production of that
eternal persistence of differentiation and identification which
"gives time" or latitude to thought. What is the thing? Derrida
asks, with Heidegger's meditations on thinghood in mind. As
Heidegger has already said in *Vorträge und Aufsätze,* the thing
is there as a holding of things in relation. Hence, "the thing
things." Because of the thing, which is to say, the thing as
indicative of the difference and identity of things, there are
things generally. In Derrida's context, the thing is in a state of
announcing its arrival into the world as thing only insofar as it
discloses itself as distanced (dis-stanced) from other things.
The thing, therefore, comes into Being only to the extent that
it has never quite fully arrived into the world as a thing-in-
itself. What is a thing? A thing is that which is coming to pass; a
thing is that which is on the way. But to see things in this sense
is to take, as Heidegger himself says in "The Thing," a "step
back." "The step back," Heidegger writes, "takes up its resi-
dence in a co-responding."[59] Derrida continues the passage
above by thinking through this corresponding as nearness.

> The essence of the near is not more near than the essence
> of red is the color red. Let us submit ourselves to the law
> of this truth, to this manifestation of essence as such
> which dominates the most powerful philosophical tradi-
> tion, until Heidegger who close to it finds the most deci-
> sive help ever in thought. Consequently, the more one is
> tempted to come near the proximity of that which is ap-

proaching, the more the wholly other—and thus infinitely distanced—of proximity buries or empties itself (*se
creuse*). As one may say of distance, there is no pertinent
opposition between the near and the far, nor any identity. Yet this bivalence of contraband or double bind affects everything: that which is, that is to say in
presenting itself, being present, comes, advances, arrives,
exists. It affects the essence of the event and the event of
essence, as much as it does indissociable semantic values
of a deterritorialized topos of the near and the far. You
intuit then what occurs in the not of dis-stance. And of
that which expends itself in this movement. And the
strange rhythm that it imprints to our discourse, to the
choice of words, to the construction of our phrases, to
the idiom of the word "pas." Rarifaction, rigorous and
strict law: it goes on to the other. It cannot be approaching as other, in its phenomenon of otherness, but in distancing itself from it and appearing in its distance of
infinite alterity as approaching. In this double step or
not, the other dislocates the opposition of the near and
the far without however confusing them. It subjects phe-
nomenal presence to this movement.[60]

The relations between Derrida and Blanchot, or between Blanchot and Heidegger, are those of a nearness in which the
subject who writes philosophy takes on the conditionality of
the thing or monument, which, as Heidegger would say, "stays
relations." But in order to see this, we must necessarily "step
back" from the subject who writes in the usual historical sense.
We must step back from the writer as monumental consciousness which is considered present-to-itself.

The step, or *pas,* then, can be understood as what Derrida in
Positions called a "mark" that does not represent a concept but,
rather, a sign for a syntactical lesion whose consequence is the
disruption of familiar conceptual economies, though by no
means their simple transcendence or destruction. Moreover,
the *pas* begins a much more explicit mode of outlining positions with respect to how Derrida believes deconstruction relates to the work of predecessors from which it has received
inspiration. In saying flatly that "Pas" formulates Derrida's

interpretation of where he fits in intellectual history, I, of course, do violence to his very delicate analyses by way of a crude metaphysical recovery, since the purpose of his analysis is to show that one can no longer pose the question in the way I just have. Nevertheless, I wish to establish that from an unreformed historical perspective a turn has been made to the issue of filiation which will become much more pronounced in *The Post Card*. Also, I wish to establish that despite the very meticulous analyses of "distance" and "arrival," "Pas" is the text wherein Derrida seems to have arrived more closely to an agreement with Heidegger than in perhaps any other of his texts, an agreement wherein the correspondence with Heidegger occurs through his paying homage to Blanchot.

Retrait *and Restitutions*

The *pas* in Derrida is, of course, exemplary of a *re-trait*. Rodolphe Gasché summarizes the meanings of this term well in the context of Heidegger in "Joining the Text: From Heidegger to Derrida" when he writes:

> The word trait (*Zug*) refers to the tracing of a way or a rift (*Riss*) which, as an in-between (*Zwischen*), opens a first relation (*Bezug*). The trait accomplishes the differential mark that allows language to name and put into relation what it names. [. . .] Second, the trait withdraws, retreats, in the very act of its tracing an in-between for a relation. [. . .] The trait comes forth only by being blotted out. [. . .] Third, the trait cannot simply be identified with this seemingly alternating movement of forthcoming and subsequent extinction, because the retreat of the trait is also what allows the trait to come forward from under its obliteration as *retrait*.[61]

In French, as Gasché also notes, *retrait* recalls terms like "recess," "withdrawal," "retrace," and "retreat." Although the *pas* can be interpreted in the context of Heidegger's *Übersteigen* in *The Essence of Reasons,* it could also be read as a *re-trait* that in coming never comes, even though it "accomplishes the dif-

ferential mark" putting the "pas (not) . . . pas (step)" into relation. The *pas* as *retrait,* therefore, would be the opening of a
relation even as what opens it withdraws into the singularity of
a word, *pas.* Moreover the "pas . . . pas" stands in a metaphorical relationship to itself even though both the tenor and vehicle
stand in the same place, the place of a pun. Like Heidegger's
use of the word *Lesen,* the *pas* conceals the trait of difference
which withdraws in its being traced, in its coming forward.
Hence, once more, the *pas* is a (not) step ahead. *"L-Entfernung*
é-loigne le lointain," or dis-stance dis-stances the distant. The *pas*
is the guide word, as Heidegger would say, of this spacing or
rift (*Riss*), which, as Derrida says in "The Retreat of Metaphor"
"n'arrive qu'a s'effacer," only comes about in being effaced. The
pas is the Heideggerian step back, the (not) step of the philosophical advance. Yet in (not)-stepping Heidegger has, in fact,
sighted the beyond or outside of metaphysical closure and of
conceptual formations which we have taken for granted at the
level not only of philosophical speculation but of ideology.

In "The Retreat of Metaphor" Derrida uses the term *retrait*
to develop a notion of metaphor that has the effect of bringing
into closer proximity the analysis of *la différance* within a Heideggerian context of conceptual relationships. And this essay,
moreover, emphasizes the paronomasic play of language as that
which resists the strategies of mimetic language. As in "The
White Mythology," metaphor is viewed in "The Retreat" as a
transference of terms, though it is discussed with respect to the
trait of difference whose effect is to reveal and conceal the
approach of meaning which is itself kept in abeyance even as it
is advanced or forwarded. Here the question is implicitly
posed: how does meaning arrive by means of metaphor? What
constitutes the "step" of metaphor as meta-lepse? Or, the "pas
de metaphor?" Certainly, the notion of wear and tear discussed
earlier in our analysis of "The White Mythology" is not so
much transcended than recontextualized along proximate
modes of conceptualization that draw their inspiration from
Heidegger, even as the idea of metaphor as writing under
erasure is kept in mind.

Addressing Heidegger's significance as a thinker, Derrida
writes,

I speak of the Heideggerian *text*: I do so to underscore by a supplementary line (*trait*) that it is not only a question for me of considering the stated propositions, the themes and theses on the subject of metaphor as such, the content of his discourse treating rhetoric and this trope, but of his writing, his treatment of language and, more rigorously, his treatment of the trait, of "trait" in every sense, and more rigorously still of "trait" as a word in his language, and of the trait as a tracing incision (*entame*) of language.[62]

Again, paronomasia. No doubt, it allows for a rapprochement or an arrival at Heidegger's writing. And this rapprochement occurs, of course, after Derrida has contested Paul Ricoeur's reading of a note in "The White Mythology" as set forth in *La métaphore vive*. Derrida points out that some of the materials he himself had not pursued in this essay pertained to Heidegger's "Der Weg zur Sprache" wherein the word *Geflecht* occurs. This word designates a "singular, unique interlacing between *Sprache* (a word I will not translate, so as not to have to choose between *langue* [language] and *parole* [speech]) and path (*chemin; Weg, Bewegung, Bewegen,* etc.). It is a question here of a binding-unbinding interlacing (*entbindende Band*) back towards which we would be incessantly steered." Heidegger's thinking on metaphor, then, becomes like an approach, or path. This is the way of metalepse, of *Übertragung*, of a carrying over toward. "We are implicated in advance, interlaced in advance when we wish to speak of *Sprache* and of *Weg* which are 'already in advance of us' (*uns stets schon voraus*)."[63] But this perception, judging from the 1960s essays touching on Heidegger, not to say "The White Mythology" of 1970, appears strongly mediated by a reading that occurred after these essays were completed, a reading of Blanchot. In footnote 29 of "The White Mythology" in Alan Bass's translation of *Margins of Philosophy*—over the interpretation of which Derrida is in dispute with Ricoeur—Derrida thinks about metaphor as transference, and thinks about the transference taking place from the sensory to the nonsensory. And he notes that such a notion of metaphorical transference exists "only within the borders of metaphysics."[64] But in "The Retrait of Metaphor,"

transference is revised to mean the interlacing of that which
is already in advance of us, with that which is to come, *à
venir*.

It is not unreasonable to assume, given the attack on what is
considered Heidegger's metaphysical and humanist vocabulary
of proximity in "The Ends of Man," that there is something
slippery in the claim of "The Retrait of Metaphor" that "I
[Derrida] could have chosen, among many other possibilities,
the one which has just been presented to me under the name of
entanglement."[65] For, what does Derrida mean by this use of
the past tense, "I could have chosen"? That is to say, *when* could
he have chosen? At the time of writing "The White Mythology"? Certainly, this is the moment Ricoeur is considering.
Yet, this is precisely the moment when Derrida could have
chosen from among the other possibilities to pursue Heidegger's notion of interlacing or entanglement with respect to
metaphor, but he would *not* have been motivated to do so.
Such a path only comes—in what we see published, at least—
after the recent reading of Blanchot. Judging from the publications, it was precisely during the late 1960s that Derrida was
not at all inclined to read Heidegger in terms of this vocabulary
of proximities. And a change occurs only with the publication
of "Pas" and, more or less at the same time, "The Retrait of
Metaphor." This marks a decided rapprochement with Heidegger that will have very important consequences for Derrida's
later work. Indeed, the "debate" with Ricoeur suggests that
Derrida is already reinscribing or turning back on himself this
new orientation as if it were unquestionably always a part of
Derrida's philosophy. One can only wonder what Ricoeur
must have thought on having the tables turned in this way.

Another essay very much in the orbit of "Pas" is "Restitutions," from *The Truth in Painting*. In many ways this is a
particularly playful and comic text that considers a well-known
Van Gogh painting of shoes discussed by Heidegger in "The
Origin of the Work of Art" and by the art critic Meyer Schapiro. The notion of "restitution" is very much considered in
regard to a coming back or *revenir* reminiscent of (one is
tempted to say, restituting) Blanchot's writings. And this is
involved in the *pas* of the shoes themselves, that "step" the

shoes cannot make even as the step is made through the process of artistic representation. This *pas* takes certain steps in Heidegger, and these steps are subjected to the *pas,* or "no," of Schapiro. Hence, Derrida, not without humor, investigates the pairing of Heidegger, who has maintained that the shoes belong to a peasant in the fields, and Schapiro, who insists that the shoes belong to Van Gogh. What a pair! But to whom are these shoes to be restored? Derrida knows that these shoes are themselves worn and torn, that possibly they have been discarded. In that case, neither Heidegger nor Schapiro's conjectures would be anything more than a wish for the thing to be animated by presence, the human subject (as *le revenant,* the ghost). Again, both Heidegger and Schapiro believe that the shoes are, indeed, a pair of shoes. There is much that is comforting in the notion of a pair. But this pair, Derrida suggests, may not, in fact, be a pair at all. Such an oversight would be forgivable in the case of Heidegger, but that a reputed art critic could not see two right or two left shoes when Van Gogh clearly paints them would be an embarrassment, to say the least.

Here, then, is Derrida's beginning for a study of a pairing which is always already divided, a symmetry harassed by asymmetry. To put it another way, Derrida views the shoes as metaphors in Heidegger's "Origin of the Work of Art" which are metaleptic in the sense that they cross over the soil or path announced by Heideggerian philosophy. Yet this crossing is necessary, because these shoes are iterated in ways that make (appropriate) and break (expropriate) pairing. For if they are exactly doubled they do not pair; if they are inexactly doubled they do pair. To make matters even more interesting, Derrida notices that Van Gogh did not paint just one canvas with representations of shoes but that there is, in fact, a series of eight of these paintings. How is the subject that Heidegger and Schapiro treat to "come back" to these meta-leptic shoes? How are these shoes to be worn in and by aesthetic theory?

If this sort of metaleptic movement makes one dizzy, Derrida ups the ante by playing off that "pair," Heidegger/Schapiro, a nonpair that turns out, of course, to be perfectly paired given their concerns. And yet, they are not by any stretch of the imagination to be paired without there being great violence done to them. Derrida, of course, is most sensitive to the fight over these shoes or their appropriation, because he knows this battle for restitution concerns a certain Jewish history. As Derrida says, "there's persecution in this tale." This persecution is relayed via a certain Professor Goldstein who had to flee Nazi Germany and who was an influence on Schapiro. And the point is that these Jewish scholars want Van Gogh's shoes to be restored to the city people, that is, to those who were persecuted by the landed *Volk* and who are to be identified, in a distant sense, to Van Gogh who was himself a persecuted figure of sorts. "There's persecution in this tale, in this history of shoes to be identified, to be appropriated, and who knows how many bodies, names, and anonymities (nameable and unnameable) this story is made of. We'll come back to this. What endures here, and what matters to me, is this correspondence between Meyer Schapiro and Martin Heidegger."[66] What matters, in fact, is the correspondence between Nazi and Jew, that correspondence which occurs in the wake of millions of dispossessed shoes stored up in concentration camp warehouses. What matters, in other words, is "restitution," or *Wiedergutmachung*. It would be that restitution which effaces the National Socialist construction of blood and soil, represented in Heidegger by the passage concerning peasant shoes in *Holzwege*. To what ghosts do these shoes return? And what ghosts return to these shoes? The laughter of "Restitutions" is steeped in the blackness of this commedia. Speaking of these shoes, Derrida says, "Several world wars and mass deportations. We can take our time. *There* they *are*, made to wait. Made to start walking, led on [*pour faire marches*]. The irony of their patience is infinite; it can be held of no account. So we've reached this public correspondence."[67] What must correspond for this correspondence to transpire? Derrida's answer is simple: the subject must correspond to the shoe, which is to say in English, the shoe must fit. That is, Heidegger and Schapiro must both see the shoes as a unified pair in order to appropriate them for an appropriate subject, be it a peasant woman or Van Gogh. Derrida, quite obviously, will see this attempt at appropriation as nothing other than a dividing of the pair, in which persecution is inscribed. For just as the Jews were persecuted by the *Volk*, Schapiro in his corresponding with Heidegger is persecuting the German philosopher, "going after him" with a vengeance, setting a "trap" for him, settling a score (but can a "score"— one thinks of a score of shoes such as this one—ever be settled?). Hence, restitution. And hence each subject gets one shoe, even if each walks badly with just one. But if this division of the pair is the disclosure of a *différance* (René Girard's thoughts are applicable here) that we call persecution, it is the *différance* of restitution which comes by way of an offering, that is to say, sacrifice.

Derrida quite ingeniously notices such *différance* in the fact that the pair of shoes depicted by Van Gogh is not really a genuine pair of different shoes that could be worn by a subject but two shoes belonging to the same foot. Without carrying out what would necessarily be a very long commentary—indeed, "Restitutions" is one of Derrida's finest and wittiest essays—one should say that in contemplating what we idiomatically call a broken pair of shoes, Heideggerian appropriation announces itself *en retrait* as expropriation. Schapiro is never able to see this expropriating horizon except from within a desire to achieve appropriation and restitution. This is why he, too, sees the shoes as a genuine pair. But Derrida knows that in those mountains of shoes collected at the death camps it would be another matter to look for pairs, that in the symmetry of the shoes of Van Gogh, themselves having survived two world wars and numbers of mass deportations, this terrifying and unspeakable expropriation of humanity has already been announced: the destiny of the Jews has been perceived as *à venir/avenir*. This is the *retrait* from within the *es gibt Sein,* the moment of expropriation from within appropriation, the destitution from within restitution. Moreover, and this is important, this holocaust is not merely a Jewish question, which is where Schapiro, according to Derrida's analysis, is so dreadfully mistaken, but is the withdrawal of Being against which both the Heidegger and Schapiro interpretations of Van Gogh stand. And for this reason these interpretations, for all their divisions or oppositions, remain a pair that are unpaired in their pairing up with persecution. In the pleonasm or paronomasia of this pairing/unpairing of shoes Derrida detects the temporal approach of a historical moment to come that has, of course, already arrived even in its eternal warning to the persecuted. A time of restitution.

With "Restitutions" in mind, we will now turn to the much later study of Heidegger by Derrida entitled *De l'esprit,* wherein the question of restitution resonates even as Derrida explores at some length the paronomasic slippage in the Heideggerian use of the word *Geist.* It is here that Derrida will, once more, turn against Heidegger, and particularly in terms of the destiny of the Jews as posited in the (dis)appropriative movement of *Geist* in the history of Heidegger's writings. Such distance-taking from Heidegger emphasizes disturbing issues that had begun to be introduced shortly after the publication of *The Truth in Painting,* though here with respect to the restitution of spirit in Heidegger's thinking and its bearing on the modern history of Germany in its relation to European Jewry. By considering *De l'esprit,* we anticipate a new phase in Derrida's thinking on Heidegger, wherein the history of the Jews in relation to European philosophy is situated in terms of a paronomasic or metaleptic reading of Heideggerian language initiated largely in the 1970s.

Heidegger's Geist

If temporality is closely associated with a paronomasic slippage of language in Derrida's essays of the 1970s, his essays of the 1980s continue such an orientation, though with respect to the historical as such. As I have already noted, some of the essays written by Derrida during the 1980s take a more negative approach to Heidegger reminiscent of attitudes taken in the work of the late 1960s. Of particular interest, in this respect, is the recent book on Heidegger, *De l'esprit,* wherein the paronomasia of spirit is considered at length: *Geist, geistig, geistlich.* We have already discussed Heidegger's early writings on being and the project in *Being and Time* which proposes by means of a temporal clue to "destroy" the conceptual apparatus of Western ontology. And we recall that during the 1960s Derrida maintains that this early Heideggerian project falls short of its aims. At the beginning of this chapter I introduced the project in Heidegger which could be said to rework the demolition of Western ontology from the vantage point of the pre-Socratic notion(s) of the *logos*. However, in *De l'esprit*, Derrida notices a much less prominent set of parallel forma- tions in Heidegger's work that, in fact, has not been generally noticed by Heidegger scholars and which is peculiarly prob- lematic. This is the consideration of how Heidegger parcels out the term *Geist* at various junctures in his career, a parceling out that has uncomfortable political implications.

"Je parlerai du revenant, de la flamme et des cendres" ("I will speak of the ghost, of the flame, and of ashes"). *De l'esprit* will speak of German history. It will discuss Heidegger's quarantin- ing of *Geist* in *Being and Time*, its placement under arrest between quotation marks. Then it will turn to the rehabilita- tion or setting free of *Geist* in Heidegger's Rectorate's Speech, "The Self-Assertion of the German University." In this speech the first words announce the coming of spirit. "The assumption of the rectorate is the commitment to the *spiritual* leadership of this institution of higher learning."⁶⁸ Important philosophical corollaries are then noticed by Derrida in *An Introduction to Metaphysics*, wherein the politics of the Rectorate's Speech is reflected through a justification of the difference between ani- mal and man, between that which has *Geist* and that which does not. After very briefly considering the study *Nietzsche* and Hei- degger's thoughts on Hölderlin, Derrida turns to Heidegger's thoughts on Georg Trakl, published in 1953, entitled "Lan- guage in the Poem," in which there is yet another manifestation of *Geist* in terms of the "difference" between *geistig* and *geistlich*. Here the earlier considerations of *Geist* are undermined even as they are recovered by the institutions of metaphysics. The study ends on an indictment of those institutions of thought which have given shelter to the historical agendas of fascism.

As in Heidegger's analysis of the *logos* in *Heraklit*, the term *Geist* is considered by Derrida as an open field of relationships in which there occurs *Ver-sammlung*, the appropriation and disappropriation of closely related thoughts that have achieved both nearness and distance from one another even as they have been gathered and strewn in the enactment of the word *Geist* over time. At one point in considering Heidegger's *Nietzsche*, Derrida will re-collect *Geist* as "*Esprit/âme/vie, Pneuma/psyché/ zoè ou bios, spiritus/anima/vita, Geist/Seele/Leben,*" which is to say, as grouped sets wherein the stability of semantic relationships founders.[69] That this *Versammlung* concerns the temporal interrelationships or correspondences between a nineteenth-century humanist endowment and its demolition by Heideggerian philosophy is crucial to Derrida, for whom one of the aims of studying *Geist* in Heidegger concerns a glossing of the complex relations between deconstruction and its supposed antagonist, humanism. When Derrida acknowledges that "l'esprit est essentiellement temporalisation," he is well aware that in order to recover the term *Geist*, one has to recollect it historically or temporally in terms of its being granted or withheld in the texts of Heidegger.[70] Whatever we choose to call *Geist*, therefore, is a function of the temporality of its transferences or translations within the cultural history of modern Germany which sought to continue and also to break with nineteenth-century tradition. In *De l'esprit* Derrida will implicitly assess the extent to which Heidegger's considerations of *Geist* and its consequences for a theory of temporality, broached in the later writings, go beyond the abrogated project of *Being and Time* wherein temporality was considered largely from the perspectives of Dasein analysis.

Whereas in *The Post Card* history is viewed as the genealogical double binds of legators and legatees, in *De l'esprit* a chronological history of political events is left intact. This is not to say that Derrida is entertaining a vulgar notion of time but that he is acknowledging the chronology of political events at the same time that he wishes to expose the relationships of philosophy and politics in terms of the Heideggerian (dis)appropriation of *Geist*. This is where Heidegger breaks with nineteenth-century *Geisteswissenschaften*, even as he reappropriates *Geist* in texts such as the Rectorate's Speech and *An Introduction to Metaphysics*. One of the main questions in *De l'esprit* is how it is possible for Heidegger, who has interdicted *Geist* in *Being and Time*, to rehabilitate humanism in texts like the Rectorate's Speech in order to encourage German politicians to become responsible leaders. This is particularly awkward, since *Geist*'s modalizations have lost an oppositional force and cannot any longer posit the human against the inhuman. In *De l'esprit* Derrida's consideration of *Being and Time* supports this point: that by undermining a Cartesian notion of the subject, a nineteenth-century conceptual armature of terms like "biologism," "race," and "nature" are also subverted. Yet, it will be difficult for Heideggerian philosophy when confronted with nazism to respond in a way that might deter fascism's crude ideological constructions.

Heidegger's *An Introduction to Metaphysics* is especially problematic for Derrida insofar as the aggressive demystification of *Geist* in *Being and Time* undergoes a retraction so that a humanist foundation can be recovered. What Derrida notices, of course, is that such a humanist reinscription marks a tactic which will be reenacted throughout Heidegger's career: the tactic of putting terms under watch or arrest—an imprisonment or quarantining of terms—that is at a later time lifted so that these terms can undergo a rehabilitation or reappropriation. It is as if in having put *Geist* between quotes in *Being and Time* and in keeping it under watch or arrest in the Rectorate's Speech, Heidegger can, in this latter text, lift the quotation marks or brackets in order to greet *Geist* as a rehabilitated word. Not only that, but Derrida suggests that *Geist* has undergone a catharsis while under arrest. In short, quarantining language allows for a purification of the word. It is here, of course, that *Geist* is disclosed in its correspondence with the *logos* as a site wherein a purification of language is at issue. This point is raised in the consideration of Heidegger's remarks on Trakl in *On the Way to Language,* though the point is also crucial with respect to *An Introduction to Metaphysics,* wherein the German language is perceived as a site in which the endowment of ancient Greek thought has itself undergone purification. In other words, even as Heidegger frees a once arrested *Geist* in order to support a rehabilitated humanist network of relations meant to counter Nazi intellectual corruption, Heidegger himself lays the groundwork for a conceptual apparatus very much in tune with a National Socialist conception wherein purification of the German language corresponds to a certain racism. *Geist,* then, is a particularly troubling word, because it serves as a metaleptic field of terminological relationships wherein the historical and political differences between nazism and humanism are ambiguously performed within the temporality or history that is Heidegger's oeuvre.

Like many of Derrida's more recent publications, *De l'esprit* is rhetorically staged as a lecture transcript wherein the occasion of delivering the analysis prohibits a full exposition or demonstration of the argument. For this reason, it is often helpful to examine the contexts of Derrida's references and, later, its intertextual references within other writings by Derrida. In Heidegger's *An Introduction to Metaphysics*, for example, one immediately notices that Derrida's argument acknowledges the extent to which the language of metaphysics against which Heidegger turned in *Being and Time* is rehabilitated when Heidegger engages a new German politics.

> We are caught in a pincers. [*Wir liegen in der Zange.*] Situated in the center, our nation incurs the severest pressure. [*Unser Volk erfährt als in der Mitte stehend den schärfsten Zangendruck.*] It is the nation with the most neighbors and hence the most endangered. With all this, it is the most metaphysical of nations [*metaphysische Volk*]. We are certain of this vocation, but our people will only be able to wrest a destiny from it if *within itself* it creates a resonance, a possibility of resonance for this vocation, and takes a creative view of its tradition. All this implies that this nation, as a historical nation, must move itself and thereby the history of the West [*Geschichte des Abendlandes*] beyond the center of their future "happening" [*künftigen Geschehens* (not in quotation marks in the German)] and into the primordial realm of the powers of being. If the great decision regarding Europe is not to bring annihilation [*nicht auf dem Wege der Vernichtung fallen soll*], that decision must be made in terms of new *spiritual* energies [*geistiger Kräfte*] unfolding historically from out of the center.[71]

If Heidegger had sought to demolish the metaphysical protocols of ontology in *Being and Time*, it is evident that in such passages as that above from the beginning of *An Introduction to Metaphysics* these protocols are reinstated: Germany is the most metaphysical of nations or peoples; it is center stage in Europe; its people must wrest a timely decision from tradition and destiny; and Germany must make its decision in terms of new spiritual energies which are unfolding from its metaphysical center. However, the passage on history also suggests that the

German people must avoid catastrophe and annihilation. The decision must be made to go beyond the center of a future occurrence. Given the materials on the *logos* which Heidegger will later develop, the suggestion appears to be made, even in such a "metaphysical" passage as the one we are inspecting, that Heidegger is calling for a decentering of metaphysics in the very act of its reappropriation as spiritual center. That is, the later pages of *An Introduction to Metaphysics* convey very much the same orientation to the *logos* that we find expanded at great length in *Heraklit,* one that, as we noticed, resisted a metaphysical recovery. Heidegger's earlier remarks on Germany, then, could and perhaps should be read in terms of the rapport between *Geist* and *logos,* wherein the "difference" works against the historical or temporal centering of Germany and the chronology of its historical destiny, which Heidegger is apparently trying to circumvent, by coming into proximity with a vocabulary from which he would like the German nation to take distance. In other words, Heidegger is trying to alter the destiny of fascist politics by disarticulating its aims and its conceptual apparatus from within.

De l'esprit does not go out of its way to stress this interpretation; rather, the study assesses the negative costs of Heidegger's rehabilitation of humanism. In doing so, Derrida will not examine the correspondence between *Geist* and the analysis of the *logos* which Heidegger considers at the end of *An Introduction to Metaphysics* but instead will consider the Heideggerian rehabilitation of humanism as a logic of confusions.

> If I analyze this "logic," these confusions, these aporias or limits of the obscure presuppositions or axiomatic decisions in which we see this logic entangled, it is to exhibit and then formalize the terrifying mechanisms of this program, all the double impediments which structure it. Is this a fatality? Can one escape such a program? I don't see any sign, at least not in "Heideggerian" or "anti-Heideggerian" discourses. Can one transform this program? I do not know. In any case, one will not transform it all of a sudden and not until one recognizes it in terms of the most twisted ruses and its most subtle resources.[72]

At issue is the relation, or correspondence, between the history of philosophy and politics with respect to the question of humanism and the risks of either deconstructing or rehabilitating humanism. Derrida wonders whether philosophy is not double binded in either instance; moreover, he tacitly considers whether deconstruction can succeed where Heidegger has failed. For Derridean deconstruction also relies very strongly on the tactic of arresting and rehabilitating terms and also takes the political tactic of destabilizing ideological formations from within rather than through outright opposition or confrontation.

With respect to the bracketing and rehabilitation of terms, one of Derrida's major points is how, through historical metalepsis, *Geist* makes various reappearances as if in its repetition one detects not only restitution but resurrection or spiritualization. "More than a value, *l'esprit* appears to designate, beyond any deconstruction, the resources of even every deconstruction and the possibility of every evaluation."[73] Of special significance to Derrida is that when Heidegger returns to the word *Geist* in a text like *An Introduction to Metaphysics,* he comes back to it as if it were a name beyond naming, or, as in the passage quoted from *An Introduction to Metaphysics* above, a locus other than the center. "The word *esprit* returns; it is no longer rejected, avoided, but utilized in its deconstructive meaning in order to designate something else which it resembles and of which it is like a metaphysical phantom, the spirit of an other spirit."[74] The metaleptic appearance of the word *Geist* is always spectral. Particularly, its return from the prisonhouse of quotation marks wherein it was under lock and key in *Being and Time* suggests not just rehabilitation but a strange analogue to a spectral return of the repressed. This is a feature of (dis)appropriation which Derrida does not believe is recognized by Heidegger: in the "destruction" of metaphysical terms like *Geist* there follows a restitution or resurrection of the spirit, a stalking of phantoms.

Already in *"Fors:* The Anglish Words of Nicolas Abraham and Maria Torok," Derrida had considered the question of spirit or of the ghost-effect in Heidegger's *What Is a Thing?* Like Heidegger, for whom the thing is disclosed as a proximity of relations wherein thinghood is established, the analysand haunted by psychological crypts has divided (disappropriated) the thing and has comprehended it in the indeterminacy of a (dis)appropriation of identificationary relationships. Moreover, in this way the analysand has expropriated or hidden the thing as present to hand, that thing being similar to a corpse that has been entombed in a crypt but whose spirit returns. "Constructing a system of partitions, with the inner and outer surfaces, the cryptic enclave produces a cleft in space, in the assembled system of various places, in the architectonics of the open square within space, itself delimited by a generalized closure, in the *forum*."[75] In *De l'esprit* Derrida argues that his major concerns in the lecture courses leading up to this study have been four-sided. But what else can this be in the context of an essay like *"Fors"* but a crypt described in terms of the partitions between the following Heideggerian problematics: that of the animal, that of the question, that of technology, and that of *Geist?* Indeed, when Derrida makes much of Heidegger's placing *Geist* in quotation marks, is it not more than simply a matter of focusing on a marginal grammatological apparatus but rather a focusing upon the "cemetery guard" from *"Fors"* who leads us away from the place where the ghost or spirit resides, who fences off Spirit?

This guard is called "the self" and "the crypt is enclosed within the self, but as a foreign place, prohibited, excluded. The self is not the proprietor of what he is guarding. He makes the rounds like a proprietor, but only the rounds." And "As for language, it inhabits the crypt in the form of 'words buried alive,' defunct words, or words 'relieved of their communicative function.'" Immediately following these observations, Derrida writes: "They [the words] no longer point to the desire via the prohibition, as in hysterical repression, which they therefore threaten to the extent that they no longer carry on the effect of prohibition. They mark, on the very spot where they are buried alive, 'preserved,' the fact that the desire was in a way satisfied, that the pleasurable fulfillment *did take place*."[76] The words in the crypt, curiously enough, are never the subject's own words but always belong to an other who is illegitimate. In thinking through Derrida's analysis of Heidegger in *De l'esprit*, one wonders the extent to which *Geist* is a similarly encrypted word. In *Being and Time,* Heidegger with quotation marks to the ready, encloses the words of an illegitimate other—the metaphysical philosopher—in a crypt or script marked by brackets, wherein *Geist* has been buried alive. *Geist,* then, is the defunct word guarded not simply by a Self but by Dasein. Yet, perhaps because *Geist* is being subject not to a hysterical repression but to a certain pleasure, the quotation marks fall away so easily in the Rectorate's Speech. Though in calling out the word *Geist,* has not Heidegger, in a way analo-gous to an analysand like the Wolf Man in *"Fors,"* protected it or kept it safe from an appropriation by others? This is the sense in which the Rectorate's Speech and, later, *An Introduc-tion to Metaphysics* could be read as a ruse wherein the cemetery guard leads the "nearest of kin" to the wrong sepulcher. Or, as Nicolas Abraham is quoted by Derrida as saying, "He stands there firmly, keeping an eye on the comings and goings of the nearest of kin who claim—under various titles—to have the right to approach the tomb" and he serves the curious "with false leads and fake graves." At the same time, a "heterocryptic ghost . . . *returns* from the Unconscious *of* the other, according to what might be called the law of *another generation."*[77] Espe-cially in the contexts of *De l'esprit* this phrase, "another genera-tion," takes on very disturbing resonances.

In guarding or encrypting *Geist* in all its various modalities, does it not return to haunt Heidegger's texts in the way the heterocryptic phantom returns from the unconscious of the law of another generation? And is not *De l'esprit* an attempt to perform a cryptonomic analysis of a *Geist* interred within a box whose four sides are defined as animal, question, technology, and spirit? "I speak of ghosts, of the flame, and of ashes," Derrida has begun. Already there he has initiated the inquiry from the place of the dead, a place that remains unnamed though we know, quite well, of what historical events it speaks. From the perspective of *"Fors,"* Heideggerian philosophy con-cerns those ghosts anticipated within Heidegger's brackets, those spirits encrypted in *Being and Time.* That such spirits may turn out to be Jewish could be unexpected, but from the van-tage point of *"Fors,"* this eventuality is not shocking, given that the spirit is always the spirit of an "other" generation.

Such a reading of *De l'esprit* takes into account that the text incorporates a vocabulary suggesting holocaust (at one point Derrida remarks that *Geist* in Hegel is equivalent to *le gaz*) and ends with some very pointed and unusually direct remarks on what has silently contributed to nazism. Moreover, Derrida specifically takes up the notion of race (*Geschlecht*) which is keyed to at least two other essays which Derrida has written on Heidegger: "Geschlecht I" and "Geschlecht II," the latter of which meditates on the monstrosity of Heidegger's raised hand, or political salute to nazism. Moreover, as I will show in the last chapter of my study, peculiar to Derrida's interrogation of Heidegger in the 1980s has been a very attenuated though persistent consideration of how to read Heidegger vis à vis Jewish history and thought. This is pronounced, for example, in "Shibboleth," where a Heideggerian analytic is applied to a consideration of Celan and the holocaust, or in a lecture on negative theology wherein a criticism of Heidegger is given at the end in place of an expected coda touching on Jewish philosophy. In other words, the study of *Geist* in Heidegger is not merely the chronological tracing of a term's deflections, rejections, and rehabilitations but the tracing of a violated spirit or ghost which stalks philosophy, a spirit which Heidegger declines to acknowledge openly in his work, but which, nevertheless, is haunting the analyses.

Let us return, in this respect, to the four sides of Derrida's script or crypt: the animal, the question, technology, and spirit. And let us think of this crypt in terms of the Jews. (1) the animal: is a Jew really human or not? (2) the question: the Jewish Question; (3) technology: the apparatus of racial extermination; (4) spirit: the ghosts of ashes and flame. To what extent is the terrifying program which Derrida has addressed above a reference to this racial transposition, a reference to the Jewish corpses which German philosophy has set apart already in the Rectorate's Speech, and what is here being called *De l'esprit?* And how does the partitioning of thought, this putting of *Geist* in quotations in *Being and Time,* anticipate such a setting apart of an "other" generation, which is to say, of the generation and genealogy of an other race (*Geschlecht*)?

Derrida, who has noted Heidegger's approach to race in *An Introduction to Metaphysics,* turns to its legatee, the study *Nietzsche,* wherein *la bête blonde* makes an appearance. Derrida recognizes that Heidegger's passages on *Rassengedanke* are to be interpreted "sur le mode métaphysique et non biologique," that is, metaphysically and not biologically. But "in thus inverting the meaning of the determination, does Heidegger alleviate or aggravate this 'thinking about race'?"[78] The metaphysics of race, already prepared for in *An Introduction to Metaphysics* may not, Derrida says, be much better than biologism. That is, by swerving away in *Nietzsche* from the crude Darwinism of the National Socialists toward a metaphysical rehabilitation of race, Heidegger still risks the fall into a suspect rhetoric, that of a terminology which only feigns opposition to a notion of "life." That this feigning concerns the way in which Heidegger raises the philosophical question about spirit ensures that *Rassengedanke* is determined most uncomfortably from the perspective of those not considered to be human who have faced liquidation.

It is not by accident that in having considered the animal, the question, and the spirit that Derrida now turns to the flame, the technology of purification. "Maintenant viens, ô feu!" It is 1942, a year significant for Jewish history, and Heidegger is lecturing on Hölderlin. "Jetzt komme, Feuer!" In the poem *Bread and Wine,* Heidegger is considering spirit as expropriation and reading the last five verses. In commenting Derrida notices, "la crémation ou l'incinération du *Beseeler,* de celui qui anime, de celui qui porte l'âme, autrement dit le don de l'esprit" ("the cremation or incineration of the spiritualizer, of the one who animates, of the soul bearer, in other words, the bearer of the gift of the spirit.").[79] Derrida knows quite well that Heidegger is addressing a poet born in the eighteenth century; however, Derrida is investigating how Hölderlin is being used for the sake of the four-cornered crypt in Heidegger's philosophy, this place where one can see cremation or incineration of the purifier, or *Beseeler.* In short, Derrida locates the catharsis of philosophical purification in a historical setting about which Heidegger has kept silent, a catharsis resonating in the questioning of *Geist*'s cryptic attributes. "Der Geist ist Flamme," Heidegger has said, and the suggestion is strong that what Derrida detects, while himself remaining silent, is a spectral phrase like *il y a la cendre* substituting for the Heideggerian *es gibt Sein.* This, of course, is a motif Derrida has developed in the double-columned essay "Feu la cendre," in which the holocaust is remembered and it is made evident that Derrida's writings recollect the holocaust through such oblique recognitions.

Without doubt a most intriguing part of *De l'esprit* is its conclusions on Heidegger's Trakl interpretation, "Language in the Poem," from *On the Way to Language,* particularly Heidegger's identification of spirit with flames and ashes wherein the question of evil is raised.

> Evil and its malice is not of a sensuous, material nature. Nor is it purely "of the spirit." Evil is ghostly in that it is the revolt of a terror blazing away in blind delusion, which casts all things into unholy fragmentation and threatens to turn the calm, collected blossoming of gentleness to ashes.

> [Das Böse und seine Bosheit ist nicht das Sinnliche, Stoffliche. Es ist auch nicht bloss "geistiger" Natur. Das Böse ist geistlich als der in die Verblendung weglodernde Aufruhr des Entsetzenden, das in das Ungesammelte des Unheilen versetzt und das gesammelte Erblühen des Sanften zu versengen droht.][80]

The English translation by Peter D. Hertz attempts a consistent translation of *Geist* and its various forms as "ghost," "ghostliness," and so on. And in the translation above he pushes the Heideggerian understatement "zu versengen droht" to conform with the reference some sentences before to "das Weisse der Asche," the whiteness of ash. Derrida's reading of Heidegger's essay on Trakl is implicitly corroborated by Hertz's translation, which enables us to consider what might not immediately come to mind: that the essay on Trakl discloses faint resonances or overtones which a sensitive ear could associate with the holocaust. In this "cryptic" essay the resonances of German address such an "event" even as Heidegger is explicitly writing about something different, namely, *Geist* in Trakl. Recalling *"Fors,"* this *Geist* could be said to disclose itself as a ghostliness from whose graves the philosophical watchman is leading us away. Of course, such an interpretation relies on the possibility, suggested by Derrida himself, that language is capable of saying something other than what we expect to hear and that we can be capable of listening with the "ear of the Other," a point developed at length in Derrida's thought on Nietzsche.[81] In *De l'esprit,* one senses that we are being asked to hear what for so many readers has been inaudible, the speaking from within a Germanic reading of German a discourse that acknowledges an "other." Derrida's analysis suggests that Heidegger's theoretical discourse on Trakl is invoking such a recognition in its attempt to deconstruct the difference between *geistig* and *Geistigkeit,* to situate Trakl's poetics beyond the difference between a Christian and non-Christian conception of spirit, which is to say, from beyond the metaphysical opposition out of which anti-Semitism is born. This Heideggerian path, as Derrida calls it, is particularly interesting in that it works against Heidegger's earlier orientations to metaphysical discourse in *An Introduction to Metaphysics* as well as its politics, which from the perspective of "Language in the Poem" is being consumed in the purifying flames of a later Heideggerian thinking on the question of being as spirit.

Yet, Derrida in sympathetically turning toward Heidegger's deconstruction of spirit also turns away from it by arguing that, in fact, this is an empty gesture wherein a Christian metaphysic is merely being recovered. In the paronomasic slippage of *Geist* which Derrida has traced in various critical points in Heidegger's career, he once more situates the relation of deconstruction to Heideggerian philosophy within the bivalence of a turning toward and away from Heidegger, one that in *De l'esprit,* historicizes and politicizes these turns in a temporal unfolding of moments wherein the question of *l'esprit* bears on the spirituality, or *Geist,* of the Germans, a spirituality that comprises a story about ghosts, ashes, and flame.

This recollection of a historical debacle, however, is made to correspond to previous theoretical developments in *De la grammatologie* whose title is somewhat mirrored in the phrase *De l'esprit.* In this sense *De l'esprit* becomes significant for us as a study that reaffirms earlier evaluations by Derrida of the Heideggerian enterprise. Indeed, Derrida's later study establishes that the spirituality Heidegger notices in Trakl is, like the *retrait* or like the *es* of the *es gibt Sein,* what *Of Grammatology* calls the *archetrace*: the *"unheard of sense"* wherein there is the "presentation of the other as such, that is to say the dissimulation of its 'as such.' "[82] In short, what *De l'esprit* demonstrates through a close reading of Heidegger's remarks on Trakl is the theoretical argument made in *Of Grammatology* wherein the trace marks "the relationship with the other." And "When the other announces itself as such, it presents itself in the dissimulation of itself." Moreover, in *De l'esprit*'s discussion of Heidegger's reading of Trakl, Derrida discloses how "the 'theological' is a determined moment in the total movement of the trace," a paronomasic movement within discourse wherein the trace is uncovered as a *retrait* which opens an ontological relation without itself being ontologically present or recoverable as something in itself. Yet, in its retreat from ontology as such, the *retrait* makes itself known at once from within and without metaphysics.[83] In so doing it may well delimit the crypt of a Heideggerian thinking which is incorporated (in Abraham's sense) within metaphysics even as it is organized to elude metaphysical recovery or incorporation. But whereas "*Fors*" requires us to acknowledge the stalking of ghosts, *Of Grammatology* points us in the direction of a trace-work. And one of the implications in *De l'esprit* is that in not having succeeded in grasping the more radical potentials of the trace, Heidegger maintains the efficacy of the ghost and its crypt.

At one point in *Of Grammatology,* Derrida says in regard to Husserlian phenomenology, with Heidegger too very much in mind,

> *This is why a thought of the trace can no more break with a transcendental phenomenology than be reduced to it.* Here as elsewhere, to pose the problem in terms of a choice, to oblige or to believe oneself obliged to answer it by a *yes* or *no,* to conceive of appurtenance as an allegiance or nonappurtenance as plain speaking, is to confuse very different levels, paths, and styles. In the deconstruction of the arche, one does not make a choice.[84]

De l'esprit's consideration of *Geist* in *On the Way to Language* is a major instance of Heidegger's admirable reluctance to make the choice Derrida notes above in *Of Grammatology* at that very moment that an awareness of the archetrace comes about. Derrida acknowledges that Heidegger already in 1953 turned against Husserlian phenomenology in precisely the sense that Derrida has outlined in *Of Grammatology*, but Heidegger still did not go beyond Husserl in the right way, because ultimately he, too, falls into making a choice. Derrida is strongly suggesting that in having refused the choice of obliging oneself to answer yes or no to the question of the trace as presence, Heidegger is still opting for a discourse in which *Geist* and its Christological apparatuses are rehabilitated and the theological recovered in a differential "movement of the trace" wherein a temporal clue of difference has been established.[85] Hence in *De l'esprit*, Derrida points to Heidegger's choice of words bearing on the archetrace: "the movement towards this more than matinal *Frühe*," "this more than vernal initiality," the what comes "before the principle of *primum tempus*."[86] Moreover, Derrida is suggesting that in not having grasped the most radical implications of the trace, even as Heidegger had glimpsed them in turning away from Husserl, Heidegger maintains a spirit animating the crypt of a philosophy in which an "other's" remains or traces are being kept safe. This is an issue to which we will have to return.

When seen in context, the quotation above from *Of Grammatology* addresses Husserl with respect to temporality, and similarly the remarks by Heidegger on Trakl also concern time, "the Aristotelian *representation* of time: succession, dimension, for the sake of a quantitative calculus, or qualitative duration."[87] Through the deconstruction of the various modalizations of the word *Geist*, Heidegger challenges such an Aristotelian notion of time by invoking through Trakl a temporality acknowledging the *Riss* which opens up a questioning of time in terms of what comes before the *primum tempus*. Yet, although Derrida acknowledges this late Heideggerian attempt to develop a radical temporal clue, *De l'esprit*, in fact, develops the critique of what Derrida sees, in the context of our investigations, as yet another major failure in the Heideggerian analysis of the relation between being and time. That is, *De l'esprit* is reflecting on an instance in the later Heidegger wherein the attempt to do violence to established metaphysical notions of being is directed toward the construction of a temporal clue (in this case, the *retrait*) which will attempt to bring to fulfillment the abrogated temporal project of *Being and Time*.

There are two major indications that, indeed, this thesis is being suggested. First, the reference to Aristotle reminds us of Heidegger's attempt to develop a theory of temporality through an examination of Aristotle's philosophy; second, the notion of *retrait* is peculiar to a vocabulary that is temporal insofar as time cannot be affirmed or denied according to the ontological choice of difference of being/nonbeing. The *retrait* is precisely that which characterizes temporality as *la différance*. Yet, just as Heidegger is deemed by Derrida's essays of the late 1960s to fall short of a radical understanding of difference, *De l'esprit* makes the same evaluation, though now of the later Heidegger for whom the term *Ereignis* can be allied with the word *Geschehen,* a metaleptic dissimulation, according to Derrida, of the word *das Geistliche*.[88]

One major difference in the way Derrida conducts his analysis in *De l'esprit* is that whereas in the 1960s matters were considered in a rather abstract set of conceptual apparatuses which were what we might call predominantly philosophical, in *De l'esprit* Derrida is indicting Heidegger and even European culture much more on a political footing. This indictment becomes very pronounced at the end of the study.

> Nazism was not born in a desert. One knows it well, but it is always necessary to remember the fact. And even if, far from any desert, it has pushed itself up like a mushroom in the silence of a European forest, it will have done so because of the shade of large trees, in the protection of their silence or their indifference, however much in the same soil. I will not bring up or count the species of these trees which make up in Europe an immense black forest. For basic reasons, their presentation defies the space of representation. In their dense taxonomy, they would carry the names of religions, philosophies, of political regimes, of economic structures, and religious or academic institutions. In short, what one calls however confusedly culture or the spiritual/intellectual world [*le monde de l'esprit*].[89]

Here not only the metaphysical tradition in its Christological manifestations but Heidegger's restrained writings about the woodland paths stand forth as shade trees which have stood silent and have given shelter to nazism. And it is these staunch vegetative umbrellas which continue to stand forth as sentinels encouraging any future anti-Semitism.

Yet, Derrida has walked the textual woodland paths of Heidegger in such a way that, as in Claude Lanzmann's *Shoah,* we sense ghosts who inhabit black forests which only correspond to Heidegger's woods, dark forests planted not so long ago by the SS, that today cover the graves of the gassed. Derrida recognizes toward the end of *De l'esprit* that throughout all of Heidegger's considerations of spirit, there is no recognition of the Hebraic notion of *ruah,* that there is nothing that speaks of the *ruah raa,* the *l'esprit malin,* or malicious mind, disclosed from the perspectives of a Jewish cultural comprehension. That is, the lengthy considerations of *Geist* shelters an evil which is not allowed to be addressed from the perspective of the Jews. And yet, as Derrida's essay keeps hinting, this Jewish outcry can still be heard, though faintly, from within the German language or a metaphysical discourse that has as one of its aims the political and spiritual suppression or silencing of the voices of the victims, the voices of the "others." To hear with the "ear of the Other" is, of course, to hear what is in the crypt or script of language, to hear in the case of Heidegger's philosophy what the ghosts or voices of history are whispering. It is to hear what from the perspective of the "traces" of the Nazi debacle is as yet unhearable or inaudible, what Derrida has called the *il y a là cendre,* the expropriative dimension of the *es gibt Sein.*

In *De l'esprit* we read, "L'esprit—en-flamme—déploie son essence.[90] Elsewhere Derrida speaks of an "écriture du feu," as if the black forest were a Heideggerian *Ge-stell* ready to burst into flames in order to cast the unholy other out. The Black Forest that is European thought therefore maintains the potential of a purifying flame even as it stands by quietly and even breathtakingly as forested glade or wooded uplands. It is here, of course, that Derrida encourages us to rethink the identities of those woodland spirits which are romantically associated with German philosophy.

This orientation to philosophy, of course, is adumbrated in *Glas,* a text made up of numerous textual crypts, wherein a number of very important counterpoints with *De l'esprit* could be developed at great length. However, we must limit consideration of these closely interconnected texts to the following observations from *Glas*.

> In order to be what it is, purity of play, of difference, of consuming destruction, the all burning must pass into its contrary: guard itself, guard its own movement of loss, appear as what it is in its very disappearance. As soon as it appears, as soon as the fire shows itself, it remains, it keeps hold of itself, it loses itself as fire.

And,

> Without the holocaust the dialectical movement and the history of Being could not open themselves, engage themselves in the annulus of their anniversary, could not annul themselves in producing the solar course from Orient to Occident. Before, if one could count here with time, before everything, before every determinable being [*étant*], there is, there was, there will have been the irruptive event of the gift [*don*]. An event that no more has any relation with what is currently designated under this word. Thus giving can no longer be thought starting from Being [*être*], but "the contrary," it could be said, if this logical inversion here were pertinent when the question is not yet logic but the origin of logic. In *Zeit und Sein*, the gift of the *es gibt* gives itself to be thought before the *Sein* in the *es gibt Sein* and displaces all that is determined under the name *Ereignis*, a word often translated by *event*.
>
> How is the event of an anniversary possible now? What gives itself in an anniversary?[91]

In *Glas* Derrida meditates at length on the absolute spirit in Hegel, but, as the passage above discloses, the meditation also includes a careful consideration of the relationships between Heideggerian and Hegelian thought. Specifically, Derrida is listening to the Heideggerian resonances within Hegel's *Lectures on the Philosophy of Religion* in which cults of light are discussed, as if Heidegger were encrypted in Hegel's writings. The word "holocaust," of course, has as its primary denotation the sacrificial fires of primitive religion, though secondarily, and in relation to modern German philosophy, one has difficulty dissociating it from the more contemporary use of the term. Given the forest metaphor in *De l'esprit*, the passage in *Glas* on the *retrait* of fire suggests Heidegger's need to meditate on the forest, or why the forest is significant as a place within which Heideggerian philosophy has been written. Yet, as the passages in *Glas* readily attest, this fire which must preserve itself as something different is a holocaustic fire. And in Heideggerian philosophical contexts this fire is being considered as that early moment before which any temporality of earliness is established. This is the "irruptive event of the [sacrificial] gift," according to *Glas,* through which the history of Being is promised or vouchsafed to mankind. In short, the holocaust has to be encrypted within philosophy for the sake of a relation between time and being through which the *es gibt,* or gift of Being, becomes thinkable. In *Glas* the sacrificial gift is an annual event, which means that even as it is performed it annuls itself in its very annulation. In *De l'esprit* Derrida considers the twenty-year anniversary of Heidegger's essay on Trakl, which could be said to annul and annulate the Rectorate's Speech. Yet, if this "event" initiates the history of Being, to what extent does it withdraw as an event appropriable within a metaphysics of presence even while giving shelter to such a metaphysics of holocaustic and temporal catharsis? Insofar as the annular annulment of the annual breaks with an obsessive notion of time that is circular and revelatory, it still works in order to perpetuate the very metaphysics it wishes to annul.

De l'esprit suggests that we may read Heidegger's essay on Trakl in this sense, that, in fact, Western thought does not deviate very much from this practice, something which can be analyzed just as effectively and in as much detail within the writings of Hegel. In other words, if Heidegger's later writings still do not succeed in sufficiently going beyond Aristotle's temporal conceptions, neither do they succeed in going sufficiently beyond the Hegelian problematic of time which Heidegger had also, in *Being and Time,* attempted to surpass. Derrida notices this already through a consideration of Heidegger's orientation to the German woods, where, he suspects, the holocaustic fire is encrypted, preserved, treasured up in the standing reserves of the woods themselves.

But it is to *"Fors"* that I would like to return. In her explanatory notes to *"Fors,"* Barbara Johnson no doubt could have added that among the word's intralingual senses, *fors* stands for "four." Heidegger has spoken on time, as we noticed, in terms of the fourth dimension, and it is this fourth dimension which Derrida has identified as the early trait in "Language in the Poem," a trait that in *Glas* is the holocaust which opens onto the history of Western ontology. That *fors* (four) suggests the relations between the four problematics which turn on the fate of the Jews in twentieth-century history and that it suggests the approach of the excluded or excepted (*fors* [except, save]), is perhaps enough initial evidence that a cryptonym could well be haunting *De l'esprit*. If such a cryptonym is plausible, it would suggest one of the paths by means of which one ought to follow the partitioning or parceling out of terms which I have identified as being paronomasic or metaleptic. Moreover, *fors*, or "four," would serve as a peculiar reinscription of the fourth dimension of Heideggerian temporality, a historical reinscription in which the event that opens onto a Heideggerian consideration of *Geist* speaks of that which a Heideggerian or humanist piety has for the most part refused to utter, an account of history from the perspective of those whose sacrifice lies outside of the problematic of spirit but whose death is required in order for the problematic of spirit to be thought. To this end Western anti-Semitism is conceivable to be a requirement of all the metaphysical institutions of thought, a requirement that Western philosophy has encrypted inside itself even as it has struggled to release itself from that burden. Specifically, with respect to Derrida's evaluation of Heideggerian thought, *fors* suggests yet another instance wherein a resistance or exception to deconstruction inheres in Heidegger's philosophy, though here the resistance is particularly distressing, since it points to the preservation of a disturbing philosophical and historical crypt, one that comes about not through a reflection on the trace, which would have had much different consequences for Heideggerian thought, but rather through the consideration of *Geist*, a term in whose paronomasic partitioning the four-sided crypt of a historical catastrophe is constituted in the binding of animal, question, technology, and spirit. As Derrida suggests in *De l'esprit*, this four-sided figure is another means whereby the significance of Heidegger's famous cancellation, or erasure, of being can be interpreted.

FOUR

ANTICIPATIONS

OF APOCALYPSE

W e have noticed that during the 1980s Derrida has posed the question of temporality paronomasically in terms of a catastrophic historical context which Heidegger would have been reluctant to acknowledge in his philosophical writings. In so doing, Derrida once more takes his distance from Heidegger even as he reconceptualizes history by way of a revisionistic Heideggerian turn toward temporality. In this chapter I develop further Derrida's more recent recasting, or revision, of the later Heidegger's understanding of language and temporality. In *The Post Card,* especially, Derrida will read Heideggerian *Ereignis* from the perspective of a literalized and technological sense of "correspondence," whose temporality accords with a philosophical intuition of catastrophe or apocalypse which Derrida associates with the "ends of man" and the "death of philosophy." In *De l'esprit* and various essays published after *The Post Card*—these include "Des tours de Babel," "Shibboleth," "Two Words for Joyce," "Geschlecht II," and "Of an Apocalyptic Tone"—Derrida turns both toward and away from Heidegger through an interrogation of the "event" that has historically delimited the notion of "ends" for Jewish thought and culture. Derrida poses this event alongside a Christian notion of apocalypse in order to deconstruct a historicist conceptualization not only of eventhood but of the difference between those events which comprise Jewish and Gentile historical relations.

The figure of Heidegger is particularly significant for Derrida, because he has initiated a vocabulary which deconstruction can appropriate and revise for the sake of disarticulating a notion of eventhood whose temporality has been eschatologi-

cally hypostasized and thereby fixed in an Aristotelian diachrony of self-contained moments. What Derrida has been
suggesting is that such hypostasization contributes to the sense
of an absolute difference between Jewish and Gentile cultures,
the border of which is historically determined in a metaphysical
understanding of the event which from a Jewish perspective
belongs to an "other" tradition that is not metaphysically comprehensible. This chapter begins with a discussion of Heideggerian *Ereignis* and Derrida's deconstructive elaboration of it,
beginning in *Edmund Husserl's The Origin of Geometry: An
Introduction*. We move then to a consideration of Heiddegger's
notion of correspondence, or *Übereinstimmung*, in *On the Way
to Language* before discussing Derrida's *The Post Card* and his
remarks on tonality and the "ends of man" in "Of an Apocalyptic Tone Recently Adopted in Philosophy." The chapter ends
with a consideration of "Shibboleth" and "Geschlecht II,"
wherein Derrida's turnings toward and away from Heidegger
are once more evident in historical or temporal contexts that
are quite disturbing from the perspective of recent Western
history. There Derrida again problematizes our ability to think
the "relation" between Heidegger/Derrida.

The Granting of Being

Without doubt, Heidegger's notion of the granting or
"sending of Being" is crucial to Derrida's later formulation in *The Post Card* of what he terms "correspondence" or
"the postal system." Given that this sending of Being is so
closely allied to the Heideggerian term *Ereignis*, the term needs
to be reconsidered from the standpoint of Derrida's more recent writings in which it is taken far beyond metalepsis or
paronomasia. Though much has been written about later texts,
like Derrida's *The Post Card*, little has been done to show their
fundamental alliance with a largely Heideggerian approach in
which the temporality of the *Ereignis* becomes of major concern in the relation between the sending and saying of Being as
posed with respect to destiny. Derrida, having established the
metaleptic temporality of language in texts such as "Pas," later
engages Heideggerian *Ereignis* more performatively through

the sending of postcards—that is, always the same card with a design by Matthew Paris. In so doing he establishes a practice in which the Heideggerian "sending of Being" achieves a destiny which Derrida will interpret in terms of a catastrophic disappropriation or apocalypse. The ends of man and the death of philosophy, themselves Heideggerian concerns, are considered at length within the mechanics or technics of a social apparatus wherein the destiny of Being is handled or forwarded. "With the progress of the post the State police has always gained ground."[1]

Such thoughts are hardly broached by Heidegger, of course, and in *On the Truth of Being,* Joseph J. Kockelmans discusses Heidegger's term *Ereignis* as the "sending of Being" or "coming-to-presence" (*Anwesen*): "Being which is granted is that which has been sent and which (as sent) remains in each one of the modifications which we find in history."[2] For Kockelmans this "sending" (*Schicken*) is to be understood not within any sort of technological apparatus like the postal system but much more metaphysically as the coming to pass of Being whose granting is necessarily temporal and therefore historical. Still, this coming to pass of Being is by no means the eschatological revelation of Being so much as what changes in the coming to pass of Being. In a very important expository passage on the Heideggerian "sending of Being," Kockelmans writes:

> History of Being, therefore, means the sending of Being. And in the various ways of sending, the sending itself, as well as that mysterious "it" which sends, holds itself back in the various manifestations in which Being "shows" itself. To hold oneself back means in Greek *epoché*. That is why we speak of epochs of Being's sending. Epoch does not mean primarily a certain period of time in the coming-to-pass of Being's truth; it means the basic characteristic of the sending itself, that is to say, this holding-itself-back in favor of the various manifestations of the gift, namely, Being with respect to the discovery of beings. The sequence of the epochs in Being's sending neither is arbitrary nor can be predicted with necessity. And yet what is appropriate shows itself in each sending, just as what is appropriate shows itself in the belonging-

together of the epochs. These epochs overlap in their sequence, so that the original sending of Being as presence
is more and more concealed in the various modifications
of the unveiling. Only the "demolition" of these concealments (destruction) will grant to thought a provisional
insight into what then manifests itself as the sending of
Being.

When Plato represents Being as *idea*, when Aristotle
represents it as *energeia*, Kant as *positing*, Hegel as absolute concept, and Nietzsche as will to power, these are
doctrines which are not just accidentally brought forth.
They are rather the "words" of Being itself as answers to
an address which speaks in the sending but which also
hides itself therein, that is to say, in that mysterious "It
grants Being."[3]

Kockelmans implicitly recognizes that the "words" of Being are
metaleptic, that the doctrines of Being are "answers to an address" through which the question of Being is transferred or
translated. Just as the translations of the Anaximander fragment cannot be thought outside of the history of the fragment's displacements and erasures, the doctrines of Being, similarly, are translations of the question of Being which make up
the history of the address of Being to mankind. Kockelmans
recognizes that in this translation of the Being question there is
displacement and erasure, or, in his terms, concealments. The
truth of Being is acknowledged, then, by way of a *correspondence*, the "belonging-together," delivered in the "sending of
Being," that is, the correspondence between the philosophical
doctrines which comprise the history of the interpretation of
Being. The epochs of history are themselves viewed metaleptically or in terms of the paronomasic, and the "sending of
Being" is nothing less than the temporal unfolding of the
epochs as *epochés* in whose sequence of displacing moments the
"sending of Being" is transmitted or carried even as it is "concealed in the various modifications of the unveiling." Destruction, then, is needed in order to grant "provisional insight"
into the sending of Being. At issue, of course, is the demolition
of metaphysics, since it is this which obscures "provisional
insight."

Kockelmans's explication of Heidegger's later philosophical positions is particularly important because it implicitly addresses the question of writing as metalepsis and as temporal clue and because it resists the kind of metaphysical recovery often manifested in the readings of Heideggerian expositors like W. J. Richardson or David Halliburton. Moreover, Kockelmans understands how the transmission of the question of Being is part of what Heidegger calls the "sending of Being" as disclosed in the epoch as *epoché,* not to mention a notion of temporality that comprehends the epoch as part of a manifold of relationships in which Being is necessarily constituted as a horizon of temporal correspondences. "Es gibt Sein" and "Es gibt Zeit," Heidegger has written, and by this he suggested that the giving of Being and of Time closely correspond. In fact, in addition to the temporal dimensions with which we are so familiar—past, present, future—Heidegger considers a fourth dimension: "proximity which brings near." Again, Kockelmans is very informative. The fourth dimension of time, "brings close to one another the coming, the having-been and the present by keeping them apart. For it keeps open the having-been by denying it its coming as present, just as it keeps open the coming (future) by withholding the present in this coming, that is, by denying it its being present. Thus, the proximity which brings near has the character of a denial and withholding."[4] Not only is the sending of Being disclosed in the granting of time's fourth dimension, but this sending is a correspondence of proximities in whose deferral of being it can be said that Being comes to pass. The belonging of Being to time and of time to Being is, as Kockelmans points out, *Ereignis:* an event/nonevent ontologically prior to Being and time granted by the undecidable (*unbestimmt*) "it" of the "Es gibt Sein," and "Es gibt Zeit."

Kockelmans's perceptive interpretation of the later Heidegger shows that the relationship between the "sending of Being," the "giving of time," and the "destiny of truth" is part of an event/nonevent structure that situates history in a very unteleological dimension, that is, the "fourth dimension" of time. If the "sending of Being" constitutes both a revealing and concealing, an assertion and concomitant withdrawal, it must also be considered in terms of a correspondence of moments whose *Ereignis* is *unbestimmt.* This is crucial for an understanding of Derrida's later texts insofar as they will concern history as a correspondence which is somewhat more literal, though, for all that, just as undetermined and unteleological. Not unlike Heidegger, Derrida, too, will focus on the "event" as an *Ereignis* in whose appropriating moment an expropriation transpires. John Sallis, in "Towards the Showing of Language," considers such a perspective from a Heideggerian point of view when he writes, "language intrinsically withdraws. . . . To think is not to oppose this withdrawing but rather to be drawn along in the withdrawal."[5] The withdrawal is itself that expropriation occurring within the appropriation of correspondences manifest in the "sending of Being" which is *Ereignis.* As Heidegger himself says, *Das Ereignis ereignet.* For Heideggerians like Kockelmans as well as Sallis, the expropriation or withdrawal of being within the "sending of Being" either poses itself as an *Aufhebung* in which Being's destiny is determined as Being, or it poses itself as a radical demolition of any notion of Being we might suppose, a transvaluation which Heidegger marked with a term at once close and distanced from that which remains unnameable, *unbestimmt,* the "it" of the "it gives," the *apeiron* of sending.

In chapter 1 we noticed that moment in Derrida's reading of Heidegger's "The Anaximander Fragment" in which presence, as the trace of the trace, became perceived as the trace of the erasure of the trace. It was here, we recall, that Derrida saw *beyond* the difference of Being and beings, a "difference" ceaselessly differing and deferring in a trace-work of *différance.* And we considered this Derridean insight within a discussion of the *apeiron* in Anaximander and how Heidegger himself interpreted it as the history which is its translation or translatability. However, there is an earlier text in which Derrida much more explicitly considers the *apeiron,* though in relation to the question of what is an event. I have left discussion of this text until now because, curiously enough, although Derrida's earlier work hinges much more specifically upon the ideas developed in "Ousia et grammè" and "La différance," his later work, especially *The Post Card,* returns to an earlier point developed in *Edmund Husserl's Origin of Geometry: An Introduction* (1962).

Ironically, it appears that in 1962 Derrida was very much ahead of himself, that he had anticipated his later work of the 1980s even before the earlier work of the late 1960s and the 1970s had been written, since in the introduction to Husserl, Derrida was considering questions raised much later concerning the definition of an "event" in terms of the correspondences of time. Concerning the context in which the term *apeiron* appears in *Edmund Husserl's Origin of Geometry*, the question is raised: "*Is there, and why is there, any historical factuality?*"[6] This question is particularly important for an understanding of *The Post Card*'s Heideggerian speculations, since Derrida is raising not only the issue of what an event is but of its temporal significance in terms of the "correspondences" of beginnings and ends. In *Edmund Husserl's Origin of Geometry*, Derrida posits a teleological consciousness through which access is given to the question of whether there is or why there is any historical facticity. "This is because the sense to which we have access is not an event's being; because this sense can always not be incarnated." Indeed, the "why" "owes its seriousness to a phenomenological certainty and through this seriousness recovers the virulence of an '*in view of what?*'"[7] The ontological asking of whether there is historical facticity, or why there is such facticity, depends upon the teleological consciousness which asks the question. This is a consciousness whose correspondences—the in view of what?—are teleologically determined as a history which does not actually question itself when it puts itself into question. Hence Derrida writes, "Teleology is the threatened unity of sense."[8]

But from a Heideggerian perspective, the question What is a fact? or What is an event? becomes much more risky, because for Heidegger facticity stands in the openness of a question, what Derrida calls, "the question of the origin of Being as History."[9] In remarking on the *apeiron*, Derrida writes,

> Ontology only has the right to the question. In the always open breach [*brèche*] of this question, Being itself is *silently* shown under the negativity of the *apeiron*. Undoubtedly, Being itself must always already be given to thinking, in the pre-sumption—which is also a resumption—of Method. And undoubtedly access to Being *and*

Being's arrival must always already be *contracted* or *drawn together*, when phenomenology begins by claiming the right to speak [*droit à parole*]. And if Being did not *have* to be History through and through, the *delay* or *lateness* of Discourse *after* the showing of Being would be but a simple misfortune [*fautive misère*] of thought as phenomenology. That this cannot be so, because historicity is prescribed for Being; that delay is the destiny of Thought itself as Discourse.[10]

What differentiates Heideggerian thinking from Husserlian analysis is the capacity of Heidegger to interrogate facticity or events as that which is not fully accessible to teleological consciousness, since it is Being as epoch which has undergone an ontological *epoché*. Subsumed under this *epoché* are the following: Being as shown under the negativity of the *apeiron;* access to Being and Being's arrival as the always already contracted or drawn together (the holding on to, the correspondence, the address); and the delay or lateness of Discourse after the showing of Being, the destiny of thought (meaning, as always, "deferred," "differed").

The *apeiron,* Derrida implies, signifies a temporal limit or arche to be understood as an "indefinite multiplicity" or "infinite implication" of an origin absolutely deferred in the delay of Being. "The Absolute is *present* only in being *deferred-delayed—(différant)* without respite."[11] This description of the showing of Being in relation to the destiny of Thought will be comprehended in terms of *la différance,* though in the introduction to Husserl's essay on geometry, Derrida situates the notion of an undecidable difference more squarely within the Heideggerian context of the ontological difference between Being and being. Yet, Derrida does not greatly develop this difference as Dasein's transcendence, as Heidegger did in *The Essence of Reasons,* even though a hint of Blanchot's *pas au-delà* (the Heideggerian *Überstieg*) is invoked as that transcendence identified with "the primordial Difference of the absolute Origin, which can and indefinitely must both retain and announce its pure concrete form with a priori security."[12] Derrida stresses that such primordial Difference is an "alterity of the absolute origin [that] structurally appears in *my Living*

Present"; moreover, "this very fact signifies the authenticity of phenomenological delay and limitation."[13] These remarks are extremely significant from the perspective of *The Post Card*, since this book is largely a writerly performance of the living present as primordial Difference of the absolute Origin and, too, the absolute End. *The Post Card*, therefore, could be seen as the praxis to the theory outlined at the finish of *Edmund Husserl's Origin of Geometry*. I will develop this later, of course, in terms of Derrida's important intertext to *The Post Card*, entitled, "Of an Apocalyptic Tone Recently Adopted in Philosophy."

At this point, however, I wish to emphasize the Heideggerian influences and connections. Clearly, at the end of *Edmund Husserl's Origin of Geometry*, Derrida has attempted, as in "Ousia et grammè," to formulate a radically undecidable notion of difference in Heidegger. However, in the Husserl study this was attempted by yoking the Heideggerian reformulation of transcendence in *The Essence of Reasons* with later Heideggerian conceptualizations of temporality. In discussing the question of thought in terms of the ontological difference between Being and beings as determined indeterminately in the Origin—the *apeiron*—it is the differentiation or correspondence of temporal moments that concerns Derrida, a differentiation which in Heidegger appears as the appropriating and expropriating proximity of moments that make up *Ereignis*, and which Derrida will reformulate as *la différance*. Near the very end of *Edmund Husserl's Origin of Geometry*, Derrida writes,

> Difference would be transcendental. The pure and interminable disquietude of thought striving to "reduce" Difference by going beyond factual infinity toward the infinity of its sense and value, i.e., while maintaining Difference—that disquietude would be transcendental. And Thought's pure certainty would be transcendental, since it can look forward to the already announced Telos only by advancing on (or being in advance of) [*en avancant sur*] the Origin that indefinitely reserves itself. Such a certainty never had to learn that Thought would always be to come.[14]

The term "transcendental" brings both Husserl and Heidegger into correspondence, marking an undecidable moment when Husserl is as embedded in Heidegger as Heidegger is embedded in Husserl. This recalls the much later "envois" of *The Post Card* wherein the student dictates to the master what the master dictates to the student. Indeed, the sentence "Difference would be transcendental" might very well signify a history of phenomenology wherein the correspondence between philosophies transgresses the determinability of the identity established between different philosophers and philosophies. In this sense the history of philosophy could be viewed as a transcendence and a transgression, since as thought, Dasein must come to understand itself in the uncertainty or undecidability of that temporal division in which is affected its relation to the difference of Being and being as the difference of philosophy itself. This, of course, would reorient Husserlian phenomenology, whose transcendentalism is that of a certainty which can look forward to an already announced telos. Already in his early critique of Husserl, Derrida embraces Heideggerian philosophy in order to challenge a notion of history which presupposes determinate differences between moments establishing a teleology wherein the correspondences between writers and ideas are linearly and progressively delimited. In fact, in considering the Heideggerian notion of transcendence, or *Überstieg*, a delimited series of teleological moments is disarticulated; though, not until the writing of *The Post Card* does such a disarticulation or deconstruction of the correspondences of the history of philosophy come about, as we will notice after an examination of correspondence, or *Entsprechung*, in Heidegger.

Heideggerian Correspondence

In *On the Way to Language*, Heidegger writes:

> Time times—which means, time makes ripe, makes rise up and grow. Timely is what has come up in the rising. What is it that time times? That which is simultaneous, which is, that which rises up together with its time. And

what is that? We have long known it, only we do not think of it in terms of timing. Time times simultaneously: the has-been, presence, and the present that is waiting for our encounter and is normally called the future. Time in its timing removes us into its threefold simultaneity, moves us thence while holding out to us the disclosure of what is in the same time, the concordant oneness of the has-been, presence, and the present waiting the encounter. In removing us and bringing toward us, time moves on its way what simultaneity yields and throws open to it: time-space. But time itself, in the wholeness of its nature, does not move; it rests in stillness.[15]

Time is what comes up, what arrives, what reaches in the rising. And this arrival occurs within what is simultaneous. The event that is time timing appears to be at once an arriving and a staying. The has-been, the presence, and the present waiting are not three determinate moments but correspondences of time which are disclosed in an encounter that is the event of encountering. Here the identity and difference between being and Being will be disclosed, and the timing of time will be understood as that difference in time which is withdrawing from its difference in its differentiation. We might say that in the *différance* of the "time times" Heidegger is delimiting the undelimitable: the *apeiron*. But Heidegger is also interested in developing the idea that giving the time times delivers us into a relation with language. "Language is, as world-moving Saying, the relation of all relations. It relates, maintains, proffers, and enriches the face-to-face encounter of the world's regions, holds and keeps them, in that it holds itself—Saying—in reserve."[16] As a relation of all relations language is also a temporal relation and constituted as the "time times." Derrida's "La différance" can be read, therefore, as an extensive elaboration of Heidegger's thoughts on language, since *différance* is that phenomenon of division in which the relation of time to language is made available for philosophical inspection. "*Différance* as temporization, *différance* as spacing. How are they to be joined? Let us start, since we are already there, from the problematic of the sign and of writing."[17] The transposition from Heideggerian Saying in *On the Way to Language* to Derridean *écriture* in "La différance" is precisely what Derrida used in the late 1960s to develop further Heidegger's temporal clue. And it was at this point that Heidegger is translated into a structuralist context wherein the sign becomes the site where the undecidability of *différance* is disclosed as the movement in time of signification. However, in the later writings, Derrida will adopt tonality as an other context from which to develop what Heidegger calls Saying. Moreover, he will comprehend this Saying in terms of the temporality of the correspondence. Again, a writerly transposition has taken place, the substitution of the letter for a voiced notion of language (Saying), but the divisibility of that writing does not occur so much at the level of the sign as it does at the level of tone where various manners of speaking or discourses are situated. In *Parages* Derrida writes, "Here there are many more discourses, none of them proposing conclusions in the form of theorems, as those raised by literary criticism, poetics, narratology, rhetoric, linguistics, semantics."[18] Hence by the mid-1980s in *Parages,* writing is viewed at the divisible level of the discourse, by which Derrida means in large part the tonality of adopting rhetorical stances. For this reason, Derrida's philosophical projects go beyond a grammatological working through, since they concern a return to a modality of Heideggerian Saying. Indeed, the more recent writings of Derrida approach Heideggerian "saying" by recognizing the temporal conditions under which such a Saying comes about or arrives at its destination. This involves the question of differentiation (*différance*), the paronomasia of language (*Pas*), the vicissitudes of "correspondence," and the divisibility of voices and synthesis of tones (*The Post Card*).

Heidegger discusses voice in the following passage, where the biblical reference to Pentecost implicitly acknowledges the divisibility of discourse, tone, speech.

> [. . .] *glossa, lingua, langue,* language. Language is the tongue. The second chapter of the Acts of the Apostles, which tells of the miracle of Pentecost, says in verses 3 and 4: [. . .] "And there appeared to them tongues as of fire, distributed and resting on each one of them. And they . . . began to speak in other tongues . . ." Yet their

speaking is not meant as a mere facility of the tongue,
but as filled with the holy spirit, the *pneuma hagion*.[19]

This quotation, from "The Nature of Language," interrogates
linguistic vocalization and asks, "But the question remains
whether the real nature of the sounds and tones of speech is
thus ever experienced and kept before our eyes."[20] Heidegger
argues that an essential property of language is tone, sound,
ringing, vibration, which, in fact, is every bit as crucial to
language as the concept of meaning. Then, Heidegger quotes
Hölderlin and specifies that in this Saying something is announced, something which has to be heard, "When the word is
called the mouth's flower and its blossom, we hear the sound of
language rising like the earth. [. . .] The sound rings out in the
resounding assembly call which, open to the Open, makes
World appear in all things."[21] Such passages can be miscon-
strued as merely comments indebted to romanticism and invoking the power of nature poetry. Especially Heidegger's
tying language to the earth or its making World appear suggests that he reads Hölderlin's poetry as a language whose
importance is its attachment to natural phenomena. However,
what language announces is merely the correspondence or
proximity of linguistic sounds, tonalities, and resonances to
natural phenomena. Heidegger insists that to read metaphorically is itself not adequate, since metaphor is still a metaphysical
or presencing agency which attaches the correspondence to a
reified comparison. Rather, correspondence means not a comparison but a filiation of that Saying which is the "relation of all
relations." And this Saying is divided, differed, and deferring.
In the correspondence of Hölderlin's words with flowers there
is not a comparison through which an identity or unity is
achieved but a correspondence that keeps word and flower very
separate, that preserves an alterity and reserve of Being in the
sound of the words themselves. Heidegger, then, breaks
strongly from the literary tradition of reading sound and sense
as a mutually reinforcing system of consonance and dissonance
whose aim is to unify meaning. Rather, Heidegger interrogates
sound or tone as an articulation or correspondence in which
elements are posed with respect to one another, as "face-to-
face," or proximate, or "nigh."

In "Beyond Intentionality" Emmanuel Levinas recasts Heideggerian thought in ways complexly germane to Derrida's philosophical projects, and Levinas considers the Heideggerian "face-to-face" in terms of a response (the correspondence, so to speak) of an ethical consciousness.

> I respond to a question more ancient than "my consciousness," a question that my consciousness could not have perceived yet which commits me, in accordance with the strange schema evident in a creature that must have been able to respond to the *fiat* of *Genesis*, before ever having been of the world and in the world, before having been capable of hearing. Dia-chrony as relation: non-relation which is relation. Non-relation in that diachrony is the multiplicity of the unassemblable which could never be counted together, whereas the terms of a relation share at least a common time and can be thought of simultaneously.[22]

Only through "the meaning of the face, of the primordial speaking that *summons me,*" is "my response or my responsibility" provoked. For Levinas, the question which is more ancient than "my consciousness" is the problematic of an *apeiron* that is seen from a Hebrew rather than a Greek perspective. The "fiat of Genesis" is a manifestation of that "face-to-face" more ancient than "my consciousness," a "face-to-face" in which diachrony is not yet history as we ordinarily understand the term. Rather, diachrony, or time, is the multiplicity of the "unassemblable which could never be counted together." And yet, this moment which is so other from moments as we usually acknowledge them concerns something of a common time, of a simultaneity of moments in which the meaning of the face (of a manifestation) summons the me and provokes a response, a responsibility. This responsibility is the "correspondence" of my consciousness to that which manifests itself in the "face-to-face," a "correspondence" which acknowledges something more ancient than "my consciousness." The "summons" in Levinas is tonal. It manifests itself even from that moment, so unlike the temporality we know, which is more ancient than "my consciousness." It resonates from the fiat of Genesis, from the "face-to-face" whose "scene" resists representation, comprehension, understanding. The resistance to representing such a scene occurs in Heidegger, too, though it concerns a responsibility disclosed in romantic poetry. In the poetry of Hölderlin, too, something more ancient than "my consciousness" is considered in terms of the "face-to-face" of language. "In language the earth blossoms toward the bloom of the sky," Heidegger says with Hölderlin's elegy "Walk in the Country" in mind. Significant for Heidegger is that in this metalepsis or transference of the earth's blossoms as repeated in the image of the sky one discovers the "face-to-face" of earth and sky and their correspondences (the symbolist tradition may be invoked here) which concern an ethical responsibility which Hölderlin has considered in the poem "Germania" as the "token of friendship," the flower of the mouth. "Departing," Hölderlin wrote, "I left a token of friendship, / The flower of the mouth behind, and lonely you spoke." The flower is subject to a transmission in Hölderlin which reveals a correspondence not only in a symbolic sense but in terms of Saying wherein the responsibility of the "face-to-face" is articulated.

In *On the Way to Language* Heidegger further explains: "In order to experience this face-to-face of things with one another in this way, we must, of course, first rid ourselves of the calculative frame of mind. The movement at the core of the world's four regions, which makes them reach one another and holds them in the nearness of their distance, is nearness itself. This movement is what paves the way for being face-to-face. We shall call nearness in respect of this its movement 'nighness.'"[23] Heidegger too relates the notion of nearness or proximity of the "face-to-face" with time. This "face-to-face" is the timing of time, the correspondence of times. Moreover, "time makes ripe, makes rise up to grow. Timely is what has come up in the rising." Yet, this rising is not simply a chronological and organic movement toward a future horizon, but it also concerns "that which is simultaneous." The simultaneity is that synchronic moment in which times have been gathered as a correspondence of times, and in the language of the poets such a disclosure of time as rising (diachrony) and as the simultaneous (synchronicity) is disclosed as Saying. In Hölderlin the world's four regions are reaching one another and yet are being held simultaneously in the nearness of their distance. They are being held in the nearness of their distance as nearness itself, as the correspondence which makes up proximity, the nearness of spaces, the nearness of times. This movement of moments— their correspondences as synchronicity and diachrony—which "paves the way for being face-to-face."[24] This "face-to-face," then, is expressed as a Saying in which our relation to language becomes "worthy of thought," or in which the destiny of the Saying focuses on that "face-to-face" wherein language becomes significant as futuricity, or memorability. The poetry of Hölderlin still speaks to us, because its Saying is destined to be memorable and significant in terms of a future horizon which manifests itself in the relations of the work's "nighness." In this sense, Heidegger quotes the following from Hölderlin's "Bread and Wine."

> Long and hard is the word of this coming but
> White (Light) is the moment.

Hölderlin's rhetorical and tonal strategies in the poem are not reducible to tropes but disclose the "face-to-face" of linguistic relationships as they concern the earth. Hence the "time times" in which the "face-to-face" is clarified involves the "space spaces" wherein is clarified the question of the correspondences of earth. Heidegger writes, "The sound of language, its earthyness is held with the harmony that attunes the regions of the world's structure, playing them in chorus."[25] Although Heidegger in part is discussing the unification and synthesis of differences, the passage mainly concerns a disseminative attunement. Such attunement is not easily subsumed under a univocal term like "tone" or "harmony" or "chorus" but broaches the "openness" of proximities which are not subject to the absolute opposition of notions like difference and identity. The harmony that attunes is both to be understood as the "face-to-face" which occurs under the auspices of a temporality which allows for both nearness and distance, but it also depends upon a sense of place or space in which the occurrence of this harmony or correspondence is itself given as a reception as well as a throwing open. For the "face-to-face" concerns not only temporal moments but the spacing without which such moments cannot be brought into relation with one another. As time times, space spaces.

The same is to be said about space: it spaces, throws open locality and places, vacates them and at the same time gives them free for all things and receives what is simultaneous as space-time. But space itself, in the wholeness of its nature, does not move; it rests in stillness. Time's removing and bringing to us, and space's throwing open, admitting and releasing—they all belong together in the Same, the play of stillness, something to which we cannot here give further thought. The Same, which holds space and time gathered up in their nature, might be called the free scope, that is, the time-space that gives free scope to all things. Timing and spacing, this Same moves the encounter of the four world regions: earth and sky, god and man—the world play.[26]

Saying is the linguistic articulation of a correspondence between a time which brings near and distances and a space which both receives and throws open. Only within these correspondences between the synchronic and the diachronic—the near and the far, the closed and the open, the same and the different, the admitting and the releasing, the belonging and the estranged—is the harmony of a world structure disclosed as Saying, or as a *Stimmung* of voices and tonalities. Saying is that articulation of space-time which is not merely a parameter for the measurement of that which is always perceived in the present givenness of a static moment offered in the now but is the "long and hard [that] is the word of this coming."

For Derrida, Saying is the coming, or arrival, of the letter which is necessarily to be comprehended in terms of its correspondence to the time and place of both its sending and reception. And like Saying, this letter or postcard traverses both synchronic and diachronic temporalities and holds them together in a correspondence wherein both the receptiveness to the Same and the throwing open upon Difference are articulated without being frozen in a static construction or now in which something takes place within spatial closure. In this sense, Heidegger has already written that "To *speak* to one another means: to say something, show something to one another, and to entrust one another mutually to what is shown."[27] However, Derrida puts this Heideggerian statement from *On the Way to Language* into practice by way of showing the postcard, by way of sending the reader a card which marks a mutual entrusting between writer and reader, addresser and addressee. But such a speaking, Heidegger would insist,

> belongs to the design of the being of language, the design which is pervaded by all the modes of saying and of what is said, in which everything present or absent announces, grants or refuses itself, shows itself or withdraws. This multiform saying from many different sources is the pervasive element in the design of the being of language. With regard to the manifold ties of saying, we shall call the being of language in its totality "Saying"—and confess that even so we still have not caught sight of what unifies those ties.[28]

Shortly following this statement Heidegger writes, "*The essential being of language is Saying as Showing,*" by which is meant the bringing of language face to face, the allowing of language to engage in a correspondence, what in Derrida is a sending of the postcard, a showing of saying to an addressee. Whether we are considering metaphor in Hölderlin or the postcard of Matthew Paris in *The Post Card,* it is a question of Saying in which something is shown as face to face, as in correspondence with one another according to the parameters of space-time as Heidegger has defined them in the passages above.

Derrida considers this correspondence, of course, in terms of the "sending of Being" which Heidegger discusses in "Zeit und Sein." Indeed, in the "Envois" of *The Post Card,* Derrida uses Heidegger's term *Schicken,* or sending, in order to discuss Heideggerian Saying not only in terms of correspondence but in the *es gibt Sein* which such a correspondence discloses. In the dispatch of September 6, 1977, Derrida explains that the sending (*Schicken*) is already to be understood as fate (*Geschick*). "If I take my 'departure' from the destination and the destiny or destining of Being [*Das Schicken im Geschick des Seins*], no one can dream of them *forbidding me to speak* of the 'post,' except on the condition of making of this word the element of an image, of a figure, of a trope, a post card of Being in some way."[29] Here *The Post Card* is made to rime with *destinal de l'être* (*destinal* is offered in place of the expected *destineé*). In this way

Derrida offers what he himself calls a "simple metaphor" of the "postal system" in which one has a place concerning "all the transference and correspondences, the 'real' possibility of all possible rhetorics." However, "would this have satisfied Martin [Heidegger]?" Derrida answers:

> No, because [Heidegger] doubtless would see in the postal determination a premature (?) imposition of *tekhne* and therefore of metaphysics (he would accuse me, you can see it from here, of constructing a metaphysics of the posts or of postality); and above all an imposition of the *position* precisely, of determining the *envoi* of Being as position, posture, thesis or theme (*Setzung, thesis,* etc.), a gesture that he alleges *to situate,* as well as technology, within the history of metaphysics and within which would be given to think a dissimulation and a retreat [*retrait*] of Being in its *envoi*. This is where things are the most difficult: because the very idea of the retreat (proper to destination), the idea of the halt, and the idea of the epoch in which Being holds itself back, suspends, withdraws, etc., all these ideas are immediately homogeneous with postal discourse. To post is to send by "counting" with a halt, a relay, or a suspensive delay, the place of a mailman, the possibility of going astray and of forgetting (not of repression, which is a moment of keeping, but of forgetting). The *epokhe* and the *An- sichhalten* which essentially scan or set the beat of the "destiny" of Being, or its "appropriation" (*Ereignis*), is the place of the postal, this is where it comes to be and it takes place (I would say *ereignet*), that it gives place and also lets come to be.[30]

For Derrida there is not simply a postal system but "les postes et les envois" (the posts and dispatches). This is a movement of signification which Derrida views as "very close" and "very far" from Heidegger. Derrida realizes that Heidegger would have disapproved of using a technical apparatus like the mails in order to talk about the sending of Being, and here, of course, the grammatological critique of the metaphysics of voice reemerges in Derrida's work, for the post office is to Heidegger's notion of sending and Saying what writing is to voice in *Of*

Grammatology. Notice, once more, how Derrida prefers to transpose Heideggerian discourse into a writerly context, such as the actual sending of postcards and all that is involved in transmitting messages by mail. Again, as in *Of Grammatology* the gambit is to recontextualize a discourse about voice in terms of a writerly apparatus that is, strictly speaking, supplementary to what we usually consider to be the significant act of expression. For the writer, such a supplement would be the sealing of a letter and its sending through the mails, or the packaging of a manuscript and its depositing at an express air service. Although this hardly sounds like a propitious context for achieving an in-depth understanding of what a text might signify, Derrida notices that the significance of a text is very much determined by the conditions of its dispatch, that one is mistaken to isolate the message from the technology or relays of its delivery. In fact, by transposing Heidegger's ontological vocabulary into the context of the apparatuses of a text's transmission or postal relays, one may deconstruct Heidegger's metaphysical recovery of Being which accompanies the project of Heideggerian demolition. This deconstruction occurs, of course, the moment that Derrida receives the Heideggerian letter or missive, the moment that, in having the message delivered to him, it becomes apparent that it has been misrouted, sent to the wrong destination, and its message misread, translated, or transposed. That is, Derrida "turns" the language of Heidegger in such a way that the discourse of the post office comes face to face with Heidegger's ontological philosophical vocabulary. Derrida writes in close proximity to the passage quoted above:

> As soon as there is [*dès qu'il y a*], there is *différance* (and this does not await language, especially human language, and the language of Being, only the mark and the divisible trait), and there is postal maneuvering, relays, delay, anticipation, destination, telecommunicating network, the possibility, and therefore the fatal necessity of going astray, etc. There is strophe (there is strophe in every sense, apostrophe and catastrophe, address in turning the address [always toward you, my love], and my post card is strophes).[31]

As soon as the arrival or thereness of the postcard is asserted there is undecidability, or *différance*. And this undecidability or difference concerns Derrida's own reception of Heidegger's missives, his seminars. Also, there is in the previous quotation the rather complex play with the notion of turning in words like *détournement, à tourner,* and *strophe,* which suggest that the relationship between addresser and addressee is subordinated to the inclinations or directions established through the process of a message's transmission, its sending. The ancient Greek term *strophe* means literally "to turn." Given the inclination of a routed message, this notion of strophe takes on apostrophic or catastrophic senses. Hence addresser and addressee are but the effects of such erratic turnings and routings, effects of the inclinations of messages en route. Part of Derrida's interest in talking at length about the postal network is that through it the existential assumptions about dialogue between selves and others are put into question. We notice, then, the extreme significance of Derrida's deconstruction of intellectual history as that which is given in the destiny of the Heideggerian sending of philosophy. That is, Derrida's problematization of his relationship to Heidegger is not a gratuitous dodge by means of which to camouflage the relation of deconstruction to Heideggerian phenomenology and ontology but is an intensive adherence to the "letter" of Heidegger's thought, a "letter" with apostrophic and catastrophic consequences. Through the medium of something as trivial as a postcard this Heideggerian "letter" is shown, a written letter or card in Derrida's context that is from a philosophical perspective—and, of course, the point of view of Derrida's oeuvre—nothing less than a writerly supplement, a marginal phenomenon. Yet these postcards themselves succumb to misroutings, tonal shifts, elliptical retreats of meaning, cancellation, abrasion, and so on. The postcards are not just apo-strophic (a turning away from) but cata-strophic (an overturning). That is, the postcards turn away from both addresser and addressee as well as possibly overturn them insofar as the postcard concerns the undecidabilities which are involved in the sending of script through the mail or the showing of the card. The "correspondence" becomes problematic as both the question of the temporality of the script's sending and its placement and/or misplacement becomes of issue.

Evident in the strategy of Derrida's sending always the same card through the mail with different inscriptions on its reverse is that the sending of the script concerns the paronomasia of writing. For it is always the same card, the simultaneity of the card, the identity of the card which is sent. And yet in this staying in place, there is difference as the card, always the same card, is spaced, divided, mailed. The temporality of the paronomasic card is, as Heidegger suggests in *On the Way to Language,* that of the correspondence between a synchronic time of the simultaneous (of that which stays the Same) and of the diachronic (that which is spaced out over past, present, future). Not only that but the card both opens a new space within which the script is to be understood in its sending of the message about Being and restricts or limits the place wherein that message is located. In this sense, the postcard is the medium in which, although a Heideggerian might least expect it, the theory of Saying is given a praxis within the technology of a writing and sending of postcards through the post.

The postcard, then, however trivial it may at first appear, functions as a supplement to the later Heidegger's thoughts on language. Indeed, the postcard is well suited to do so, because the dispatch is a space which cannot be disentangled from the duration of its being transmitted, that is to say, its being written, sent, received, read, and so on. Yet, as Derrida says, the postcard is at once very close and very far from Heidegger. The postcard is close to the extent that through Derrida's writing Heideggerian philosophy is dictating the script as well as its own self-consciousness about the technology of its correspondence and the capacity for its own self-conscious deconstruction of its own thought. At the same time, the postcard is remote from Heidegger because the script is being sent backward in time to Heidegger himself, to an addressee who has passed away, a destination which the card can never reach. This is an "address" without which philosophy would be dis-continued, since our capacity to think at all depends upon our ability to address people who have passed away—Plato, Aristotle, Descartes, and so on. In this sense yet another correspondence is achieved, a correspondence with the dead. And, of course, it is to the dead that Derrida is dictating and through the dead that deconstruction necessarily must pass.

Yet, in this context one is so removed from Heidegger that the distance in which Heidegger himself has been withdrawn gives another perspective on the "sending of Being" and its "event" in terms of the genealogical correspondence between legator and legatee, father and son, one lover and another. In *The Post Card* the temporality of genealogy is constituted as a correspondence or appropriation of moments wherein filiation is at once established and broken. This complements an understanding of Heideggerian thought that does not reflect a static or presenced structure lifted out of time and evaluated as a thing in itself, since this would be merely a traditional historical approach. Rather, Derrida is complementing an understanding of Heideggerian thought as the performance of time according to a correspondence of historical proximities—for example, the proximities established in intellectual history—in whose sending or delivery the history of Being (or genealogy, for Derrida) is deconstructed. In *The Post Card,* only by appropriating or holding on to Heidegger can Derrida demolish the historicity of this hold. But for this to occur, the addressee of Derrida's address must not only be held but held back, subjected to a withdrawal or concealment, so that he can be inscribed into his own problematic of how Being is both disclosed and withdrawn at the same time. Given the "holding back" which occurs as Derrida lays "hold" of Heidegger, it is certain that the letter, dispatch, or postcard "sent" to Heidegger will miss its address, and hence Heidegger's philosophy, in being missed, will fail to reach its "destiny," which is the philosophical afterlife it lays claim to in deconstruction. In this "face-to-face" of the taking "hold" of Heidegger, the legatee, Derrida, disinherits as he inherits the legacy. This is the event of an intellectual history in which *Ereignis* as appropriation and dis-appropriation takes place, the history or temporality of an *Ereignis* whose destiny thwarts the expectations of academic philosophers for whom, despite the content of any philosophy, its history appears teleologically predetermined in a conceptual apparatus which from a Heideggerian perspective has been demolished. In this sense, Derrida's turning *Ereignis* back on the destiny of Heideggerian philosophy is anything but unauthorized from the position of the legator, Heidegger. Rather, given the Heideggerian legacy, always already deconstructing itself as legacy, the philosophy of Heidegger is posed as problematic for the one who would wish to take up where Heidegger left off, since from the perspective of the later Heidegger it would be a metaphysical trap to inherit or lay hold of that in whose *Ereignis* a laying hold (*lesen*) is itself undermined.

In *The Post Card* Derrida complicates matters considerably by situating himself between Heidegger and Freud, which is to say, in their "correspondence" or their "face-to-face" encounter as thinkers. With respect to Heidegger and genealogy this has the peculiar consequence of a correspondence that is quite perverse given Heidegger's antipathy to Freud and psychologism. And this correspondence, of course, occurs through a third term, the psychoanalytical consideration of a pornographic scene in which two homosexual philosophers are founding the Western tradition. Derrida's friends Cynthia Chase and Jonathan Culler have "staged" a moment when Derrida at Oxford comes across a postcard with a design by the medieval artist Matthew Paris, whose design shows Plato dictating to Socrates. The way in which Plato stands behind the behind of Socrates—this strategic modification of the Heideggerian "face-to-face"—suggests to Derrida not only that Socrates is writing what Plato dictates but that the "position" of these figures suggests that they could be considered homosexual lovers. Derrida suggests that such a sexual positioning of dialogue may be paradigmatic for philosophy, generally, and this marks the correspondence, then, of not only Plato and Socrates, but also of Heidegger and Freud, and Heidegger and Derrida. Speaking of the couple Heidegger and Freud, Derrida writes:

> Here Freud and Heidegger, I conjoin them within me like the two great ghosts of the "great epoch." The two surviving grandfathers. They did not know each other, but according to me they form a couple, and in fact just because of that, this singular anachrony. They are bound to each other without reading each other and without corresponding. I have often spoken to you about this situation, and it is this picture that I would like to describe in *Le legs*: two thinkers whose glances never crossed and

who, without ever receiving a word from one another, say the same. They are turned to the same side.[32]

This odd correspondence that does and does not take place— or which takes place behind the backs of Heidegger/Freud— follows the logic of the post, or of the "postal principle," which, in Derrida's context, is inherently a "pleasure principle." In part, this "postal principle" suggests that temporally the most intimate relationships occur "too late," that the pleasure principle inherent in the coupling of figures like Heidegger/ Freud takes place in the genealogical imagination that is intellectual history, a history Derrida is himself constructing from the perspective of a deconstructive genealogy that does violence to our chronological apprehension of time.

Indeed this sort of genealogical investigation of temporality is further complicated if one takes into account Ned Lukacher's interesting observation that Derrida makes the involuntary association of Heidegger with "some old Jew from Algiers," probably either his philosophy teacher at the lycée who taught him Plato's *Dialogues* or, and this is more problematic, his father. "Isn't the joke finally that Heidegger is a kind of father; that in this old photograph of Heidegger [which Derrida found in a photograph album of Heidegger], Derrida sees the head of his father?"[33] Given Lukacher's interesting hypothesis in *Primal Scenes*, it is evident that in the charged (if not amorous) correspondences between Derrida and Heidegger genealogy undergoes violation. The *es gibt Sein* which is disclosed in the temporality of the patriarchal line is threatened at that moment when the figure of Heidegger corresponds with Derrida's father, though only in the logic of the "post," wherein couplings have only a fantasmal influence over us. Lukacher argues in *Primal Scenes* that however much Derrida wants to overcome his filiations, the fathers (not only Derrida's real father and Heidegger, but Freud, too, is involved as "the old Jew") return from within his writings as ghostly mutterings: "Derrida's history of writing and Heidegger's history of Being are efforts to account for the radicality of the temporality of language. They are attempts to account for a silent, unidentifiable voice in the text that is always pregiven, prior to the oppositions of identity and difference, subject and object, a mark, a trace, a trait, a *retrait* in the text that veils itself, withdraws into itself, and forgets all about itself."[34] In Derrida the scene of intellectual filiation "comes to signify an ontologically undecidable intertextual event that is situated in the differential space between historical memory and imaginative construction, between archival verification and interpretive free play."[35] In this space of the undecidable correspondence of intertexts, voices begin to haunt the Derridean enterprise, and according to Lukacher, Derrida begins to stalk Heidegger the way Hamlet stalked the ghost of his father on the battlements of Elsinore.

As Lukacher recognizes, the correspondence between philosophical couples, rather than being wholly concretized as writing (or letter), manifests itself as a tonality, or *Stimmung,* that is epiphenomenal, resonant, de-centered. And the question of tone emerges most forcefully in "Of an Apocalyptic Tone Recently Adopted in Philosophy," a codicil to *The Post Card,* which suggests that tone is what remains after an intellectual history has been violently disrupted from within a Heideggerian mode of Saying that negates its own preeminence as speech even as its tonalities achieve an undetermined destiny in the work of an other where it is necessarily mis-laid. What Lukacher notices, of course, is that such tonality also reflects what from the Freudian perspective of *The Post Card* could be called trauma, which Derrida himself refers to when he writes in *The Post Card* that "The Wolfman died 7 May. A little bit of me is gone. Had I told you that I am also Ernst, Heinele, Sigmund, Sophie, and HAlberstAdt . . . ? This is the story that I write myself, *fort:da* and 4 + 1 (*à suivre*)."[36] Yet this "trauma" is by no means to be considered a "crisis" but rather part of a "catastrophe" whose tonalities make up epiphenomenal correspondences in which the destiny of the sending of Being's destruction accompanies the delivery of an ending in which *es gibt Sein.* This "tone" or "voice" of correspondence is nothing if not the modification of a Heideggerian notion of Saying in which *Ereignis* can be detected, an *Ereignis* whose temporality Derrida has reconceptualized in terms of the "post."

Although a Freudian reading of *The Post Card* might lead one to conclude that Derrida has so thoroughly double bound the problematic of intellectual filiation that intellectual history as we know it becomes unthinkable, the Heideggerian materials suggest that we are necessarily considering an existential project that must interpret the "sending of Being" as an appropriation and disappropriation of relations that are not given in a genealogical paternally determined moment but in the encounter of heteronomous moments wherein *Ereignis* is disclosed in relation to the coming and passing of Being as a proximity of relations whose determinations can be detected in terms of "family romance." If Derrida transposes this sending into the transmission of the word or language through the *techne* of the post and the context of the family, it is to demonstrate better the extent to which the Heideggerian notion of the sending of Being has been reconsidered from the perspective of the "post" of the philosophical correspondence.

In *The Post Card* emphasis falls upon intellectual history as a temporality or genealogy of the transference through which the sending of Being is not only heteronomously received in different epochs as the unconcealment of truth but is comprehended as the event of a critical performance whose time is experienced as an autobiography of disarticulated and rearticulated moments, what Derrida in *Edmund Husserl's Origin of Geometry* was ironically calling "my living present." *The Post Card*, then, reflects the performance of philosophy as the "sending of Being" transmitted through the autobiographical consciousness of a philosopher who dwells upon thought not as an idealistic set of conceptual relationships but as a genealogy wherein the philosopher's own being takes place as that which has been destined in what Gregory Ulmer might call the "post-age" of biological and historical time.

An interesting consequence of this autobiographical reflection will be that, by way of inheriting and accepting the legacy of Heideggerian thinking through which Being has been "dispatched" (sent and subjected to demolition), Derrida will not only carry forward what Heidegger recognized as the demolition of metaphysics and the unconcealing of a Heideggerian "temporal clue," hence focusing on the notion of what comprises that "event" in which the "ends of man" can be thought, but will also dismantle the underpinnings of an intellectual history by means of which this very act of deconstruction can be genealogically thought within Western tradition. This dismantling plays havoc with those aspects of attachment and detachment that would characterize deconstruction as a distinct philosophy within a teleological history of intellectual developments. It would, in effect, bring to fruition those thoughts on the event and transcendence which Derrida had so near the beginning of his career, even though it frustrates the attempt of anyone trying to put deconstruction in a historicist framework, since the inheritance of Heidegger's legacy is itself what comprises the deconstruction of the correspondences between legator and legatee, the relation between one body of thought and another. What characterizes this deconstruction, however, is special attention to the event not merely as Heideggerian *Ereignis* but, as we will see, as catastrophe or, as Blanchot has put it, *l'écriture du désastre*.

The Tonality of Apocalypse

"Of an Apocalyptic Tone Recently Adopted in Philosophy" is a "supplement" to *The Post Card,* an apocalyptic missive that missed its destination, and there once again Derrida addresses the Heideggerian temporal clue from the perspective of the later Heidegger in *On the Way to Language.* In this essay, too, the question of tone or tonality refines and revises the Heideggerian notion of Saying in its relation to the "face-to-face" and *Ereignis.* However, "Of an Apocalyptic Tone" marks an important turning point, or cata-strophe, in Derrida's deconstructive projects insofar as it turns even more radically away than *The Post Card* does from the explicit orientation toward a grammatological gesture in whose performance the question of tone or voice is mediated. In fact, "Of an Apocalyptic Tone" is astonishing in that it does not reject tone or voice in even its most oracular and metaphysically staged moment: that point at which it announces the ends of man (*les fins de l'homme*). It is as if voice were suddenly unbracketed in the phenomenological sense, as if a deconstructive taboo were suddenly lifted. In part, the strategy of lifting the ban on voice is that Derrida's essay is largely a defense in which those who accuse deconstruction of hermeticism, mystification, literariness, or general craziness ("not serious philosophy") are countered with a devastating critique of the degree to which those who believe in a neutral, objective, or rational "tone" are themselves mystified, since they unthoughtfully compress and focus textual effects which, in fact, cannot be easily disentangled from a metaphysical and theological context of intuitions, postures, and styles. Yet another aspect of Derrida's "Of an Apocalyptic Tone" concerns the strategy of transposing Heideggerian thinking into a Judeo-Christian context, that is, placing contemporary philosophy within the context of "sacred history" with its decidedly Hebraic legacy. Just as in *The Post Card* there is the curious relation between Socrates and Plato, in "Of an Apocalyptic Tone" a similar relation exists between the Jewish and Christian traditions, one in which the Jewish tradition is being informed or spoken to by a Christian tradition that is inherently anterior to it. Closely allied to this aspect of the essay is Derrida's concern with the notion of translation, the "difference" between the terms *Gala* and *Apokalupsis*. What is involved here is the transmission of an apocalyptic tone which does "not exclude dissonances, gaps, deviations, or inadequacies." Lastly, "Of an Apocalyptic Tone" is intended as part of *The Post Card*'s tonal performances, its "tonal changes," and it plays into the writings of Maurice Blanchot in which that tone is also located and mimed by Derrida. In fact, at the end of "Of an Apocalyptic Tone," Blanchot's writings or tonalities will be specifically invoked, something which ties or corresponds this text with Derrida's recent *Parages,* in which essays on Blanchot are collected. Given my orientation to "Of an Apocalyptic Tone" it will be necessary to bracket Derrida's response to Kant which has its own very complex textual history and which has been well explained by Irene Harvey in *Derrida and the Economy of Difference.*

My focus, of course, is on the question of time and how it is disclosed in the *Ereignis* that is tonality. At one point in "Of an Apocalyptic Tone" Derrida writes:

> If, in a very insufficient and only just preliminary way, I draw your attention to the narrative sending [*envoi*], the interlacing of voices and *envois* in the dictated or addressed writing, I do so because great attention no doubt would have to be given this differential reduction or gearing down of voices and tones that perhaps divides

them beyond a distinct and calculable plurality—at least in the hypothesis or the program of an intractable demystification of the apocalyptic tone, in the style of the *Lumières* or of an *Aufklärung* of the twentieth century, and if we wanted to unmask the ruses, traps, trickeries, seductions, and engines of war and pleasure, in short, all the interests of the apocalyptic tone today. We do not know (for it is no longer of the order of knowing) to whom the apocalyptic dispatch [*envoi*] returns: it leaps [*saute*] from one place of emission to the other (and a place is always determined *starting from* the presumed emission); it goes from one destination, one name, and one tone to the other; it always refers [*renvoi à*] to the name and to the tone of the other that is there but as having been there and before yet coming, no longer being or not yet there in the present of the *récit*. And there is no certainty that man is the exchange [*le central*] of these telephone lines or the terminal of this computer without end.[37]

The apocalyptic tone is an oracular tone through which something has been sent, a tone that comes unannounced, out of nowhere, or more accurately that somewhere unmoored from a distinct sender and receiver. It comes in terms of a temporal disclosure, its *Ereignis,* a time of synthesized and corresponding tones which are directed toward a future in which something is to be given, in which "it comes." The dictation of the dispatch, the interlacing of the voices, and the division of tonalities are themselves part of a *télé*-pathie, as Derrida calls it, consisting of disembodied resonances which are carried *along with* that discourse one calls philosophy. These resonances are like a semantic fallout, effects of a catastrophe or big bang in the future anterior. This is the big bang of the "He War" discussed in "Two Words for Joyce," or the destruction of the Tower of Babel, or the catastrophe which is the holocaust, or the threat of nuclear liquidation which is to come in who knows what sort of calamity. This is not to say that the apocalyptic tone is reducible to perceptions of social catastrophe, but that the catastrophe, as such, is sent as part and parcel of this tone which concerns the "ends of man," *les fins de l'homme.*

This tone, whatever we deem it to be, is ethical insofar as it brings us "face to face" with a time which can only be distantly recollected or barely anticipated, a time of reckoning. We recall from discussion of the Anaximander fragment that reckoning is one of the horizons of the *apeiron,* and Derrida investigates this reckoning in terms of the violent emission whose dispatch escapes our ability to comprehend it in terms of day-to-day communication in whose speech acts we often invest an un-critical trust. "Language," Emmanuel Levinas has written, "is perhaps to be defined as the very power to break the continuity of being or of history."[38] Derrida interrogates this notion in terms of considering language from the standpoint of tonal resonance whose synthesis is, in fact, but a bundling or bond-ing of tones which are by no means homogeneous or harmo-nious and by no means "given" all at once. For these tonalities exist only in proximity to one another, a proximity which reveals itself as other, as from an other place. The apocalyptic tone is always already there, carried through various discursive relays and media, and yet its arrival is sudden and unpredict-able. It comes like a telepathic dispatch, the sudden knowledge of something thought by an other, a knowledge that is no proper knowledge. We do not know, for it is no longer of the order of knowing, Derrida says. Rather, we detect. We pick up—who knows how?—residues, resonances, overtones, hints, premonitions, after-shocks, echoes, traces of an "event" that is not locatable, discernible, empirically given: *les fins de l'homme* and, too, the death of philosophy.

Contrary to Heidegger, whose thoughts on language and voice touch upon the term *Stimmung* (attunement), Derrida's "Of an Apocalyptic Tone" engages tonality as *Verstimmung* (untuning). For the tonality of the apocalyptic is not merely blended in with other tonalities but is also dissonant, noisy. When Kant attacks those "mystagogues" who announce the death of philosophy and the ends of man, opposing the model of the voice of reason whose tone is neutral, objective, and mezzo forte, he assumes that tone can be reduced to the point of view of the speaker, to the presence of the oratory and the rhetorical strategies behind it whose motivations are clearly expressed by the will of the speaker. That is, for Kant, tone is always univocal. Tone is reducible to one voice, the presence of the voice that speaks with undivided attention. Kant, in short, cannot recognize tonal difference. But "how do we distinguish the voices from the other in itself, in oneself?"[39] This is the question Kant never asks, the question that the metaphysics of voice refuses to pose. The voice of reason, as Kant calls it, is precisely that strategy used to dampen the proliferation of strident and stray tonalities, the strategy used to enforce a univocal tone. Derrida's "Of an Apocalyptic Tone," however, is an inquiry not into the rhetoric of an apocalyptic tone but into the difference and divisibility of tonalities and how their detection in the voice(s) of the oracles poses a threat for the metaphysics of a reasoned voice.

Were it simply a matter of polyphony or of polylogue one could simply invoke Heidegger's discussions of voice in *On the Way to Language*. However, there is the complex question of how the bundling of tonalities reaches us from beyond the self's epistemological apprehension of the world as a historical relation involving knowledge of the past and foreknowledge of the future. In this sense detection of the ends of man concerns the event of the arrival of tonalities which are recognized from beyond the being of our Dasein, whose recognition takes place outside, beyond, or exterior to us even as we ourselves are thinking it. The *Ereignis* which is the tonal dispatch manifests itself as a sudden arrival of a message that has been thought from beyond our being, from beyond the "ends of man." And this beyond is itself nothing less than a temporal clue that beckons from a proximity to the time of an end out of which Dasein necessarily constitutes itself from a theological vantage point within a tonal manifold of discursive relations.

Citing Maurice Blanchot's *Le dernier homme*, Derrida writes:

> With you, beloved voice, with you, last breath of the memory of all human happiness, allow me still this commerce of a single hour. Thanks to you I delude my solitude, and I penetrate into the lie of a multiplicity and a love, for my heart loathes believing that love is dead; it does not support the shudder of the most solitary of solitudes, and it obliges me to speak as if I were two.

Commenting on this question, Derrida adds,

"As if I were two": for the moment he thus sends himself this message by acting *as if* he could still really appeal to it. This impossible destination signs, stamps the death of the last man, inside and outside him. He knows him beyond the *as if*.[40]

In other words, the moment of the last man's death is not a moment that is focused on him as subject or self but as a dispatch or sending whose place of origin is situated in an "end" that has not yet occurred. Yet this origin, this end, what is it? Derrida discusses it in terms of the apocalyptic approach of a temporal horizon, of an eschaton. "Whoever takes on the apocalyptic tone will be asked: with a view to what and to what ends? In order to lead where, right now or in a few minutes? The end is beginning, signifies the apocalyptic tone. But to what ends does the tone signify this?"[41] The oracular voice is one that approaches us from these ends of man, one that arrives, is dispatched, sent.

That the apocalyptic tone is divided, bundled, or *Unverstimmt* concerns its proximity to an end in which Being undergoes what Heidegger would call demolition, the eradication of those concealments out of which the everyday experience of Dasein is made up, that experience which in Kant is narrowed to the voice of reason, or what we might in a more popularized vocabulary call the commonsensical. What is appropriate shows itself in the sending of an apocalyptic tone, and this appropriate *what* is the deconstruction of a chronological notion of selfhood in history which places emphasis upon the separability of moments and the experience of a now as now. Rather, the apocalyptic tone manifests an *Ereignis* reflected in a belonging-together of different times or epochs as intuited outside the univocal and centered consciousness of one who experiences life in that same time wherein life is lived. Rather, hearing the call of an apocalyptic dispatch would mean the capacity to live in a multiplicity of temporal disclosures beyond the *as if* of fictional identifications or empathic constructions, beyond that doubling of a self which would still be self.

The apocalyptic tone comes from the end: unspecified, concealed, withheld. It arrives telepathically, as if one always knew this end were there. Hence Derrida writes, "The end is soon, it is imminent, signifies the tone. I see it, I know it, I tell you it, now you know it, come. We are going to die, we are going to disappear. And this death sentence, this stopping of death [*arrêt de mort*] can only judge us."[42] This end, Derrida notes, is acknowledged as Babel, as the dispersion of languages, the diaspora of peoples. This is the effect of the arrival of a name, in the beginning, an arrival that the Father marks with a catastrophe: destruction of the tower, demolition of the name, deconstruction of a determinate relation between the Father and his chosen. For Derrida it is as if the apocalypse of the New Testament were always already inscribed in Genesis, as if the beginning cannot be understood without recourse to knowing what is the *fin de l'homme*. How is this end translated? How is this beginning translated? How are we as practitioners of philosophy to translate ourselves into sacred history and sacred history into philosophy? What Babel proffers itself in the division philosophy/theology? And to what extent is this division itself a shifting of tones, an apocalyptic and catastrophic moment, as perceived from the standpoint of the ends of man or the ends of philosophy?

Philosophy, and especially Heideggerian and post-Heideggerian philosophy, cannot be thought responsibly without turning to this fundamental issue of translatability whose meaning depends upon the arrival of the dispatch sent from that which is beyond, the dispatch which says, "I am going to come," "I am in the process of coming," "I am on the point of going to come." These statements are themselves dictated from the end by Jesus, dictated "from behind, in the back of John, like a *shofar*." The disclosure is sent to John on Patmos, sent through the medium of a bearer or angel, a pure messenger. "And John transmits a message already transmitted, testifies to a testimony that will be yet that of another testimony, that of Jesus; so many sendings, *envois,* so many voices, and this puts so many people on the telephone line."[43] The sendings and voicings from the end, are they not part of the demolition of that metaphysical or idolatrous voice which reduces consciousness to the monologic and the self-certainty in self as that which is always present to self, or simply present in time? The sending of the apocalyptic tone is that dispatch which reveals the belonging-together of dispatches and tones, which reveals the problematic of translation as that which demands relaying, displacing, sending, forwarding, returning, circulating, and so on. In this sending of Being, then, one can say, "It grants Being." As Kockelmans noted in Heidegger the question of time concerns the coming, the having been, and the present as a proximate relation which denies the present or presence in any static sense. The *es gibt* means, as Kockelmans is quoted above as saying, that "it keeps open the coming (future) by withholding the present in this coming." For Derrida this withholding is not marked by an absencing but by an other directedness or exteriorization of one's consciousness of Being such that Being in its openness or coming can be intuited in its *Ereignis* in that granting constituted by tone. In terms of the correspondence of tones and times, the coming of the sent dispatch, the withholding of the self as that which is present-to-self, we can make the transition or translation from philosophy to theology and back again, a translation which demystifies Kant's absolute difference between the voice of reason and the voice of the oracle.

Toward the end of "Of an Apocalyptic Tone" Derrida returns to his earlier formulations of *écriture* by suggesting that the apocalyptic tone is inherently a kind of writing or postal inscription.

> And if the dispatches (*envois*) always refer to other dispatches without decidable destination, the destination remaining to come, then isn't this completely angelic structure, that of the Johannine Apocalypse, isn't it also the structure of every scene of writing in general? This is one of the suggestions I wanted to submit for your discussion: wouldn't the apocalyptic be a transcendental condition of all discourse, of all experience itself, of every mark or every trace? And the genre of writings called "apocalyptic" in the strict sense, then, would be only an example, an exemplary revelation of this transcendental structure.[44]

If so, then the apocalypse reveals the revelation, the self-presentation of an apocalyptic structure of language, and "of the experience of presence." But this experience is that of "the divisible dispatch (*envoi*) for which there is no self-presentation nor assured destination."[45] Perhaps alluding to his essay on Mallarmé, entitled "The Double Session," Derrida discusses the dispatch as if tone could be folded into itself, its divisions neither a mark of separability nor of continuity. This divisible nondivisibility dismantles dominant contracts, bonds, attachments, lineages; it is a divisibility of the dispatch which ensures a diaspora of peoples and a shattering of churches into splinter groups. The message or dispatch given or sent from the temporal horizon of end(s) divides and mixes the bonds that we make with that which is revealed, that "I shall come: the coming is always to come." In this message, always mediated by a messenger, the belongingness established between the one who receives and the one who sends is threatened at the moment of its revelation.

In the traversal and transference of this "I shall come," the event of the Coming is not so much defined as preceded by an anticipatory call in whose divisibility the event that is the end disarticulates itself before thought: "The event of this "Come" precedes and calls the event. It would be that starting from which there is any event, the coming, the to-come of the event that cannot be thought under the given category of event."[46] Given this call as divisible and displaced, as undecidably anticipatory yet antecedent to itself, Derrida determines that the place, the time, and the advent of the apocalyptic "no longer lets itself be contained simply in philosophy," and therefore it cannot be held in the conceptual structures of onto-eschato-theology, and metaphysics. That is, in making the translation from theology to philosophy and back, there is the disclosure of a sending of Being in whose dispatch as tone—the belongingness of anticipatory and antecedent moments concerning the *fins de l'homme*—the relation between philosophy and theology is transcended by that which cannot any longer be thought according to the difference of what is within and without Occidental conceptual systems. That is, thought considered from the perspective of this translation between philosophy and theology is a thinking about that which is "beyond" even such difference.

At the end of "Of an Apocalyptic Tone" Derrida more openly acknowledges the Heideggerian aspects of his argument as filtered through the concerns of "Pas" on Blanchot, a text which itself focuses on the word *Viens* ("Come"). Derrida writes:

"Come" (*Viens*) beyond being—this comes from beyond being and calls beyond being, engaging, starting perhaps in the place where *Ereignis* (no longer can this be translated by event) and *Enteignis* unfold the movement of propriation. If "Come" does not try to lead or conduct, if it no doubt is an-agogic, it can always be led back higher than itself, anagogically, toward the conductive violence, toward the authoritarian "duction." This risk is unavoidable; it threatens the tone as its double.[47]

Heidegger, like Kant, resisted the raising of tone. As is well known, in Heidegger's work tone is especially quiescent. Yet, such a resistance to stridency, is it not itself saturated with an apocalyptic tone already destined or "coming" to Heidegger's writing from the "end of philosophy" and the *fins de l'homme,* a "coming" that cannot come from a voice, from a self that says I, a subject that is determinable? Is it not in a certain disclosure of the "face-to-face" that Heidegger's quiescence, like that of Blanchot's, recognizes the catastrophe which is the end, a catastrophe always already divided from itself, as the timing of time, the spacing of space?

"Come" cannot come from a voice or at least not from a tone signifying "I" or "self," a so-and-so (male and female) in my "determination." "Come" does not address itself, does not appeal, to an identity determinable in advance. It is a drift [*une dérive*] underivable from the identity of a determination. "Come" is *only* derivable, absolutely derivable, but only from the other, from nothing that may be an origin or a verifiable, decidable, presentable, appropriable identity, from nothing that may not already be derivable and arrivable [*arrivable*] without "rive" (without the source, spring, *rivus*).

This is

an apocalypse without apocalypse, an apocalypse without vision, without truth, without revelation, *of dispatches* [. . .] without last judgement, without any other eschatology than the tone of the "Come" itself, its very difference, an apocalypse beyond good and evil.[48]

The apocalypse without apocalypse would be an apocalypse exterior to itself in whose proffering or coming the apocalyptic is itself expunged or ended. This is the end of the end, the end of the end of the end, and so on, a paronomasia of folded endings, the "timing of time" repeated infinitely, transferred without end. End without end would be an end supplementary to or outside the end, an end in whose ending the end is made undeterminable, the destiny that is the end of man wholly unappropriable in its necessary appropriation by an apocalyptic tone. "The *without*, the *sans* marks an internal and external catastrophe of the apocalypse, an overturning of sense [*sens*] that does not merge with the catastrophe announced or described in the apocalyptic writings without however being foreign to them. Here the catastrophe would perhaps be *of* the apocalypse itself, its *pli* and its end, a closure without end, an end without end."[49] Given such an end, the apocalypse is always here and yet never arrives, is affirmed without coming, anticipated in the absence of its Being. Catastrophe, according to Derrida, is situated here, since it is this end of the end which overturns, even to the point of reversing the arrow of time. Moreover, it is a catastrophe in which the revelation or disclosure of the end of the end is spoken, a disclosure in which the apocalypse itself as a manifestation of a law of genre is overturned and deconstructed by a tonality of the *without* where end under erasure is end(ed) and end(ing).

Venturus Est

Derrida's consideration of the "ends" of man is mediated not only by Maurice Blanchot but also by the much more elusive Emmanuel Levinas about whom Derrida has written two major pieces, "Violence and Metaphysics" and "En ce moment même dans cet ouvrage me voici." At the end of "Violence and Metaphysics," Derrida writes:

The Greek miracle is not this or that, such and such astonishing success; it is the impossibility for any thought

ever to treat its sages as "sages of the outside," according
to the expression of Saint John Chrysostom. . . . In wel-
coming alterity in general into the heart of the *logos,* the
Greek thought of Being forever has protected itself
against every absolutely *surprising* convocation.

Are we Jews? Are we Greeks? We live in the difference
between the Jew and the Greek, which is perhaps the
unity of what is called history. We live in and of difference.[50]

This difference is what motivates the discussion of the two
terms *Gala* and *Apokalupsis* in "Of an Apocalyptic Tone," but
perhaps even more important is the notion of exteriority which
Derrida wishes to reintroduce from "outside" the Greek tradition, an exteriority that is discussed, though somewhat un-
satisfactorily for Derrida, by Levinas in his formidable philosophical treatises. Because Derrida has consistently maintained
the view that one cannot merely go beyond a philosophical
tradition like Western thought and simply disarticulate it from
a position exterior to it, the difference "Jewgreek is greekjew"
(the phrase is taken by Derrida from Joyce's *Ulysses*) offers that
site of possible destabilization in which the notion of "ends"
can be interrogated from within the philological interplay of
last things: *Gala* and *Apokalupsis.* Levinas himself, in a key
essay, "La trace de l'autre," writes that "Occidental philosophy
coincides with the unveiling (*dévoilement*) of the Other (*l'Autre*) where the Other, in manifesting itself as being, loses its
alterity."[51] Western thought, Levinas says, represents a horror
of the other as truly Other; which is to say, Occidental thought
is allergic to that which is exterior to its conceptual apparatuses. Indeed, such a resistance to exteriority is expressed in the
Western formulation of Being as intrinsically available to consciousness and comprehensible within a system of relationships
that can be accounted for by the reason that consciousness is
capable of thinking. Levinas, therefore, in moving beyond Occidental thought considers a movement beyond Being that
cannot return to its philosophical points of departure (consciousness) and that cannot be recovered under the rubric of
identification (reason, system, logocentrism). Derrida's concern with letters or missives in *The Post Card* parallels Levinas's

orientation to Being in that the letters are an example recalling the trajectory of biblical epistles disclosing "apocalyptic" dimensions of closure or ending which go beyond a notion of Being recoverable under the rubric of identification or the return to points of departure. This is itself the "apocalyptic tone" which in its *Verstimmung,* or "untuning," is what announces the "death of philosophy" as "the possibility for the other tone, or the tone of another, to come at no matter what moment to interrupt a familiar tonality."[52]

John's Apocalypse is itself a dispatch which John hears "as a dictation [of] the great voice of Jesus."[53] And this scene of dictation recalls for Derrida Matthew Paris's scene of dictation between Socrates and Plato. "Write and send, dictates the voice come from behind, in the back of John, like a shofar."[54] Here, too, the "time" of the dictation is problematized in that Derrida notices that the scene of dictation presupposes that Jesus "comes" prior to his "arrival" announced in the phrase "I shall come." That is, the time of the coming is already curiously divided into an event that approximates a Heideggerian *Ereignis* where moments are at once appropriated and expropriated in a correspondence which Derrida will situate in the apocalyptic scene of writing as represented by St. John the Divine, a "correspondence" conditioned by the "transmission" of voices. "So John is the one who already receives some letters [*courrier*] through the medium yet of a bearer who is an angel, a pure messenger. And John transmits a message already transmitted, testifies to a testimony that will be yet that of another testimony, that of Jesus; so many sendings, *envois,* so many voices, and this puts so many people on the telephone line."[55] In terms of this "correspondence" or "transmission" the "face-to-face" is established as linguistic paronomasia, which is to say, that Saying in which the "time times" is disclosed as the "face-to-face." A quotation from Chouraqui's translation of John's Apocalypse reads,

> If you do not stay awake,
> I shall come like a thief:
> you will not know at what hour I shall come to you.

Commenting, Derrida writes:

I shall come: the coming is always to come. The *Adôn,* named as the aleph and the taw, the alpha and the omega, is the one who has been, who is, and who comes, not who shall be, but who comes, which is the present of a to-come, a future [*à-venir*]. *I come* means: I am going to come, I am to-come in the imminence of an "I am going to come," "I am in the process of coming," "I am on the point of going to come." "Who comes" (*o erkhomenos*) is translated in Latin by *venturus est.*[56]

In the paronomasic interplay on the word "Come" (*Venez*), Derrida has "interlaced" the rhetoric of arrival or coming in Blanchot's *L'attente l'oubli,* which itself "corresponds" with John's *envois,* and allows for the Heideggerian formulation of the "time times" (that which arrives, which reaches in the rising) to be developed in a theological context foreign to Heidegger's ontological discourse. Certainly in the "I am going to come" there is the correspondence of temporalities disclosed as an "event" of an encountering, that is, the reception or *Ereignis* of the apocalypse as transmitted in the divisibility and simultaneity of dispatches which is itself announced in the "saying" or "verse" "I shall come." Already the beginning of John's Apocalypse says that whosoever reads the record is blessed, for "the time *is* at hand," the time in which, as is said in chapter 3, "I come quickly." Yet, what does it mean to say that "the time *is* at hand"?

In terms of the paronomasia disclosed by the word "come," such a time is not at hand in the usual sense we have of a now; rather, such a time *is* in terms of a Heideggerian *Ereignis,* wherein moments of temporality "correspond," though here quite literally as the Derridean *Envoi.* Simply put, Derrida's "Of an Apocalyptic Tone" dwells on the multiplicity and multiplication of apocalyptic dispatches which are given or sent through St. John the Divine in order to show that the "destination" or "ends" of this transmission are themselves plural, divided, unassimilable. The "I shall come" is not temporally determinable as an arrival that can be expected to occur at a particular moment which we can accurately predict in chronological or everyday terms, because the "I shall come" is, like the

Heideggerian *es gibt Zeit* or *es gibt Sein,* an ontological and temporal clue concerning the approach of Dasein before the "face-to-face" whose time is always already at hand even in its withdrawal. In the "I shall come" the "face-to-face" is not only disclosed from within the temporality of a paronomasic discourse—"I shall come," I am going to come," and so on—but in terms of an other that is truly Other in the sense formulated by Levinas, which is to say, that which does not return to its points of departure and which breaks with our capacity to find an identification within it.

One of the chief departures that Levinas takes from Heidegger is in the commitment to the idea that ethics precedes ontology. Indeed, it could be said that Judaism, in general, takes this posture in contrast to Christianity, because Judaism does not privilege the ontological question of what is the nature of God's existence, only to subordinate ethics to such theological interrogations. Rather, Judaism focuses on the laws of the sacred texts, because these laws establish an ethical responsibility between members of a Jewish community and the All High, an ethical condition which does not seek to represent the deity's existence in either a set of religious dogmas for the many or a philosophical theology for the few. Levinas's readings of the Talmud are especially indicative of this perspective, because they suggest that in the verses selected from the Talmud one finds examples of how an ethical responsibility is disclosed in what is called by Levinas the "face-to-face," in which the closure of metaphysics or ontology is preceded by a much more disruptive and violent relation that opens onto the "beyond of Being"; here the "correspondences" between self and other— Levinas also refers to Same and Different, illeity and alterity— are established in what is their violent and unrecoverable destruction or demolition.

In "La trace de l'autre," Levinas develops the thesis that in one's encounter with an other (*autrui*) who shows his or her face there is revealed the trace of the Other (*l'Autre*), which is that of the holy. In the "face-to-face" there is disclosed a relation to difference unrecoverable as an experience of morality, which can be represented as something identical to itself. That is, in the "face-to-face" a totality of relationships is ruptured for the sake of a disclosure of the infinite. In *Ethics and Infinity,*

Levinas cites Blanchot as a kindred thinker when he writes about the *écriture du désastre:*

> In Blanchot it is no longer being, and it is no longer "something," and it is always necessary to unsay what one says—it is an event which is neither being nor nothingness. In his last book, Blanchot called this "disaster," which signifies neither death nor an accident, but as a piece of being which would be detached from its fixity of being, from its reference to a star, from all cosmological existence, a *dis-aster*. He gives an almost verbal sense to the substantive disaster. It seems that for him it is impossible to escape from this maddening, obsessive situation.[57]

Levinas's conception of the trace of the Other is tied to this notion of one's existential recognition of ethics as an opening onto a dis-aster which is that "piece of being which would be detached from its fixity of being," that which is neither being nor nothingness. In "La trace de l'autre," a text crucial for Derrida, Levinas discusses this "disaster" as a third term, the excluded middle, as he calls it, of being and nothingness: *au-delà de l'Etre*. Given the contexts of our study, of course, this is apparently a kindred term to Heidegger's *Überstieg* and Blanchot's *le pas au-delà*. That is, the *au-delà de l'Etre* marks the deconstruction of transcendence, though it does so from the side of what lies beyond, rather than, in the case of both Heidegger in *The Essence of Reasons* and Blanchot in *Le pas au-delà*, from the side of Dasein. It is *au-delà de l'Etre* that the trace of the Other is detected, a trace which is "not a sign like any other" for it "also plays the role of the sign. It may be taken as a sign." Moreover, this trace "signifies *outside* all intentionality of making signs and *outside* of any project in which it would be sighted." Because this is a "trace-work," it follows that the "outside" of Being is not only differed from itself, always already exterior to itself (paronomasically an exterior to an exterior to an exterior, etc.) but differed as a deferring.[58] Hence the *au-delà de l'Etre* is itself that "end of the end" that Derrida is addressing in "Of an Apocalyptic Tone." Moreover, the trace is, in Derrida's context, a performance of the sign that is nothing less than a tonality transpiring in an ethical relation, the "I shall come," which constitutes what Levinas, after Blanchot, would see as the "dés-astre" and what Derrida is calling the "cata-strophe."

At this point, the influence of Levinas upon "Of an Apocalyptic Tone" can be more clearly outlined in terms of how it modifies Derrida's orientation to Heidegger and, too, how it affects the question of temporality as inherited from the Heideggerian tradition. The question of tone, although it marks within a Heideggerian context a notion of correspondence, is, in Levinas's context, a question of the trace of the Other or the *au-delà de l'Etre*. From the Heideggerian perspective the correspondences suggest those synchronic and diachronic aspects of temporality as *Ereignis* in which the "face-to-face" is disclosed in its various manifolds of temporal and spatial proximities. But from the Levinasian perspective the contextualization of tonality as trace suggests a breaking of correspondences from the horizon of the *au-delà de l'Etre* and an understanding of temporality in terms of the "without" or "outside" in which the trace of the Other, always *au-delà de l'Etre,* functions to differ and defer the end and in so dividing it appears to intuition as a disaster or catastrophe. This catastrophe is conveyed in the words, "I shall come," precisely because this phrase is articulated from the perspective of the *au-delà de l'Etre*. For in the wake of the trace of the Other the end is always deferred, divided, shifted, differed, and yet, for all that, imminently on the way, dispatched, sent, given. In the "I shall come" an ethical relation arrives or comes even before ontology with its most fundamental questions. That is, like Levinas, Derrida turns against Heideggerian philosophy in a way that is cata-strophic or even apo-strophic. Like Levinas, he poses the radical indeterminacy of an ethical responsibility before (in front of) ontology and in so doing reverses the priorities of Heideggerian thought. Also, by studying a Christian scripture, Derrida, by having recourse to a Hebraic perspective, allows for the catastrophe which is apocalypse to have cata-strophic consequences for the historical relationships between Christianity and Judaism, since Derrida's analysis with its Levinasian orientations welcomes alterity into the heart of the *logos* and exacerbates the question raised in "Violence and Metaphysics," "Are we Jews? Are we Greeks?" For "we live in the difference between the Jew and the Greek, which is perhaps the unity of what is called history." But this "difference," as we have seen, is one that "comes" from the outside, a "difference" which does not follow from ontology and its Heideggerian problematization of Being and beings but which constitutes itself in the ethical relationship between the me and the other (*autrui*) in which is disclosed the *au-delà de l'Etre*. This beyond or otherwise than being points to that trace of the Other (*l'Autre*) in whose wake the relation between a me and a him (or her) may be intuited. This relation more than merely implies the establishment of a responsibility concerning, in Derrida's context, the catastrophic relationship between Christian and Jew. This catastrophe involves not only an overturning of the received historical relations within which Judaism is considered as different from Christianity but a *revelation* of the end as enfolded and divided in the *Ereignis* that is the indifference of *Gala/Apokalupsis*, an indifference wherein the infinite deferral of the end announces itself in the traces of a *désastre*. Both the horizons of liquidation and fecundity are given in this *désastre* as phenomenological clues, allowing us to intuit our way back to the prehistory of the Hebrew self. Levinas writes in *Otherwise Than Being or Beyond Essence,*

> But in the "prehistory" of the ego posited for itself speaks a responsibility. The self is through and through a hostage, older than the ego, prior to principles. What is at stake for the self, in its being, is not to be. Beyond egoism and altruism it is the religiosity of the self.

Again,

> [The ego] is a being divesting itself, emptying itself of its being, turning itself inside out, and if it can be put thus, the face of "otherwise than being." This subjection is neither nothingness, nor a product of a transcendental imagination. In this analysis we do not mean to reduce an entity that would be the ego to the act of substituting itself that would be the being of this entity. Substitution is not an act; it is a passivity inconvertible into an act, the hither side of the act-passivity alternative, the exception that cannot be fitted into the grammatical categories

of noun or verb, save in the said that thematizes them. This recurrence can be stated only as an in-itself, as the underside of being or as otherwise than being. To be oneself, otherwise than being, to be disinterested, is to bear the wretchedness and bankruptcy of the other, and even the responsibility that the other can have for me. To be oneself, the state of being a hostage, is always to have one degree of responsibility more, the responsibility for the responsibility of the other.[59]

In the "I shall come," of the correspondence of the Other, the ego who hears listens to the tonalities from the "otherwise than being," the *au-delà de l'Etre,* and as such "listens to Being" (this is Heidegger's phrase) from the perspective of the beyond or hitherside, wherein the being of the self or ego is perceived as empty or divested of itself. This is what Derrida implies within a Levinasian context by the phrase *les fins de l'homme.* That is, Derrida, in considering the beyond, exterior, or outside of Being as the apocalyptic end announced in the "I shall come," himself arrives at the "ends" of man, where the self accedes to a primordial ethical relationship of which the apocalypse or catastrophe, in its very overturning of the difference, ontology/ethics and Christianity/Judaism, is what Derrida calls the "catastrophe of the apocalypse" or "apocalypse without [outside] apocalypse." This deconstruction of the concept of the "end" not only does violence to conceptions of Heideggerian eschatology in which the destiny of Being reaches its fulfillment as revelation of truth but also does violence to a Christian eschatological reading of John's Apocalypse by suggesting that the end of time and the coming of the Messiah are themselves infinitely divided and deferred in their very arrival or dispatch. Moreover, it suggests that the "good news" or "correspondence" which makes up New Testament scripture not only withholds revelation, apocalypse, and the end in its very bringing of history to a close but is little else than a tone or trace "without sender or decidable addressee, without last judgment, without any other eschatology than the tone of the 'Come' itself, its very difference, an apocalypse beyond good and evil."[60] Such statements are not, to the contrary of what some Christian readers will suspect, expressions of a deep-seated atheism but an interpretation of Christian apocalypse from the standpoint of the *au-delà de l'Etre* as developed by Levinas in a Judaic context. It is here that a "subject" unthinkable from within Occidental tradition is intuitively reunited with a pre-history that occurs "outside" of Greek logocentrism where the Other as radically Other cannot be thought, an "outside" where the self is divested of that ontology which precludes the ethical understanding of its responsibilities before the alterity of the Other.

Toward a Hebrew Ereignis

In contrast to "Of an Apocalyptic Tone," Derrida interrogates the correspondence of tonalities in "Two Words for Joyce" from the perspective of the Old Testament. "Two Words for Joyce" first appeared in *Post-Structuralist Joyce* (1984), and an expanded version has since appeared in *Ulysse Gramophone* (1987). In "Two Words for Joyce," Derrida explores tonality as the metalepsis or paronomasia inherent in Joyce's *Finnegans Wake,* namely in the phrase "he war." One of the consequences of this exploration will be the discovery, within the largely untranslatable Joycean language, of a nihilism in the relation of Being and time that counters Heidegger's more teleological and even unifying sense in essays like those on Anaximander that the history of Being as transferred in language passes through a metaleptic current of translations in which, despite a history of "misreadings," the question of Being in relation to time uniformly unfolds. Such translation occurs by way of metaphorical structures in whose appearance truth is deferred, though, in fact, that truth as the process of translation or metaphorization is continually manifesting itself. Insofar as such metaphorization occurs through the metalepsis or exchange of one translation for another, a *retrait* is established in the extension or presencing of a linguistic moment even at the very time of its absencing and retraction.

In "Two Words for Joyce," Derrida will show that one can locate texts addressing the relationship of being, time, language, and translation (or metaleptic transmission) that disarticulate the attunements of these various relations. For in "Two

Words for Joyce" attention is paid to the tonalities of diaspora as Joyce has brought them into semantic relation by means of the possibility/impossibility of a transference or translation of words across linguistic boundaries. Such transference occurs by means of a correspondence of sounds, which is to say, by means of the appropriation and disappropriation of tonalities which pass or do not pass across national linguistic frontiers, a phenomenon analogous to what Derrida in *The Post Card* calls the *tranchfert* and which, in another essay, is more closely approximated in the title "Shibboleth." In "Two Words for Joyce," Derrida will argue that Joyce's right perception of such a disarticulation not only culminates in a very violent reading of these relationships with respect to history as catastrophe, a theme we have already noticed in "Of an Apocalyptic Tone," but that this violence is inherent in a Hebraic reading of the question of being, time, language, and translation as evidenced in Genesis. "Two Words for Joyce" strongly suggests that through a careful reading of *Finnegans Wake* one can sight a possible means whereby to criticize Heidegger's notion of *Ereignis* (the coming of the event) as predicated too much on a notion of unity concerning the various moments of appropriation and expropriation.

As if remembering "Pas," Derrida begins the essay, "It is very late, it is always too late with Joyce, I shall say only two words." That these two words are themselves about a temporal, existential condition—"he was"—serves as a clue to the gradual slippage within language whose effect is to disarticulate the unity of a temporal moment, or manifold. Concerning Derrida, of course, is the matter of distanciation, the proximity of the words "he war" from one another as well as what that means in terms of those to whom the "he war" is addressed. Not only that, but the distance affects the question of translation, the proximity or distance of words to one another. To recall a quotation above from "Pas," "the proximity of the near is not near, not proper to itself." Indeed, the question in Joyce concerns this proximity or properness of language to itself. As we will notice, this proximity is itself to be considered in terms of the step/not, or *pas,* the *retrait* of transcendence or, to put it another way, of translation. "What are these two English words? They are only half English, if you will, if you will hear them." The question here, clearly, is not only of time and being but of language as trans-lation, of an English that is only half English and half something else. Speaking of this phrase, "he war," Derrida writes:

> I spell them out: HEWAR, and sketch a first translation: HE WARS—he wages war, he declares or makes war, he is war, which can also be pronounced by babelizing a bit (it is in a particularly Babelian scene of the book that these words rise up), by Germanizing, then, in Anglo-Saxon, He war: he was—he who was ("I am he who is or who am," says YAHWE). Where it was, he was, declaring war, and it is *true*. Pushing things a bit, taking the time to draw on the vowel and to lend an ear, it will have been true, *wahr*, that's what can be kept [*garder*] or looked at [*regarder*] in truth.
>
> He, is "He," the "him," the one who says I in the masculine, "He," war declared, he who was war declared, declaring war, by declaring war, was he who was, and he who was true, the truth, he who by declaring war verified the truth that he was, he verified himself, he verified the truth of his truth by war declared, by the act of declaring, and declaring is an act of war, he declared war in language and on language and by language, which gave languages, that's the truth of Babel when YAHWE pronounced its vocable, difficult to say if it was a name . . .
>
> I stop here provisionally, through lack of time.[61]

Clearly, toward the end of this quotation Derrida's reading of Joyce is almost entirely paronomasic, and he is particularly sensitive to the fact that only through the slowness of the unfolding of time can such an interpretation be pulled out or pulled through the phrase that Joyce has written in the *Wake*. Particularly in terms of the repetition of the pronoun, the meaning shifts. The "he war" takes on significance as a transmission of a declaration of being ("he war"/"he was") and of truth, the declaration of the truth of being in whose transmission this truth is verified as the "war," that modality of Being in whose contemplation language itself is pluralized and pulverized. This is the declared "war" (the "was" of being) in lan-

224 Anticipations of Apocalypse

guage, on language, and by language, the "war" that gives languages. The "he war," in other words, can be transmitted only in terms of this declaration of war through the name, this declaration of a war on language. Yet, as we shall see, this "war" is itself an *Ereignis* which holds itself back, since its declaration is untranslatable, undeclarable. In this sense the declaration is a *pas* marking a step-that-is-and-is-not. "L'Entfernung é-loignant," Derrida says in the Babelizing or Joycean language of "Pas." In Joyce himself this distancing of distance is precisely given in the hybridized language of "he war," a phrase that produces a radical slippage of signification, perhaps one of the most radical Derrida has ever considered in his essays.

The phrase "he war" comes from the last full page of the first section of part 2 of *Finnegans Wake,* in which pantomime begins at twilight. Throughout this particular part of the *Wake* Joyce makes references to events which occur in Genesis. For example, "We've heard it aye since songdom was gemurrmal" ["Sodom was Gemorrah"] (251.36). There is a passage on Noah's ark —"O! Amune! Ark!? Noh?!" (244.26)—and toward the end of the chapter a mention of Babel. This occurs after the pantomime or theater in the chapter comes to an end with the thunder of the father, H.C.E.

Byfall.
Upploud!
The play thou shouwburgst, Game, here endeth. The curtain drops by deep request.
Uplouderamain!
Gonn the gawds, Gunnar's gustspells. When the h, who the hu, how the hue, where the huer? Orbiter onsewers: lots lives lost. (257.29–36)

Here, "Byfall" is German for *Beifall,* or applause. "The Day Thou Gavest, Lord, Is Ended: 'The darkness falls at thy behest'" can be substituted for "The play thou . . . request" "Uplouderamain" might be "applaud louder, man!"; Gunnar refers to the stage manager Michael Gunn, and "gustspells" to "godspells," or "Gospels." "Orbiter onsewers" could mean "arbiter's answers" and "lots lives lost" suggests "Love's Labors Lost," the "lost wife of Lot," or "lots of lives lost." There is also the paronomasic "When the h, who the hu, how the hue, where

the huer?" This sentence marks not only the falling of the
curtain and the dissolution of the biblical stories into a kind of
babble, but the dis-integration of language under the recognition that the gods are gone. And one wonders, is the paronomasic play on the "he war" in Derrida not inherently addressing this dissolution, "When the h, who the hu, how the
hue, where the huer?" Indeed, the text suggests that theology is
merely mime, theater, performance—language merely reenact-
ing itself, mumming itself, metaleptically unfolding itself. At
the end of the chapter from part 2, we have nothing else than
Götterdämmerung. "Gwds with gurs are gttrdmmrng," Joyce
writes (258.1–2). And, we hear them rumbling in the distance.
Yet this hectoring rumble also invokes covenants.

> Yip! Yup! Yarrah! And let Nek Nekulon extol Mak
> Makal and let him say unto him: Immi ammi Semmi
> [Heb.: My mother, my nation, my name]. And shall not
> Babel be with Lebab? [Heb.: Lebhabah: hearts] And he
> war. And he shall open his mouth and answer: I hear, O
> Ismael, how they laud is only as my loud is one [Gen.
> 17:20: "And as for Ishmael, I have heard thee: Behold I
> have blessed him, and will make him fruitful and will
> multiply him exceedingly; twelve princes shall he beget,
> and will make him a great nation"]. (258.9–13)

If the "gwds . . . are gttrdmmrng," a covenant is being made
with Abraham in which Ishmael (he is clearly Shem in Joyce's
terms, whereas Shaun is Isaac) accedes to greatness. Yet, it is
Ishmael who will be "a wild ass of a man, his hand against every
man and every man's hand against him" (Gen. 16:12), and it is
Ishmael who will be the father of the nomadic tribes—the
outcast, who will speak a different tongue from the Hebrews.
Although Derrida does not acknowledge it, Ishmael is also a
very plausible subject for the "he war" of Joyce's text, which, in
terms of Shem and Shaun, represents the fratricidal conflict
between the two brothers. It is between these two brothers, at
once so similar and different, that the "he war" transpires, and
in it that two persons are doubled, paronomasically repeated:
Shem and Shaun. "He war," in this sense, represents the division of the same, the limit/nonlimit of a difference between
peoples, the tribes of Ishmael, the people of Isaac.

However, Derrida's reading of the "he war" focuses on the effects of God's Being which are not determinable in terms of differentiation. That is, in the declaration of the name of God in the "he war," language, which is incapable of determining its meaning, will necessarily be sacrificed, pluralized. This, Derrida argues, is the effect of the "he war" on the language of the *Wake* itself, on a text whose "differences" cannot be reduced to "difference." Hence Derrida's reading of the phrase focuses on the "fission" of the text. "[Joyce] repeats and mobilizes and babelizes the (asymptotic) totality of the equivocal, he makes this his theme and his operation." Or, again, "[Joyce subjects] each atom of writing to fission in order to overload the unconscious with the whole memory of man: mythologies, religion, philosophies, sciences, psychoanalysis, literatures."[62] Still, implicit in this interrogation of the "he war," or war on language, is that Derrida's reading will necessarily touch not only on Babel and translation but on the violence which accompanies the necessary division or casting off from the father. If the nation of Israel is being invoked in this passage as something to be established, the reference to Ishmael in the "he war" looks proleptically, by way of example, to the fate of Abraham's son as if it were an allegory for the casting out and destruction of the Hebrews and of Israel by the Roman Empire. Like Ishmael, the Jews will find themselves not only cut off from Israel but cut off from the Father, and, already after Babel, subjected to speak in tongues that are "other." In the "he war," then, Joyce recognizes the condition of a Leopold Bloom within the immediate context of a language that has been pluralized or pulverized, not to mention a historical context in which every man's hand is against him. Of course, this is, for Derrida, everywhere implicit in the meaning of "he war," what we notice as part of a doubled identification or accompaniment, to the declaration of God's presence in the "he war." That is, in the figure of Ishmael and, more generally, in the question of Israel's history, the being cast off from God, the distance to the Godhead, or absence or eclipse of God becomes stressed. In the assertion of God's "he war" the assertion of presence is superimposed on the "he war" of Ishmael, which asserts absence, eclipse, or distance. The "he war," then, becomes the phrase in which both of these horizons of God's Being are inscribed or vocalized.

Derrida's reading of the "he war" stresses the disclosure of God's Being in terms of the appearance of a phenomenon as phoneme or, as he playfully puts it, "phone-menon." By paronomasically reinscribing the "war" of "he war" between two languages—English and German—the revelation of Being is always already described within the war of language—its *Wahrheit,* past, and violence which comprise its Being as language. In terms of these linguistic overlays, the question of the "event" or "phenomenon" not only of God's Being but of language is problematized within the tonalities of linguistic slippage, comprising an iteration that is not recoverable as mere assertion of Being, that is to say, of idea, energeia, positing, absolute concept, or will to power. In Joyce, this *epoché* of Being occurs through the paronomasia of the event or phenomenon of declaration or donation by way of the "he war," which is to say, by way of a violent slippage of the vocative, not to mention of *écriture.*

In the landscape immediately surrounding the "he war," we are, if such a present is possible, and this place, at Babel: at the moment when YAHWEH declares war, HE WAR (exchange of the final R and the central H in the anagram's throat), and punishes the Shem, those who, according to Genesis, declare their intention of building the tower in order to make a name for themselves. Now they bear the name "name" (Shem). And the Lord, the Most High, be he blessed (*Lord, loud, laud . . .*), declares war on them by interrupting the construction of the tower, he deconstructs by speaking the vocable of his choice, the name of confusion, which in the hearing, could be confused with a word indeed signifying "confusion." Once this war is declared, he was it (*war*) by being himself this act of war which consisted in declaring, as he did, that he was the one he was (*war*). The God of fire assigns to the Shem the necessary, fatal and impossible translation of his name, of the vocable with which he signs his act of war, of himself.[63]

The giving of the name or assertion of the "he war" is, like the *es gibt* in Heidegger, an assertion concerning the time of being. With respect to this biblical moment, the relationship between time and being appears extremely violent and deconstructive, since the assertion by the all high of the time of its being amounts to nothing else than a declaration of "war" (*Wahrheit,* the having always already been, combat) in which language not only succumbs to paronomasia but to utter disruption. The time of being is revealed, in this context, as a time asserted from within the metalepsis of language, that is to say, the confusions inherent in its translation or *Übersetzung* of the word "war." As in Heidegger's reading of the ancient Greek texts, in the Bible, once more, Being and time are not disclosed within language as univocal or logocentric meaning; rather, being and time are disclosed as the most radical violence to language insofar as violence is disclosed in an "event" that not only appropriates but expropriates in a mysterious and "undetermined" manner. This is what Blanchot would view as the "secret of an ancient fear" determined and undetermined through time, what we have quoted in the previous chapter from *Le pas au-delà* as "the step beyond which is not achieved in time, which would lead beyond time, without this beyond being atemporal." In Joyce this "beyond" is the "war," the "was" of the "he," the "was" or "war" under whose secret or untranslatable sign we live with an ancient fear, the fear of the "he war" (he was; he wars).

The indetermination, secrecy, and dreaded violence of the "he war," then, functions in Derrida as an allegory of reading for the *es gibt* in Heidegger. Whereas Heidegger stays clear of a theology directly addressing religious history as told in the Bible, Derrida ventures, through Joyce's *Wake,* to recover a reading of the *es gibt Sein* by way of referring to the relationship between God, language, and his chosen people. In Joyce's text, the God of fire donates or gives to Shem (the Shem: or, name) a name that is unnameable, substituting, as it were, one name for another. In so doing, God gives a signature that cannot be translated, transmitted, or transferred. Through this untransferrable name the relationship between time and being is disclosed not merely as something that belongs to an event of giving, but, as well, to an event of withdrawing. This is where a more orthodox reading of Heidegger's *es gibt Sein* becomes crucial, since it stresses in the giving of Being a withdrawal or retraction, what Derrida calls the *retrait*. This expropriation from within the "event" of being's involvement with time is treated by Heidegger often as merely an occlusion, conceal-ment, or veiling. And when Heideggerians, for example, talk about destruction, this Heideggerian approach is often devel-oped in terms of the "demolition" of "concealments" from which Being will emerge more clearly to Dasein.[64] Yet, in Derrida's reading of Joyce, one hidden motive for the inter-pretation Derrida chooses to give the *Wake* concerns the vio-lence that is concealment or expropriation itself. In this case, as is obvious, the sending of the message by God is anything but merely an establishment of presence, the revealing of Being. In the "he war" it is as if the presence of the present were itself being expropriated, retracted, demolished. And the Shem, the name, will suffer by way of a terrible linguistic catastrophe, a story that cannot be fully told or made present, since the de-struction of the Tower of Babel means the destruction of the ability to tell of the things as they once were. After the destruc-tion, all that can be said is "he war," which is to say, in Heideg-ger's terms, "es war." This is the epoche of Genesis, then, the *retrait* at the beginning. Evidently, this *retrait* involves time as that which asserts the presence of something even as it denies the present of presence, the presencing of presence.

Unlike Heidegger, Derrida discusses the articulation of be-ing, time, and language in terms of a historical and theological catastrophe, the identification of a people in terms of its rela-tion to a name in whose reception a confusion of tongues and destruction of institutions results, the "he war." "Once this war is declared, he was it (*war*) by being himself this act of war which consisted in declaring, as he did, that he was the one he was (*war*)." In this paronomasia of the "I am who I am," being, time, and language are disclosed as breaking with the logic of difference and identity, and the "war," then, consists in the disarticulation of temporal moments of difference and in the assertion of being, time, and language, or what Heidegger would have called *Ereignis,* that manifold of appropriating and expropriating moments in which the relationship of being and time is revealed as plural, open, and violently disruptive with respect to the metaphysical comprehension of meaning. "The palindrome ('And shall not Babel be with Lebab? And he war . . .') overthrows the tower but plays too with the meaning and the letter, the meaning of being and the letters of being, of 'being,' BE,EB (baBEl/lEBab), as it does with the meaning and the letter of the name of God, EL,LE."[65] Here language is evidently the conduit through which the violence of the event of the bringing into proximity of time and being is reflected in Joyce's text. There is, for example, the metalepsis of BE,EB or of baBEl/lEBab in which "lebab" is not only a palindrome for babel but a Hebrew word meaning "heart" as well as a derivative of two Irish words, *leaba,* meaning "bed," and *leabhar,* meaning "book." Babel repeated backward as palindrome signifies the book, the bed, and the heart of the Shem which are disclosed within the violence that has already occurred to language, the "event" of declaring the Being of the All High which "war." Indeed, in terms of the war within language the "event" of the "he war" is reflected as linguistic collision and as intralingual collusion, though it is in terms of the slippages between tower and bed, heart and book, that Joyce yokes ancient Hebrew history with that of the Celts. For in Ireland, too, people have experienced the catastrophe of ruined towers (see, for example, W. B. Yeats's "The Black Tower") and of the destruction by conquerors of an originary language, something Joyce refers to satirically in the Mutt and Jute episode of the *Wake.* Here, as everywhere in the *Wake,* the "event" of linguistic destruction cannot be localized but is itself inappropriable, even as its effects are only too much felt.

Here even Derrida restricts the ramifications of the event of Babel to its biblical source, since, as he says, his time is itself limited, and pursues further the question of time in relation to the "he war": "For the 'he war' also tells of the irreplaceability of the event that it is, which is that it is, and which is also unchangeable because it has already been, a past without appeal which, before being, was. So that's war declared: before being, that is being a present, it was: was *he,* the late god of fire. And the call to translate rejects you: thou shalt not translate me."[66] The event of naming Being is close to that of Blanchot's *pas au-delà,* a step/not beyond, a moment which tells of the irreplaceability of something that is, which is that it is, and which cannot change, since it has already been, and yet a moment which is not exactly simultaneous with the already been. The name, in other words, is a trace structure which negotiates between was and is, a *différance* of moments that cannot be reduced to the kind of difference in which a division between presence and absence can be instituted, in which a notion of being takes place that imitates human being or Dasein, rooted as it is in the finite change of temporal moments, past, present, future. "He war" is quite other and untranslatable. It defies linguistic incorporation, with its temporal horizons, and therefore confuses that language, disrupts it in its very transmission, its dispatch. The *différance,* certainly, concerns this curious impasse of the "dispatch" which cannot be "dispatched." "In the beginning, difference, that's what happens, that's what has already taken place, that's what was when language was act, and the tongue [*la langue*] writing. Where it was, *He* was."⁶⁷ If the "event" of the "dispatch" is disseminated in terms of the overlapping of national histories, the event is also restricted because not accessible to a philosophy of presence or presentations. This is a past without appeal that, before being, was. Unrepresentable and yet inscribed, always already before being and yet giving the name "I am," unlocatable event and yet irreplaceable moment, the "he war" is a violent defiance of Western metaphysics.

   Certainly, the indeterminacy of the "he war" approximates that of our recognition of Anaximander's notion of the *apeiron* which also concerns, in Heidegger's view, the question of transmission or translation. In Heidegger's reading of the fragment of Anaximander, we recall that its relation to being or truth passed through the trans-lation or meta-lepsis of the text through history, that being was disclosed in this slippage of the text by Anaximander through so many philosophical hands. In Derrida's reading of Joyce, however, the history of such a transmission of being through language as told from a Hebraic perspective, the "and he war," stresses rather the impasse of the philosophical or prophetic dispatch, the untranslatability of the question of being and the linguistic violence this broaches. Given Joyce's reading of Babel, not to mention of Ishmael, one can read the Heideggerian account of being as textually disclosed through history in a much more nihilistic if not deconstructive manner, in terms of the heavenly signature which declares war on mankind through the double bind of sending a dispatch or declaration which is impossible for the addressees to under-stand or trans-late. "He war," or the Being of him that war marks that nihilistic moment of being as catastrophe which accompanies the election of a people. "He war" not only marks the problematic of the relationship of being, time, and language as one that cannot be synthesized or unified into a comprehensible structure but also marks the violence to which a chosen people will be subject: their establishment and casting out. The destruction of Babel and the confusion of languages already is deeply involved with this catastrophe which cannot be separated from the time of the Hebrews, the history of the Jews. Here the temporality of Being as the All High comes into proximity with the history of God's chosen, a history of human being and a temporality of sacred Being that is everywhere marked by a violent disruption that prohibits the coalescing of meanings into a coherent manifold of relationships even while language itself is subject to a metaleptic movement in which clues to being, time, and meaning are revealed.

Heidegger in "Over 'The Line'" wrote that the oblivion of Being affects its essence as well as the way in which we interrogate that essence through language. Derrida's reading of Joyce involves not only this question of the oblivion of Being—what amounts to the "he war"—but of how this oblivion involves Dasein as the Shem, as those to whom this oblivion has been transmitted in the heart of Babel such that the book of the Hebrews is itself destroyed and disseminated in a diaspora of words about the nature of God's being. Whereas Heidegger could discuss the restoration of metaphysics in "Over 'The Line'" through an understanding of the line between being and nothingness, Derrida argues that Joyce reveals this line as an impasse within which translation, transference, and comprehension are thoroughly double binded.

> But the God of Babel had already tortured his own signature; he was this torment: resentment *a priori* with respect to any possible translator. I order you and forbid you to translate me, to interfere with my name, to give a body of writing to its vocalization. And through this double command he signs. The signature does not come after the law,

it is the divided act of the law: revenge, resentment, reprisal, revendication *as* signature. But also as gift and gift of languages. And God lets himself be prayed to, he condescends, he leans over (Loud/low), prayer and laughter absolve perhaps the pain of signature, the act of war with which everything will have begun. This is art, Joyce's art, the space given for his signature made into the work. *He war,* it's a counter-signature, it confirms and contradicts, effaces by subscribing.[68]

If for Anaximander the being question was to be considered in terms of justice and injustice in accordance with the "assessments of time," for Derrida this "assessment" is nothing other than that conveyed through the transference of a signature tortured by its author, an "assessment" that also transpires through time, since it is the time of sacred Being and human history which is intimately bound with the transference of the name of the eternal. This "assessment" is the "he war," the violence, the torture, the reprisal that occurs in donation of a name which prayer partly assuages and partly abets. The "assessment"—is it not the catastrophe of a Being and a being whose differences and identities remain unstable, incomprehensible, unsynthesizable, incommunicable? This is the shadow under which Dasein writes, or, more accurately, the condition of Joyce's *Wake,* the sign of an ancient fear that has swamped Joyce's text in a war in which language becomes what Blanchot calls the *écriture du désastre.*[69]

The *Wake,* for all its hilarity, is a book of the dead, perhaps, in more than one sense, a book about the end of the book, a writing about the end of writing, and a text about *les fins de l'homme.* Although such pronouncements on the *Wake* may sound commonplace enough, Derrida has demonstrated with respect to Joyce's metaleptic writing the degree to which his book of the dead can be interpreted to expose a nihilism within the Heideggerian notion of the *es gibt Sein* that serves to deconstruct Heidegger's philosophy by way of exacerbating or collapsing its structure without at the same time exiting that manifold of philosophical relations. That we encounter the slippages of time in the "event(s)" of Joyce's language is extremely pertinent from our perspective in this study, since it shows in yet another way the degree to which Derrida's philosophy shadows the time project that Heidegger had undertaken. Whereas it might be assumed that many of Derrida's recent essays have become merely occasional pieces, it has to be remarked that in essays like the one on Joyce, there is clearly the carrying forward of an ongoing critique of Heidegger's handling of time from within a textual site which serves to disarticulate the overall manifold of relations upon which Heidegger's philosophy depends. Certainly, in the occasional essay on Joyce, Derrida makes a remarkable move: by considering the *es gibt* from the standpoint of Hebrew theology or biblical history, as mediated by Joyce, he liberates the violence that is always already implicit in Heidegger's own reflections.

If George Steiner, in his *Martin Heidegger*, reflected on why it was that Heidegger never directly addressed the modern catastrophe that was the holocaust, Derrida, in "Two Words for Joyce," listens for the resonances of holocaust in modern literature and philosophy by means of a radical trans-scription, translation, or *tranchfert* that brings into relation Heidegger's *es gibt Sein* and Joyce's "he war." The effect of this move is not to impugn Heidegger's morality—this is what seems to be at issue in Steiner—but to demonstrate from the standpoint of philosophy and its engagement with literature that, indeed, Heidegger's writings are addressing modern Jewish history, that the holocaust can be heard from within the tonalities produced by bringing Heidegger and Joyce into correspondence, or temporal attunement. That, in fact, Derrida is self-consciously writing his texts in order to demonstrate a point such as this will become even clearer in the writings of the 1980s which follow "Two Words for Joyce," particularly the essays on the term "Geschlecht" in Heidegger and the question of the date in the poetry of Paul Celan.

Dating Catastrophe

Again, like "Of an Apocalyptic Tone Recently Adopted in Philosophy," "Two Words for Joyce" also helps to situate a certain reading of *The Post Card*, much like other writings, such as, "No Apocalypse, Not Now (full speed ahead, seven missiles, seven missives)," "Des tours de Babel," "Télépathie," "Feu la cendre," and "Shibboleth." In "No Apocalypse, Not Now," which was delivered at a symposium on nuclear criticism, Derrida develops the missile or weapon within the context of an apocalyptic dispatch, and he points out not only that the temporality of such a dispatch is itself nuclear—that is to say, quantized in small units—but that even here the apocalypse is held in abeyance even as it may be realized. In "Des tours de Babel," Derrida again discusses the transference of God's name which culminates in that name's *retrait,* the occurrence of which is accompanied by catastrophe: the ruin of the Tower of Babel, and diaspora. This is an instance of an Old Testament dispatch to be compared with the New Testament dispatch which reads "I shall come." Most certainly, "Of an Apocalyptic Tone," "Two Words for Joyce," "Des tours de Babel" and "Shibboleth" ought to be considered as part of a series of essays which have a profound bearing not only on how we are to reinterpret language, transference, dispatch, and temporality but on how one is to understand the significance of sacred history with respect to post-Heideggerian thought.[70] The essay "Télépathie" belongs to *The Post Card,* though it was dropped from the initial publication of the *envois.* And it, too, touches on notions of apocalypse and makes the daring admission that philosophy is a telepathic process in which ideas are picked up by the writer as if he or she were a medium. This idea intensifies Heidegger's notion of historical transference, as in the example of the Anaximander fragment's numerous translations, and blends it with the work on the notions of dispatch, posting, relay, destination, which occurs in *The Post Card.* Derrida's essays "Feu la cendre," "Shibboleth," and his essays on *Geschlecht* (gender, race) in Heidegger touch on catastrophe and the historical from a perspective much different from that developed in our consideration of the tonalities of apocalypse. Yet, these pieces, too, engage an ethics wherein the question of ends is posed. Again, temporality and the relationship between Jewish and Gentile culture is a crucial relay in the understanding of Derrida's philosophical developments in such texts.

Aside from *De l'espirit* two important recent essays touching on Heidegger are "Shibboleth" and "Geschlecht II: Heidegger's Hand," wherein the question of the temporality of catastrophe is posed in such a way that Derrida again approaches Heidegger even as he turns away from his thought. In "Shibboleth" Derrida turns toward Heidegger when he considers the dating of Paul Celan's poetry as a "correspondence" of time wherein the event of catastrophe is re-collected even as it is estranged from itself. The poem "speaks of this date only insofar as it is freed, as it were, of its debt—and of its date."[71] In the giving of the date of the poem the date undergoes a withdrawal. Thus while preserving its memory, Celan carries the time of the date beyond the singularity of its mere presencing as event present to itself.

The date in Celan's poetry corresponds to a Heideggerian *Ereignis* in which temporality is held together as a relationship of events whose encounter "suggests the random occurrence, the chance meeting, the coincidence or conjuncture which comes to seal one or more than one event *once*, at a given hour, on a given day, in a given month, in a given region; and encounter as it suggests an encounter with the other, the other ineluctable singularity for which the poems speak and which may in its very otherness inhabit the conjunction of one and the same date. It happens."[72] Temporality is given in this happening, in this conjunction of the event in its *différance* wherein the difference between the singularity and the multiplicity of events is deconstituted and reaffirmed. Most disturbing is that Celan "calls this multiplicity by the very strong and very charged name of 'concentration.'" That is to say, in the Heideggerian appropriation of time the recollection of disappropriation or expropriation comes about through use of the term *Konzentration*.

> I understand the word *concentration,* which can become a terrible word for memory, *at once* both in that register in which one speaks of the gathering of the soul or of "mental concentration," as, for example, in the experience of prayer [. . .] and in that other dimension in which concentration gathers around the same anamnetic center a multiplicity of dates, "all our dates" coming to conjoin or constellate in a single occurrence or a single place.[73]

Although Heidegger is never directly mentioned, the discourse in which Celan's consideration of the date is situated draws so heavily on the vocabulary of the late Heidegger that one cannot ignore this allusive structure in relation to the development of a notion of time or the date wherein the catastrophe of the holocaust can be remembered as that which overflows the borders of what many would prefer to view as a single event whose exceptional horror stands in modern history like a tragic parenthesis or ellipsis from which all people would like to claim distance and immunity. Yet, through a consideration of Heideggerian *Ereignis* one achieves, from within modern German philosophy itself, a notion of the catastrophic event whose anniversary is ours and not ours, in whose giving of the date our being is also given and withdrawn. By way of Heidegger the holocaustic date in Celan marks the possibility of our grasping or re-collecting the event not as singular but as that which has and will continue to recur, even if it is the recurrence of that which cannot chronologically return. "A date," Derrida writes, "is a specter." And as such it haunts memory but also constitutes it as a spectral haunting of that which returns despite its having passed away forever. This is conceivable because

> a date is not something which *is there*, since it withdraws in order to appear, but perhaps *there are* (*gibt es*) dates. I will associate for the moment, in a preliminary and disorderly way, the values of the given and the proper name (for a date functions like a proper name) with three other essential values: 1) that of the missive [*envoi*] within the strict limits of the epistolary code; 2) the re-marking of place and time; 3) the signature, for if *data littera* is the initial letter, it may nonetheless come, as date, at the letter's end and in either case, whether at the beginning or the end, have the force of a signed commitment, of an obligation, a promise or an oath (*sacramentum*). In its essence, a signature is always dated and only has value on this account. It dates and is a date.[74]

The temporality of the date is, as in Heidegger, associated with correspondence and sending, though here, as in *The Post Card*, Derrida considers the date in relation to missive and signature, which is to say, in relation to a dispatch or signed commitment wherein the addressee learns that his or her time is up, that the end has come. The term "shibboleth" is itself a "concentration" of terms wherein a manifold of dates or endings are given in terms of the *différance* between deliverance and nondeliverance, between those who gain passage from catastrophe and those who do not. Yet, in Celan this word concentrates an undecid-ability of passage wherein the temporality of catastrophe resists commemoration even as it has left its traces or marks within the words or recollections of Celan's poems. "I will not cite all the tears, the ashes, and the rings which Celan has ciphered," Derrida writes. Yet,

> We have been speaking all this time of dates coded by the conventional grid of the calendar [. . . .] Precisely because of the ring [the calendar], the commemorated date and the commemorating date tend to rejoin and conjoin in a secret anniversary. The poem is this anniversary, the giving of this ring, the seal of an alliance and of a promise. It *belongs* to the same date as what it blesses, gives and gives back again the date to which it belongs and for which it is destined.[75]

The "belonging" or "correspondence" of the dates is itself that temporal circling which allows and forbids passage between events and in so doing deconstitutes the event as singular moment even while it inhibits the identification of events through time as a unifying medium of chronological moments. Hence Derrida writes, "I will not speak here of the *holocaust,* except to say this: there is the date of a certain holocaust, the hell of our memory, but there is a holocaust for every date, somewhere in the world at every hour."[76] That is, the event that is the holocaust cannot be subsumed except in terms of a Heideggerian interplay of temporal dimensions wherein the "event" is given in its appropriative and dis-appropriative moments. Certainly, if Heidegger himself never addressed the holocaust at length in his own writings, Derrida offers in place of this ellipsis or elision a manner by means of which Heidegger is allowed to speak the password, "shibboleth," the word that provides him passage out of a correspondence or trafficking with a certain German culture. "Shibboleth," then, could be read as an apologetics for Heideggerian thought insofar as Heideggerian *Ereignis* allows us to think the holocaust outside of the historicist perspectives to which nazism itself was naively bound.

But if Heidegger is approached in order to disclose wherein his mode of philosophical reflection takes its distance from certain German cultural relationships, there is another Derridean reading of Heidegger given relatively close in time to "Shibboleth" which puts Heideggerian thinking "on watch." In "Geschlecht II" Derrida studies the photographed posture of the writer who raises his hand.

> (Since then I have studied all the published photographs of Heidegger, especially in an album bought at Freiburg when I had given a lecture there on Heidegger in 1979. The play and the theater of hands in that album would merit a whole seminar. If I did not forgo that, I would stress the deliberately craftsman-like staging of the hand play, of the monstration and demonstration that is exhibited there, whether it be a matter of the handling [*maintenance*] of the pen, of the maneuver of the cane that shows rather than supports, or of the water bucket near the fountain. The demonstration of hands is as gripping in the accompaniment of the discourse. On the cover of the catalog, the only thing that overflows the frame, that of the window but also of the photo, is Heidegger's hand.)
>
> The hand is monstrasity [*monstrosité*], the proper of man as the being of monstration. This distinguishes him from every other *Geschlecht* . . .[77]

And, in another place, "*Monstrer* is *montrer* (to show or demonstrate), and *une monstre* is *une montre* (a watch)."[78] What "cata-strophe" do we "watch" in the de-monstration that is the raising of Heidegger's hand, and particularly in terms of *Geschlecht*? And what does our "watch" tell us when we see Heidegger's pious raising of the pen? At what "time" or epoch is this raising of the hand set? And in whose interests has this raising of the hand been? In the interests of whose *Geschlecht*? In the interests of whose historical and apocalyptic monstrosities? It would be here, of course, that one will have once again to read *Glas,* but the gestures of the death knell resound loudly enough in "Geschlecht II." "Not only does man's hand point out and show, but man is himself a sign, a monstrous sign [*un monstre*]." And, "the man that speaks and the man that writes with the hand, as one says; isn't he the monster with a single hand?"[79] The hand, indeed only the outstretched single hand, of Heidegger gives something (the gift) though it also takes something away, and in this *retrait* of the hand's outstretched gesture the monstrous is itself given in what Heidegger calls the *es gibt Sein*. Derrida focuses in "Geschlecht II" on the hand's relation to race ("we are prowling around the nationalist thing and the thing named *Geschlecht*"),[80] on the incipient and problematic visual pun of Heidegger's photographed raised hand on the cover of the *L'Herne* special issue on Heidegger in which Derrida's "Geschlecht I" appeared (this essay focuses on the question of *Geschlecht* as sexuality), and on the raising of the philosopher's hand as Nazi salute. When Derrida speaks of this raising of the hand, this saluting of the monstrous by the "monstrasity" of showing the hand as an offering of a gift, one wonders whether there is not the unhappy pun between the English word "gift" as "present" or "offering" and the German word *Gift*, which means "poison." "Rather this thought of the hand belongs to the essence of the *gift*," which would be to say, to the essence of poisoning, of extermination.

But to return to our major point of focus, how are we to consider this Derridean turning toward and away from Heidegger in the de-monstration of horror as it relates to the notion of correspondence as "concentration" in "Shibboleth" and as it relates to the salute of the hand in "Geschlecht II"? As in the earlier essays, it is apparent here, too, that Derrida's readings of Heidegger punctuate or temporalize his own approaches to the texts of another insofar as these readings suggest various moments wherein the historical relation between Derrida and Heidegger is disclosed. As in "Of an Apocalyptic Tone," "Des tours de Babel" and *Ulysse gramophone: Deux mots pour Joyce,* the approach to Heidegger is made by way of a cultural encounter with Judaism and an interrogation of the question of catastrophe that is itself extremely alien to Heideggerian thought. And yet in bringing Heidegger into close proximity with these alien concerns, Derrida demonstrates that the "event" we might call Heideggerian thinking is not dialectically unifiable in terms of an oppositional structure but, rather, is composed of very heterogeneous formations whose moments correspond to one another without reconciling themselves along a determinate border wherein one can easily "take sides." These "formations" are indicative of the convergence of particular thoughts in certain times which have historical significance. Yet, it is Derrida's genius to have shown that such significance is not easily gathered under a singular interpretation or paradigm and that it is far less easy to "take sides" on Heidegger's philosophy than many have assumed.

Something very similar is reflected in Celan's poem "Engführung," which also invokes Heideggerian thinking and whose title breaks the temporality of a history that would be able to determine the sides against which historical catastrophe can be delimited. For "Engführung" refers not only to the hemming in or closing off of options for victims of the holocaust but also can be read from the side of nazism as the straightening up or bundling together of the social order. Throughout this poem on the holocaust—it also recalls Hiroshima—Celan writes numerous lines which can be read from the perspectives both of victims and of victimizers, something which the English translations of this poem have not taken into account. Hence Celan too has engaged in a de-monstration (an un-monstration) of catastrophe wherein the event is deconstructed as a unified set of temporal relations upon which we might assume it would be easy ethically to take sides. Celan demonstrates or subverts an ethico-historico account by focusing not only on the destruction of a Jewish experience of worldhood—of being in the world—but on the destruction of worldhood more generally as a temporal manifold of relations which poses itself in the possibility of re-membering or reconstructing a place. The destruction or catastrophe that brings about an unworlding of worldhood is disclosed as a space of opposing forces within which the differences between sides is cut along various lines by using the same marks. And here no "shibboleth" or password might give us safe passage out of catastrophe, since this catastrophe is not an event capable of being extricated from time, generally, because its worldhood has been entirely annihilated, even though after the catastrophe there are things and landscapes still remaining. But mere place cannot substitute for worldhood, since worldhood depends upon an ethics of belonging or corresponding between people. In "Engführung" these correspondences between even the opposed sides have been so disarticulated that the destruction of world has preceded the very violence by which we can assert its having taken place. When Celan writes, "Etwas / lag zwischen ihnen," for example, it is this something which lies between which occupies the zone of the "untrüglichen Spur" wherein the catastrophe retreats and hushes itself up in the meadows of the dead where nothing any longer corresponds.

> Jahre.
> Jahre, Jahre, ein Finger
> tastet hinab und hinan, tastet
> umher:
> Nahtstellen . . .

As if anticipating Derrida's remarks on the hand, Celan notices how capable a finger is of feeling or prowling around the sutures of monstration. But whose finger is this? Is it the finger of one related to the victims or the finger of one who likes to reopen the wound? What is the ethical nature of the fingering of that which is monstrous? From what side of the *Engführung* does it come forth? Of course, metaphorically this finger is time or the historical itself which touches. But of whose history or time is this touching a part? As if to develop this thought Celan writes:

> Wie
> fassten wir uns
> an—an mit
> diesen
> Händen?[81]

In what way do we grasp one another with these hands? As one is driven toward certain moments, how is one going to take hold of an other? From what side of the givenness of events does one act? Or what does the hand give, offer, hold out, given the exigencies of time? "Und es kam." "And it came," it arrived, it happened, it fell due. Or, as Derrida puts it, "Il y a là Cendre."

In Derrida's "Geschlecht II" and "Shibboleth" the taking of

political sides on the philosophy of Heidegger occurs in a way similar to Celan's painfully ambivalent cutting across border-lines which delimit the oppositional boundaries and definitions of historical catastrophe. Although Heidegger is viewed momentarily, in one essay, as the monster with raised hand, in the other he is seen as giving access to a more profound understanding of holocaust than one might have assumed was possible for a thinker who on the surface of things appears to be so unsympathetic to the issue. In this "difference" Heideggerian philosophy encounters itself as its own "shibboleth," which is to say, as that password which does and does not allow for that correspondence between a Gentile and a Jewish historical problematic wherein time can be reckoned, as Levinas puts it, otherwise than being.

For Derrida, of course, the point is not to pass over in order that sides can be reaffirmed but to recognize the impediments or aporias of the notion of there being a passage or passageway which might be considered the way to a beyond of Being. In large part, this aporia is what could best be set as a roadblock to a certain anti-Semitism which is predicated on the metaphysics of "difference" between Jews and Gentiles. This is particularly significant with respect to Heidegger, since it is in contemplating this German thinker that the Jewish Derrida deconstructs those antinomies whereby the laws of difference, what Derrida has elsewhere called apartheid, can be catastrophically instituted as pogrom or holocaust. That this institution of difference will recur as catastrophe if not radically deconstituted has become painfully self-evident in the 1980s, especially for European Jews. Nevertheless, in the appropriation of Heidegger, Derrida dis-appropriates the very notion of historical difference through which anti-Semitism can be thought, disarticulates the catastrophic dispatch put into circulation by the metaphysics of theological difference, the "face-to-face" of the Jews and the Gentiles.

Though it may be somewhat premature to advance an opinion, it is not very unlikely that one of the aims of Derrida's recent thoughts on Heidegger has been to deconstruct the historical conceptual conditions whereby anti-Semitism becomes thinkable. This tactic is what Levinas would consider the *au-delà*, or beyond, of a metaphysical "face-to-face" encounter wherein the relationships between self and other are metaphysically recoverable at the level of mere presentation or positioning. Rather, the *au-delà* of the "face-to-face" is the beyond of adequation between self and other, the beyond of containedness, and "it is in this," Levinas writes, "that the signification of the face makes it escape from being."[82] Again, "Ethics isn't comprehensible as the corollary of a vision of the world, as founded upon being, knowledge, or upon categories or existentials."[83] With respect to temporalization, Levinas has said:

> I am trying to show that man's ethical relation to the other is ultimately prior to his ontological relation to himself (egology) or to the totality of things that we call the world (cosmology). The relationship with the other is *time:* it is an untotalizable diachrony in which one moment pursues another without ever being able to retrieve it, to catch up with, or coincide with it. The non-simultaneous and nonpresent are my primary rapport with the other in time. Time means that the other is forever beyond me, irreducible to the synchrony of the same.[84]

Indeed Derrida's relationships with Heidegger are non-simultaneous in this temporal sense, and particularly in texts like "Shibboleth" and "Geschlecht II," it is in the temporal passing beyond the metaphysics of the "face-to-face" that Derrida establishes an ethics wherein responsibility is disclosed in the absence of there being an a priori correlation of values wherein morality is pre-given. Rather, Derrida in contemplating Heidegger deconstitutes the totality of relationships which is the history or synchronized temporality wherein Jewish and Gentile cultures have come into an antagonistic relation that is perceived as pre-given. This deconstruction of the totality or synchronization of temporal moments is itself ethical insofar as it establishes that our relations to an other come prior to those ontological relations wherein ethics withdraws under the pressure of an ontico-historico synchronization. In short, by deconstructing the genealogy of deconstruction, Derrida situates philosophy upon ethical principles very much in sympathy with Levinas, for whom such thinking is a "thinking beyond the thematisable correlative; this mode of thinking the Infinite without equalization and, moreover, without returning to itself, is a putting thought into question by way of the Other."[85]

This *disproportion du rapport* with the Other opened by reflection is itself "le *dehors* plus extérieur que tout extériorité ou la transcendance ou la durée infinite n'arrivant pas ni n'allant à terme" (the outside more exterior than any exteriority, transcendence, or infinite duration neither going to nor arriving to term). To think this "outside" of Occidental ontological protocols is not, as Derrida too has noted in a recent lecture, part of a negative theology. "The transcendence of the Infinite," Levinas writes, "is not recoverable in propositions however negative they may be."[86] To think beyond Being is not to negate it, to position theism against atheism, but, rather, to work beyond the symmetry of such a difference, wherein ethics is subordinated to ontology and belief in Being comes to stand for an ethical posture. Christian anti-Semitism has relied heavily on a propaedeutics of belief founded on the metaphysical difference of theism/atheism (belief/nonbelief), and it is in terms of this difference that "catastrophe" has been theologically determined and politically enacted as war with infidel nations, the burning of heretics, and persecution of the Jews. It is here, of course, that the "ethical" dimensions of metaphysical difference become most dubious.

Derrida, in approaching Heidegger, deconstructs such an ethical propaedeutic by disarticulating those corollaries whereby the principle of a metaphysical or ethical difference is no longer conceivable and hence inoperational as a foundation for anti-Semitic action. Also, such a disarticulation reorients our perception of time insofar as it fulfills Levinas's conviction that time is given in the relation where relationality is withdrawn, in that proximity where the diachronic encounters itself as the noncoincidence of moments which defy the arrow of time. It is here that everything coincides with respect to an In-finite that holds itself open as a totality of relations whose correspondences elude the correlatives of the ontological difference between Being and beings. This, then, is the shibboleth Levinas and Derrida uncover in Western ontology, the shibboleth of difference and identity in whose gathering the fate of the Jews has been determined under Western eyes.

FIVE

THE THESIS

OF TIME AS

TIME OF THE

THESIS

In Derrida's "The Time of a Thesis: Punctuations," the interrelation between philosophical and literary writings is never too far from being raised, and in this context Derrida will wonder, "Should one speak of an epoch of the thesis? [. . .] Should one speak of an age of the thesis, of an age for the thesis?"[1] In part, these questions remind us that to write a thesis is to assume that natural language ought to be treated as a formal system, or, in Derrida's vocabulary, as a logocentric construct. Is the age for such a thesis past? Is there a time wherein the philosophical attitude concerning the difference between philosophy and, say, literature comes to an end? Or can one say, as Kant did, that the offenses of the imagination are unbridled lawlessness?

In speaking of a time of the thesis, Derrida refers to his own age (his existential experience of time), to the fact that he is a bit overdue in defending his academic thesis at the Sorbonne, namely, after he has established himself many times over as a major philosopher. "Allow me to begin by whispering a confidence which I shall not abuse: never have I felt so young and at the same time so old." Both the autobiographical significance and the general condition of ambivalence or dividedness interests me. Existentially, the remarks strongly suggest that Derrida rejects an experience which pretends it is fully present to itself in any particular time, in what we might call a certain age. And this divisibilty of experience in time relates to Derrida's resistance to completing the thesis, a resistance which is to philosophy itself.

> Between youth and old age, one and the other, neither one nor the other, an indecisiveness of age, it is like a discomfiture at the moment of installation, an instability, I will not go so far as to say a disturbance of stability, of posture, of station, of the thesis or of the pose, but rather of a pause in the more or less well-regulated life of a university teacher, an end and a beginning which do not coincide and in which there is involved once again no doubt a certain gap of an alternative between the delight of pleasure and fecundity.[2]

This ambivalence or bivalence characterizes the relation between deconstruction and Heideggerian philosophy, too, insofar as it is a binding of something older with something younger, what in Derrida's essays feels "like a discomfiture at the moment of installation, an instability." This kind of bivalence is, in fact, noticeable at many other points in "The Time of a Thesis: Punctuations." And at one point it occurs with reference to Heidegger himself. Speaking of those writers who have been particularly interesting to Derrida, we read:

> It is also true that the living thinkers who gave me the most to think about or who most provoked me to reflection, and who continue to do so, are not among those who break through a solitude, not among those to whom one can simply feel oneself close, not among those who form groups or schools, to mention only Heidegger, Levinas, Blanchot among others whom I shall not name. It is thinkers such as these to whom, strangely enough one may consider oneself most close; and yet they are, more than others, other. And they too are alone.[3]

These remarks reflect more than moods. They also reflect Derrida's conviction that one cannot position oneself in relation to such writers in a way that a thesis would result. For the position that a thesis would take is inherently threatened by a bivalence of proximities, a bivalence which finds its approaches to figures like Heidegger multiplied and contradictory. Implicitly Derrida is asking to consider how a thesis can take place in the instability of a relation to other figures. And he wonders how, given this instability, one can write within an academic framework wherein discourse is regulated by the notion of the thesis. "It was already clear to me that the general turn that my research was taking could no longer conform to the classical norms of the thesis," nor, Derrida adds, did he think his work fit very well the laws regulating scholarly discourse. "The very idea of a thetic presentation, of positional or oppositional logic, the idea of position [. . .] was one of the essential parts of the system that was under deconstructive questioning."[4]

Of course, when philosophers talk about the agon of reason or about true statements, they are invoking the notion of a thesis with a determinate position or "thetic presentation" that ensures decidability within a formal method of analysis that can distinguish between truth and falsehood. When a philosopher like Rudolf Carnap discusses the definition of a theory, we can expect a definition such as, "A theory is *axiomatized* when all statements of the theory are arranged in the form of a deductive system whose basis is formed by the axioms and when all concepts of the theory are arranged in the form of a constructional system whose basis is formed by the fundamental concepts." However, in *The Logical Structure [Aufbau] of the World* Carnap is not so much interested in the fundamental concepts as in the structure of theory as a *constructional* system of relationships. Hence Carnap writes, "We shall maintain and seek to establish the thesis that *science deals only with the description of structural properties of objects.*"[5]

In "The Time of the Thesis" Derrida explains that when he first contemplated writing a thesis he chose the topic of "the ideality of the literary Object," which, from a Husserlian perspective, would have described the structural properties of certain objects as constituted in the consciousness of them. But in *Speech and Phenomena* we are given profound glimpses of why such a thesis could not be written: for in Husserl the ideality of any linguistic object is predicated on the ideality of speech whose words "must remain *the same* and can do so only as an ideality." Or, "in certain cases there is the ideality of the object itself, which then assures the ideal transparency and perfect univocity of language; this is what happens in the exact sciences."[6] The difficulty with such ideality is that it presupposes a correspondence or relationality of words to "objects" (in their widest senses), which remain the same and are "scientifically" repeatable like a laboratory experiment in physics. Derrida points out that the "being" of such relationality—one thinks of a formal system like Rudolf Carnap's "constructional" system of relationships—"depends entirely on the possibility of acts of repetition. [. . .] Its 'being' is proportionate to the power of repetition; absolute ideality is the correlate of a possibility of indefinite repetition."[7] The notion of a thesis, then, would be precisely that of a position that stays the same within a system whose repetitions or repeatability guarantee its place. Tradition, then, could be defined as the temporality within which these repetitions transmit and reactivate fundamental positions or, as Derrida says, origins. "For Husserl, historical progress always has as its essential form the constitution of idealities whose repetition, and thus tradition, would be assured *ad infinitum,* where repetition and tradition are the transmission and reactivation of origins." Derrida notices that this ideality in Husserl is already presupposed by Plato as an "ethico-theoretical act that revives the decision that founded philosophy in its Platonic form."[8] In other words, an infinitely repeatable and demonstrable truth, axiom, or thesis is inherently founded on a notion of both ideality and valuation (ethics) which is worked out at length in *The Republic.*

What Carnap calls a system of relations is never anything less than a Platonic ideality insofar as these relations, if they can be admitted as true, must be demonstrated to be iterable, permanent, or *present.* And this introduces what in *Speech and Phenomena* is Derrida's own "thesis": that the ideality of speech as an "object" for philosophical speculation depends upon the notion of its "being" as "presence." Here, of course, we already see the influence of Heidegger on Derrida, for *Speech and Phenomena* could be read as Derrida's successful attempt to demonstrate why and how Heidegger's philosophy dismantles the idealistic presuppositions (or metaphysical ground) of Husserlian phenomenology. Not the least of these presuppositions is that a thesis can survive the present moment. "To think of presence as the universal form of the transcendental life is to open myself to the knowledge that in my absence, beyond my empirical existence, before my birth and after my death, *the present is*. [...] The relationship with *my death* (my disappearance in general) thus lurks in this determination of being as presence, ideality, the absolute possibility of repetition."[9]

The longevity of the thesis or of those relationships or correspondences which determine the power of any theory depend upon an existential assumption, that one's ideas can live on or persist, as if they occurred in a temporality always already present to itself. In other words, there is an ideality of the subject which props up the ideality of the object as an invisible theoretical relation. Logic, structure, relation, valuation, and thesis are but manifestations of an existential assumption about the ability of the subject to transcend its temporality as an entity that is always "there" in a present moment. Hence we can write phrases like "Shakespeare thinks . . . ," or "Rousseau forgets . . . ," or "Heidegger doesn't realize . . ." as if texts and their positions could be recalled or restored in an eternal present moment. In *Speech and Phenomena*, however, we are asked to relinquish this view and consider a time of the thesis that is inherently divided or differed and deferred from itself. This divisibility already is introduced into the dismantling of logic as a unitary structure.

> We have experienced the systematic interdependence of the concepts of sense, ideality, objectivity, truth, intuition, perception, and expression. Their common matrix is being as *presence*: the absolute proximity of self-identity, the being-in-front of the object available for repetition, the maintenance of the temporal present, whose ideal form is the self-presence of transcendental *life*, whose ideal identity allows *idealiter* of infinite repetition.[10]

Most interesting is that as Derrida concludes his study of Husserl we are asked to contemplate not Heidegger but Hegelianism, which "seems to be more radical, especially at the point where it makes clear that the positive infinite must be thought through (which is possible only if it thinks *itself*) in order that the indefiniteness of *différance* appear as such."

Moreover, and this is where Derrida's reading of Hegel is indeed radical, "this appearing of the Ideal as an infinite *différance* can only be produced within a relationship with death in general," which is to say, with a relationship between life and death that breaks with the usual absolute distinction we make between what is present and what is absent.[11] By this point in our study we should be able to detect a feint when we see one, and the turn to Hegel at the end of *Speech and Phenomena* is quite clearly a turning away from Heidegger, whose works have in and of themselves suggested the critique of presence whereby Husserlian phenomenology comes to grief. Yet, this "relation" to Heidegger is divided or parceled out by means of propping the discussion on Hegelian thought. But this dividing of the thesis or critique of presence between Heidegger and Hegel is itself the maintenance of the thesis as that which is never recoverable as a position which is present to itself as itself. Rather, the turning away from Heidegger and toward Hegel suggests a repetition of the thesis in yet an other, wherein the thesis is at once leveled and raised. And this leaves Derrida not so much the holder of a thesis but as a subject who is de-positioned in the dividing or parceling up of a thesis between Husserl, Heidegger, and Hegel.

Of course the Hegel reference should not be viewed as some kind of rhetorical trick designed merely to undermine the notion of thesis through the tactics of differentiation, for in the reference to Hegel, Derrida enlists the idea of a dialectical overturning wherein thought passes beyond "absolute knowledge" at that moment when its transcendental closure caves in upon itself, when "this infinite absolute appears to itself as its own death."[12] Here the work of Hegel is being appealed to in order to radicalize the Heideggerian dismantling, and one suspects this is the case because immediately after these references to Hegel there follows a paragraph in which Heidegger is being invoked in terms of how we should read the history of representation before that time when conceptions of presence or ideality were established, in the time of the pre-Socratics.

In "Cartouches," from *The Truth in Painting*, Derrida considers Gérard Titus-Carmel's "Pocket Size Tlingit Coffin" and wonders how or if the "thesis" of the work is posed. What is the relationship between the thesis and its example? What is posed as true and how is such truth represented? In large part, "Cartouches" outlines the death of the thesis as it takes place in a most literal example: the Tlingit coffin. To this extent Titus-Carmel is a "thanatographer."

> With respect to the paradigm, precisely. He is not content with dealing with [*traiter de*] sepulcher, dead man, and remains, and, to this end, with joining on their paradigm. No, it is the paradigm which he does down, and to death. His paradigm does not show a coffin, it shows itself in *its* coffin, last dwelling *of the* paradigm finally laid in earth.
>
> Titus-Carmel cadaverizes the paradigm. Hounding its effigy, feigning the feigning of it in a series of simulated reproductions, he reduces it, he transforms it into a tiny piece of waste, *outside the series in the series,* and henceforth no longer in use.
>
> He does without it ([*no*] more paradigm, [*no*] more coffin, one more or less), he puts an end to it.[13]

Important for Derrida is that Titus-Carmel "learns to go without" that model or thesis which would form the basis for the 127 drawn caskets which supplement the sculpted model and its cartouches. The coffin is the site where the thesis is foreclosed even as it is inherently divided like the spoils of war. The thesis is nothing less than the divisibility of the utterance or expression, the multiplication of the example, the repetition which allows for a fixation on a particular content to become possible. The sculpted model is neither the basis for the drawings nor a supplement to them. Rather, it is a simulacrum whose condition of thesis or ground for representation is subjected to a dissemination of inscriptions or represented embodiments whose attempt to fill in the coffin only serves to hollow out the veracity of its taking place as object, thing, or work.

In "Restitutions" the seriality of representation and the divisibility of the artistic thesis is further explored with respect to the readings of Van Gogh's paintings of shoes, readings which once more concern the endless divisibility of a thesis in light of a pair or pairs of shoes which complicate the possibility of any one thesis being posed, from a thesis to step forth. Both "Cartouches" and "Restitutions" suggest, then, that to pose a thesis is to participate in what Derrida calls "identificationary ingenu-ousness." And yet, something is nevertheless "given" in these representations of shoes. But what does the work intellectually pose before us? What does the work present? In "Restitutions" presentation is both constituted and deconstituted as an "inter-lacing." That is, the conflict between Meyer Schapiro and Mar-tin Heidegger over the interpretation of Van Gogh concerns an interlacing of positions wherein something is given by the paintings of the shoes that is not recoverable as the truth of a representation; rather, it is disclosed as an interlacing of repre-sentational correspondences wherein a notion of truth emerges as a horizon on which the notion of the thesis is both posed and deposed. "I've arrived late. I've just heard the words 'abyss' 'offering,' or 'gift.' *It gives* in the abyss, it gives—the abyss. There is, *es gibt,* the abyss. Now it seems to me that *The Origin* can also be read as an essay on the gift [*Schenkung*], on the offering: one of the three senses, precisely, in which truth is said to come to its installation, its institution, or its investiture [*Stiftung*]."[14]

The point is not that there is no thesis to be talked about but that the work is only too capable of giving us a thesis, that in Heidegger's or Schapiro's writings a thesis is relayed or sent, a thesis which comes about through a consideration of a work in which the thesis is itself constituted even as it is withdrawn in an abysmatics of pairings, doublings, and multiplications. If there is a thesis, here, it is what Derrida calls a "conceptual mechanism," or *Begriffsmechanik.* But this mechanism operates precisely through the giving in Heidegger and Schapiro of examples, in the re-presentation of the shoes which are para-digmatic. Yet, of what are they examples or paradigms? Derrida argues that the shoes disclose relations between "couples of determinations superimposed on the thing."[15] This is the "schema" which Heidegger uses to accompany the representa-tion of the shoes, a schema not so very unlike those 127 draw-ings Titus-Carmel drew in order to interlace his thanatography of the coffin.

> Without it [the schema] we would understand nothing
> of the passage about such-and-such a work by Van
> Gogh, nothing of its differential function, and nothing

of its irreducible equivocality either. I called it a schema: basically, and in a barely displaced Kantian sense, it's a hybrid, a mediation or a double belonging or double articulation. The product [*Zeug*] seems to be situated between the thing and the work of art (the work is always a work *of art* in this context: *Werk*). It shares in both, even though the work resembles [*gleicht*] the "simple thing" more than does the product. The example of the shoes guides the analysis of this schematism when it is first set in place.[16]

The shoes exemplify a paradigm and in so doing establish a framework of relationships which break with the frames of conventional notions of representation. Such a framework is what Derrida calls the schematism, a term converted from Kant's *Critique of Pure Reason* into a Heideggerian key, wherein the notion of the painting occupies an intermediate zone between mere thing and work. This "inter-posture" of the painting inhibits an easy translation between thing (shoe) and work (representation).

> The intermediate mode is *in the middle* of the other two, which it gathers and divides in itself according to a structure of envelopment which is difficult to spread out. Here, first of all, is the schematism of the product. For example: shoes *in general*. I pick out and emphasize a few words: The product [*Zeug*], for example the shoe product [*Schuhzeug*] rests, as ready [*fertig*, finished] in itself as the thing pure and simple, but it does not have, as does the block of granite, this *Eigenwüchsige* [. . . .] On the other hand the product also shows an affinity [*Verwandtschaft*] *with the work of art, inasmuch as it is produced* [*hervorgebracht*] by the hand of man. In spite of this, the work of art in its turn, by its self-sufficient presence [*in seinem selbstgenügsamen Anwesen*], resembles (*gleicht*) the thing pure and simple, referring only to itself (*eigenwüchsige*) and constrained to nothing (*zu nichts gedrängten*)]. (. . .) Thus the product is half a thing, because determined by thingliness, and yet more than that; at the same time it is half work of art, and yet less than that.[17]

Derrida's argument is that Heidegger's correspondences which construct the "schematism" or framework of the work do not merely surround the work like an exterior critical border but comprise an interlacing. We recall that for Kant the "schematism" was "some third thing, which is homogeneous on the one hand with the category, and on the other hand with the appearance, and which thus makes the application of the former to the latter possible."[18] For Derrida this schematism is comprehended as the correspondences or interlacings between various modalities of the painterly work as object for consciousness. "Tight interlacing, but one which can always be *analyzed,* untied *up to a certain point.*" The "thing" is itself a network of interlacings of interpenetrating correspondences—product, work of art, thing—which do not admit of simple distinctions, since they do not admit themselves to consciousness as merely three different "things." As in "Cartouches," Derrida uses the literal figure of the represented object—here the shoe—to reflect this Heideggerian understanding of mimetic binding.

> We shall articulate this *strophe* of the lace: in its rewinding passing and repassing through the eyelet of the thing, from outside to inside, from inside to outside, *on* the external surface and *under* the internal surface (and vice versa when this surface is turned inside out like the top of the left-hand shoe), it remains the "same" right through, between right and left, shows itself and disappears (*fort/da*) in its regular traversing of the eyelet, it makes the thing sure of its gathering, the underneath tied up on top, the inside bound on the outside, by a law of stricture.[19]

The law of stricture is itself the thesis, which is to say, that which binds us and by which we are bound. But this thesis operates by way of the stitch, or suture. It laces up or ties the thing together as if the thing were never anything less than a product or thing like a shoe which is made or stitched up by a worker or cobbler. Yet, such a workerly binding or stitching is merely a perspective on the thing offered through the process of interlacing itself wherein the thinghood of the thing is unthinged. An indeterminacy between the thing and its unthinging is connected in "Restitutions" to the Freudian notion of the fetish, which, as Derrida showed earlier in *Glas,* presents itself at once as autonomous object or determinate undivisible thing and, at the same instance, as that which is infinitely divisible and spatially indeterminate, given that it cannot decide the difference between interiority and exteriority. Again, notice how the literal image serves as binding.

In *What Is a Thing?* Heidegger argues that "truth is a fitting to things, a correspondence (*Übereinstimmung*) with the things," and he interrogates this notion of correspondence in terms of the structure of truth as an assertion about the verity of things.[20] The idea that truth fits our perception of things, Heidegger argues, is not self-given but is itself a cultural assumption made in ancient Greek times. What, then, is the coherence of the essence of truth in its relation to the essence of things to which it is bound? What is the law of stricture by means of which the truth of an assertion is attached to the truth disclosed by the thing? "How does the proposition, the interpretation, come to present the measure and model of how things in their thingness are to be determined?" And "Truth consists in the predicate's belonging to the subject and is posited and asserted in the proposition as belonging."[21] This propositional nature of discourse establishes the notion of thesis as determinate position with respect to how things are or how they belong according to a structure of truth which fits our perception of things. Kant's notion of the schematism is an epistemological framework which guarantees the possibility of achieving such a structure of truth, or, as Kant says, "the schema is therefore the determination of the representation of a thing at some time or other." It is, in fact, "the agreement of the synthesis of different representations with the conditions of time in general."[22]

The thesis, of course, accords to this agreement of the synthesis which is given at some particular moment in a chronological sequence of time. Indeed, "the schemata are thus nothing but *a priori* determinations of time in accordance with rules. These rules relate in the order of the categories to the *time-series,* the *time-content,* the *time-order,* and lastly to the *scope of time* in respect of all possible objects."[23] The verity of the thing, therefore, depends upon the compression or agreement of time to what might be called a present moment from which all other moments can be ameliorated. In "Restitutions," Derrida has sympathetically approached Heidegger in order to push further the idea that notions like the Kantian schematism depend upon numerous assumptions about the givenness of things as things and a bifurcation between thing and thought, that the schematism makes up a classical notion of framing wherein a classical notion of the thesis or proposition is embodied. By emphasizing terms like "binding" or "interlacing," Derrida de-constructs the thing as thing and demonstrates its philosophical and psychological sutures whose relays deconstitute the synthetic senses of time that a figure like Kant needed to posit in order to clear the way for the time of the thesis.

In *The Post Card* Derrida directly addresses the thesis in terms of interlacing temporal differences exemplified by the couple life/death. And he considers Freud's *Beyond the Pleasure Principle* in a section called "Athesis": "The issue rather is *to rebind* [*relier*], but precisely by means of the analysis of the notions of binding, *nexum, desmos* or stricture, the question of *life death* to the question of the *position* (*Setzung*), the question of positionality in general, of positional (oppositional or juxtapositional) logic, of the theme or the thesis."[24] The emphasis, therefore, falls upon an "overflow [of] the logic of the position" and "the impossibility of a resting point." The a-thesis drifts, moves, travels "from a shore, a border, a coast with an indivisible outline."[25] These shores of the a-thesis are acknowledged again in *Parages* where Derrida discusses the two coasts of the transatlantic between which seminars have been divided, the thesis parceled out, where shores come into and pass out of view.

Given these thoughts on the a-thesis, it would appear that our consideration of the relation between Derrida and Heidegger must necessarily be that of an interlacing or invaginated returning of texts that deconstitutes any historicist attempt to reconstitute the relation between thinkers as that which can be posited as some Thing to be known and grasped as a thing in itself. This avoidance of positioning which detaches Derrida from the ideology of the thesis, much like the dynamics of intellectual filiation (the "S" and "P" of *The Post Card*), are not to be considered as merely clever attempts to double bind the relation between deconstruction and Heideggerian philosophy by setting up undecidable road blocks in the path of chronological understanding. Rather, these approaches acknowledge a multiplicity of relationships running between complex formations of knowledge that cannot be reduced to the "difference" of theses with impunity, that cannot be localized to the historical philosophical framework of a tradition of great minds wherein each thinker is reducible to a thesis or set of basic principles that either follows from or differs with the thoughts of predecessors and followers. That is to say, Derrida resists becoming the last chapter in the history of philosophy, which will inevitably be followed by the thought of someone else. This detachment from the philosophical tradition is not merely critical in the sense that it delimits a distance through which one canonizes oneself in tradition; rather, this detachment is an attempt to break the spine of tradition as a teleological structure that reduces philosophy to just so many things to be serially apprehended. In other words, deconstruction's a-thesis is itself part of a strategic set of relays whose aim is to expose the asynthetic within the agreement of thought reached by way of a temporal synthesis of moments. The a-thesis, rather, opens up correspondences which overrun the borders of synthetic agreement and historicist positionings insofar as they assume a temporal synthesis such as that expressed by Kant.

This opening up of correspondences paradoxically distances deconstruction from Heideggerian philosophy even as it historically fulfills the destiny of Heidegger's work. This is evident when one considers the very fine chapters on Heidegger's earlier handling of temporality by Henri Birault in *Heidegger et l'expérience de la pensée.* "In its last endeavor, the thought of Heidegger is neither positive nor negative, nor even indifferent to affirmation or negation. Rather it is *suspending.* It is the thought of the suspension of being which holds us in suspense between earth and sky, between death and the gods."[26] This suspension is itself a temporal opening wherein the destiny of history becomes thinkable as that which transpires in the opening of what time makes potential. The suspension between the positive and the negative, the affirmation and the negation, is not a positioning or synthesis of moments so much as it marks a correspondence of moments wherein a destiny comes to pass in the availability or opportunity of various relationships that are always already dis-positioned though by no means deprived of relationality. This reflects, as well, the insight of Emmanuel Levinas, who reinterpreted the Heideggerian problematic of time as that which "signifies the *always* of non-coincidence, but also this *always* of the *relation*—of the aspiration and of the wait: a connection more binding than any ideal line and which diachrony cannot sever."[27]

Conclusion

In *The Philosophical Discourse of Modernity*, Jürgen Habermas advances the thesis that Derrida's philosophy is an "orthodox" Heideggerian project dwelling on the "contours" of "temporalized *Ursprungsphilosophie*." "Heidegger purchases the temporalization of *Ursprungsphilosophie* with a concept of truth made historically dynamic, but deracinated." And Habermas adds, "When one lets oneself be as affected by the circumstances of contemporary history as Heidegger does, and nonetheless progresses, as if with the force of gravity, into the dimension of essential concepts, the truth claim of inverted foundationalism becomes rigidified into a prophetic gesture."[28] By "inverted foundationalism" Habermas is referring to Heidegger's substituting a temporalized or dynamic notion of origination for an origin atemporally fixed and static. Habermas calls this more dynamic notion of foundationalism the "self-temporalizing dispensation of Being," and both Heidegger and Derrida use it to deconstruct the atemporal and spatial foundationalist notion of the philosophy of the subject. However, as "self-temporalizing" this inverted foundationalism is incapable of dialectics and therefore constitutes an "absolutely unmediated" notion of the sacred by which is really meant a temporalized understanding of deconstructed Being that must be accepted on faith alone.

Anyone who is familiar with Frankfurt School thought will immediately hear the admonitions by Herbert Marcuse of Heidegger's existential philosophy, admonitions Marcuse published in "The Struggle against Liberalism in Totalitarianism" in 1934. Speaking of conceptual naturalism, Marcuse wrote that its formulations "announce the characteristic tendency of heroic-folkish realism: its *deprivation* of *history* to a merely temporal occurrence in which all structures are subjected to time and are therefore 'inferior.' "²⁹ Heideggerian existentialism, as Marcuse argues, valorizes Being and in so doing leaves philosophy "exempt from any rational standard or norm lying beyond it; it is itself the absolute norm and is inaccessible to any and all rational criticism and justification."³⁰ That Heideggerian existentialism is being yoked together by Marcuse's study with the right-wing ideology of the folk suggests that already in this early and penetrating reading of Heidegger, Marcuse was addressing what Habermas calls an inverted foundationalism. Already in Marcuse's terms, this represented the degradation of history through a temporalized notion of Being that worked against the significance of the historical "event" per se. Of course, Marcuse thinks that such temporalization leads to a static or spatial foundationalism and that the Heideggerian invocation of Being leads to reification and, again, dehistorization. Habermas's term "inverted foundationalism" suggests something exactly analogous: that the temporalization of Being is, finally, antithetical to a dialectical and dynamic notion of history wherein people are intellectually empowered as agencies of social change. That Derrida, in Habermas's view, merely extends a right-wing politics of the 1930s, as discussed by Marcuse, is implied throughout Habermas's analysis. "As Schelling once did in speculating about the timelessly temporalizing internesting of the past, present, and future ages of the world, so Derrida clings to the dizzying thought of a past that has never been present."³¹ In other words, Derrida, like Heidegger, drew from the wellsprings of German romanticism in order to employ temporality for the sake of degrading a consciousness of history and disempowering the social subject.

Habermas's thesis is that Derrida wants to improve on Heidegger's analyses by transposing the vocabulary of Being into the vocabulary of a radicalized Saussurean linguistics. In this manner a temporalized *Ursprungsphilosophie* is made manifest in language, which is then taken up in order to deconstruct discourses which are said to have a foundational basis. Because, in Habermas's view, a temporalized *Ursprungsphilosophie* is not dialectical—we may recall Derrida's numerous essays which attempt to undermine Hegelian dialectics —it is therefore incapable of manifesting truth claims that are verifiable or valid, since without dialectics this so-called inverted foundationalism cannot conceptually engage anything other than itself and, as a consequence, cannot be affected or transformed. Like any foundational category it must always remain at once self-identical and yet uncompromisingly other or off-limits. Habermas, in assuming that this inverted foundationalism must have its roots in religion, says that in Derrida "only religious connotations furnish any points of support—but they are immediately rejected as ontotheological remnants."[32] In other words, Derridean deconstruction is contradictory, in Habermas's view, because it depends upon the very metaphysics that it vigorously seeks to expunge by means of a deconstructive purification of metaphysical language, both within and outside itself. If Derrida is more up to date than Heidegger, it is because Derrida, in Habermas's view, turns to language as a means of concealing a shaky foundationalism grounded in the temporalization of Being. Habermas, then, sees Derrida merely as a follower or lackey of Heidegger. "Derrida's deconstructions faithfully follow the movement of Heidegger's thought."[33]

I have summarized Habermas's main objections, which, of course, implicitly pay homage to Marcuse, in order to point out that, from our much fuller appreciation of the various moments sighted in both Heidegger and Derrida, such a reduction to a single thesis about temporality is itself rather crude in that it necessarily ignores many of the subtle complexities and interrelations which we have discussed, not the least of which is the deconstruction of the type of thesis whereby Habermas binds Derrida to Heidegger, as if it could be assumed that they share a common foundation. Indeed, I am suggesting that Habermas himself is the one who introduces the undialectical cornerstone by means of which he then accuses both Heidegger and Derrida of backhandedly recovering the very metaphysics they propose to dismantle. If one merely notices our chapter divisions it should become very clear that, in fact, what Habermas is pejoratively calling a temporalized *Ursprungsphilosophie* is far from being undialectical, ahistorical, irrational, or merely mystical. In fact, what we see in Derrida's temporalization of his turnings toward and away from Heidegger as it inheres in the history of Derrida's writings on Heidegger is precisely a very critical establishment of the a-thesis that energizes numerous dialectical relationships between Derridean and Heideggerian thought while, at the same time, resisting a singular dialectical opposition between the figures Heidegger and Derrida, which would resolve their philosophical engagement into precisely the kind of foundational thesis that Habermas is attempting to make, as if the differences and identities between Derrida and Heidegger could be easily shaped into a static, foundational point of view from which someone outside of this relationship could mount a critique aimed at killing two birds, as it were, with one stone.

What is particularly important is that the a-thesis is not a "no-thesis" but the metaleptic or temporalized interplay of dialectical moments wherein a Heideggerian turn is exacerbated by Derrida by means of a turning toward and a turning away from. Here the Heideggerian conception of a hermeneutic circle is performed by means of a philosophical turning that inheres within a relationship to an other whose intellectual history cannot be recovered according to a crude dialectics of influence anxiety or the like. Rather, this history is a complex hermeneutical mobilization of oppositions and identifications that, thanks to the hermeneutical circle, or turn, bring multiple conceptual formations into a metaleptic and temporalized relation wherein the Being question is not sacralized or made foundational but instead is situated in the process of a historical and critical enactment in which conceptual sides are taken and positions mobilized through what is called the time of the thesis. What separates Derrida from Habermas is that Derrida is willing to let the thesis take its time as a gradual unfolding of arguments that takes place in and as real time, which is to say, history, whereas in Habermas the thesis simply is set forth in a textual now or simple present in which a critique is mounted in a hit-and-run manner, its consequences recorded as something definitive which has been done in the past and to which students of Habermas can return if they wish to understand the foundational truth which in Habermas's opinion binds Heidegger to Derrida.

If the a-thesis appears radical, it is not because Derrida by sleight of hand has cheated us of dialectics and has offered in its place a temporalized *Ursprungsphilosophie*. Rather, it is because the a-thesis takes place in intellectual history within the real time that is Derrida's intellectual career and in terms of which the dialectical relationships are paronomasically played out in an abrasion of positions whose wear and tear takes time. Whether we have time in a postmodern culture for such a philosophical enactment of a meticulous unfolding in time of intellectual relations which are not reducible, merely, to any one major thesis or point of contact which might release a thinker like Derrida from the hold of Heidegger is a question that one might well ask. Certainly, Marcuse in the 1930s would not have felt that history allows us the luxury of a philosophical reflective time that literally spans decades. And it is according to this political sense of crisis in some of the Frankfurt School thinkers that they inevitably are led to some discomfort with thinkers who take their time with time or, more accurately, history.

In fact, this is what Heidegger himself did as a thinker, and the instances of metalepsis we have noticed are evidence of this taking time with time. For this reason it is violently reductive to fix Heidegger's reflective coordinates at a date like 1933, in the way Habermas does, as if Heidegger became fully manifest as a thinker in an article expressing sympathy for Hitler written for the *Freiburger Studentenzeitung*.[34] My point, of course, is not that one should overlook such writings or discount their significance in and of themselves as political symptoms of Heidegger's thought during the 1930s, but that one also has to comprehend such texts within the much broader historical sweep of Heidegger's entire oeuvre wherein the turnings toward and away from National Socialism are themselves not easily recoverable according to a foundationalist dialectic such as the Frankfurt School thinkers produce. That is, the temporalization of Heideggerian thought itself progresses through various turnings, some of them political, which, as Derrida has shown in *De l'esprit*, take their time in the iteration of the vocabulary of metaphysics and in so doing disclose a large range of oppositions and identifications wherein philosophy's proximities to politics breach a simple ideological closure of the sort that Habermas is seeking.

If the sort of philosophical temporalization enacted by Heidegger de-emphasizes actions as always and forever rooted in a present where outrage or admiration is to be statically fixed, it also intensifies our understanding of history as something other than what Marcuse saw in terms of a reduction of events to sporadic and localized moments fixed in a present and deprived of the long-range consciousness of historical and political consequences. That is, Heidegger's temporalization of thought brings events into a complex set of correspondences whose effects, though less immediately concrete, are nevertheless of a long-range nature and as such manifest an endurance or persistence of relations through time which a politics of the immediate historical event lacks, a politics Habermas invokes when he comments that Heidegger's writings about the Führer transpire in the historical shadow of the KZ installations. Although Derrida himself apparently feels uncomfortable with much that he finds in Heidegger, he acknowledges and appreciates the time of Heideggerian reflection and is willing to let that time gradually play itself out in a significant historical unfolding of intellectual relationships which we find chronicled in the essays and books of Derrida. Of course, how or in what way this temporality bears on the "meaning" of Heideggerian philosophy is not given in the thesis on time but in the time of the thesis, and it is in this sense that any reflection on Heidegger and Derrida must necessarily be a reflection on the relationship of time and language.

NOTES

(All English translations are mine unless otherwise indicated in the Bibliography.)

Introduction

1. Heidegger, *Being and Time*, p. 63.
2. Heidegger, *Basic Problems of Phenomenology*, p. xvi. Italics mine.
3. Heidegger, *Basic Problems of Phenomenology*, p. 332.
4. Heidegger, *Basic Problems of Phenomenology*, pp. 22–23.
5. Gasché, *The Tain of the Mirror*, p. 113.
6. Gasché, *The Tain of the Mirror*, p. 119.
7. Gasché, *The Tain of the Mirror*, pp. 119, 120.
8. Derrida, *The Post Card*, p. 267.
9. Derrida, *The Post Card*, p. 267.
10. "Deconstruction in America: An Interview with Jacques Derrida," *Society for Critical Exchange*, no. 17 (Winter 1985), p. 23.
11. Derrida, *De l'esprit*, p. 35.
12. Richardson, *Heidegger: Through Phenomenology to Thought.*
13. Heidegger, *The Question concerning Technology and Other Essays*, p. 41.
14. Marx, *Heidegger and the Tradition*, pp. 173–175.
15. Blanchot, *L'entretien infini*, p. 390. Certainly for Blanchot, the notion of "turn" is perhaps uppermost in the context of Nietzsche's *Wiederkehr*, that "repetition (or return) which produces its own detour" (p. 410). Without doubt, Blanchot's understanding of the "linguistic turn" in Heidegger comes by way of a reading of Nietzsche's eternal return, and Jacques Derrida will reenact this reading when in *Eperons* he discusses the styles of Nietzsche by way of Heidegger. See Derrida, *Eperons*.
16. Derrida, *Of Grammatology*, p. 23.
17. Ricoeur, *The Conflict of Interpretations*, p. 224.
18. See Gadamer, *Philosophical Hermeneutics*, pp. 235–236. Gadamer focuses on Heidegger's interrogating the notion of essence in the context we are considering, and Gadamer argues that essays like the "Letter on Humanism" are largely complementary to the extent that

the language question teleologically develops problematics already set up in *The Essence of Reasons*. Gadamer's reading reflects a general tendency in the German scholarship on Heidegger to give innovative priority to the earlier writings and to study how Heidegger modified by means of terminological translations or the raising of auxilliary issues those positions delineated in texts like *Being and Time* and *The Essence of Reasons*. Here an organic model of Heideggerian interpretation suggests itself.

19. Kockelmans, *On Heidegger and Language*, p. xi.

20. Heidegger, *The Essence of Reasons*, pp. 38–39.

21. Heidegger, *An Introduction to Metaphysics*, p. 51.

22. Thomas Sheehan, "Heidegger's Philosophy of Mind," p. 313. Sheehan sees the turn as "the overcoming [. . .] or surpassing of metaphysics' forgetting of appropriation." This definition would characterize the later Heideggerian notion of *Ereignis*, though I would say it is inappropriate in the context of the Leibniz study, which Sheehan is explicitly citing as the place where the turn occurs. The Heidegger passage is quoted from *The Metaphysical Foundations of Logic*, p. 158.

23. Heidegger, "Letter on Humanism," p. 205.

24. Levinas, *Otherwise Than Being or Beyond Essence*.

Chapter One

1. Derrida, *Dissemination*, p. xv.

2. Derrida, *Of Grammatology*, p. 158.

3. Derrida, *Of Grammatology*, p. 158.

4. Heidegger, *Early Greek Thinking*, p. 51 (*Holzwege*, pp. 336–337).

5. Heidegger, *Early Greek Thinking*, p. 51.

6. Derrida, *Margins of Philosophy*, p. 66.

7. Derrida, *Margins of Philosophy*, p. 67.

8. Heidegger, "The Origin of the Work of Art."

9. Heidegger, *Early Greek Thinking*, pp. 16–17.

10. Heidegger, "The Anaximander Fragment," pp. 16, 17.

11. Diels, *Die Fragmente der Vorsokratiker*, p. 89.

12. Heidegger, *Early Greek Thinking*, p. 57 (*Holzwege*, p. 342).

13. Heidegger, *Early Greek Thinking*, p. 26.

14. Heidegger, *Early Greek Thinking*, p. 30.

15. Heidegger, *The Question of Being*, pp. 50–51.

16. I'm especially grateful to Stavros Deligiorgis for pointing this out to me.

17. Heidegger, *What Is Philosophy?* pp. 69– 71.
18. Derrida, *Positions,* pp. 49–50.
19. Derrida, *Of Grammatology,* p. 6.
20. Gasché, *The Tain of the Mirror,* p. 116.
21. Gasché, *The Tain of the Mirror,* p. 118.
22. Derrida, *Margins of Philosophy,* p. 227.
23. Heidegger, "Logos," p. 73.
24. Derrida, "The White Mythology," p. 228.
25. Heidegger, "Who Is Nietzsche's Zarathustra?" p. 67. I have chosen the translation by Bernd Magnus over that by David Krell, in *Nietzsche,* vol. 2 (New York: Harper and Row, 1984), because it allows for more separability or "difference" in its language. Phrases like "the belonging together of Being" in Magnus are more helpful than Krell's "coherence of Being" from my vantage point.
26. Heidegger, "Who Is Nietzsche's Zarathustra?" p. 69.
27. Derrida, *Margins of Philosophy,* pp. 233, 241, 243.
28. Olafson, *Heidegger and the Philosophy of Mind,* p. 78.
29. Olafson, *Heidegger and the Philosophy of Mind,* p. 82.
30. Heidegger, "The Anaximander Fragment," p. 22.
31. Heidegger, "Who Is Nietzsche's Zarathustra," pp. 72–73.
32. Derrida, "The White Mythology," p. 268.
33. Nietzsche, "Rhétorique et langage: Texts traduits, présentés et annotés par Philippe Lacoue-Labarthe et Jean-Luc Nancy."
34. Rey, *L'enjeu des signes,* pp. 25, 90.
35. Derrida, "The White Mythology," p. 271.
36. Heidegger, "The Anaximander Fragment," p. 26.
37. Martin Heidegger, *Grundbegriffe,* vol. 51, pp. 94–122. It is likely that Jacques Derrida did not have access to this manuscript at the time he interpreted "The Anaximander Fragment" in the late 1960s. Throughout this book I assume that materials are not genuinely accessible until published and therefore do not enter into speculation about whether Derrida knew about certain features of the seminar which he drew from or was influenced by.
38. Kirk and Raven, *The Presocratic Philosophers,* p. 117.
39. Kirk and Raven, *The Presocratic Philosophers,* p. 111.
40. Quoted in Sweeney, *Infinity in the Presocratics,* p. 6. For a much fuller exposition on the scholarship concerning the Anaximander fragment, see Sweeney's book. In large part, I'm drawing from Sweeney's work, selecting those aspects of the history he documents relevant to our concerns.
41. Sweeney, *Infinity in the Presocratics,* p. 7.
42. Sweeney, *Infinity in the Presocratics,* p. 9.
43. Heidegger, "The Anaximander Fragment," p. 57.

44. Heidegger, *Grundbegriffe*, p. 96.
45. Heidegger, *Grundbegriffe*, p. 99.
46. Heidegger, *Grundbegriffe*, p. 116.
47. Halliburton, *Poetic Thinking*, p. 164.
48. Heidegger, *The Question of Being*, p. 91.
49. Derrida, *Margins of Philosophy*, p. 23.
50. Derrida, *Margins of Philosophy*, p. 23.
51. Derrida, *Margins of Philosophy*, pp. 23–24.
52. Derrida, *Margins of Philosophy*, p. 24.
53. Derrida, *Margins of Philosophy*, p. 24.
54. Derrida, *Margins of Philosophy*, p. 25.
55. Derrida, *Margins of Philosophy*, p. 25.
56. Derrida, *Margins of Philosophy*, p. 25.
57. Derrida, *Margins of Philosophy*, pp. 25–26.
58. Derrida, *Margins of Philosophy*, p. 26 (translation slightly amended).
59. Derrida, *Margins of Philosophy*, p. 26.
60. Derrida, *Margins of Philosophy*, p. 13.
61. Derrida, *Margins of Philosophy*, p. 13.
62. Derrida, *Margins of Philosophy*, p. 13.
63. Derrida, *Of Grammatology*, p. 22.
64. Derrida, *Of Grammatology*, p. 22.
65. Derrida, *Of Grammatology*, p. 23.
66. Derrida, *Of Grammatology*, p. 23.

Chapter Two

1. Derrida, *Margins of Philosophy*, p. 38.
2. Derrida, *Margins of Philosophy*, p. 41.
3. Derrida, *Margins of Philosophy*, p. 42.
4. Derrida, *Margins of Philosophy*, p. 43.
5. Derrida, *Margins of Philosophy*, p. 44.
6. Derrida, *Margins of Philosophy*, pp. 45–46.
7. Aristotle, *Physics*, p. 78.
8. Aristotle, *Physics*, p. 79.
9. Aristotle, *Metaphysics*, p. 87. The passages are taken from Book Delta. Many of the metaphysical categories which both Heidegger and Derrida consider are defined by Aristotle in this section, and hence Book Delta may function for us as an important glossary of metaphysics.
10. Aquinas, *Commentary on Aristotle's "Physics,"* p. 263.

11. Derrida, *Margins of Philosophy*, p. 56.

12. Derrida, *Margins of Philosophy*, pp. 66–67.

13. Sheehan, "'Time and Being,' 1925–27," p. 183.

14. Sheehan, "'Time and Being,' 1925–27," p. 185.

15. Heidegger, *Basic Problems of Phenomenology*, p. 249.

16. Derrida, *Positions*, p. 45. In citing this text, I only wish to point out how generalized the deconstruction of number becomes in terms of the Derridean project as a whole.

17. Derrida, *Dissemination*, pp. 296–297 and 294.

18. Said, "Abecedarium Culturae," p. 381.

19. Heidegger, *Basic Problems of Phenomenology*, p. 287. Because of the awkwardness of the translation, I include the original from *Die Grundprobleme der Phänomenologie*, pp. 406–407.

20. Deleuze, *Différence et répétition*. See chapter 2 of Deleuze's book for his remarks on time and chapter 5 for his remarks on number. Especially useful is Deleuze's conviction that "repetition is not a repetition of elements or of successive and exteriorized parts, but of wholes coexisting at various degrees or levels" (p. 367). That these levels of repetition are differentiated in such a way that the levels resist synthesis even as they achieve stability and reference with one another is crucial to Deleuze's means of deconstructing the notion of a scientific cognitive subject.

21. Heidegger, *The Metaphysical Foundations of Logic*, pp. 196–197.

22. Heidegger, *The Metaphysical Foundations of Logic*, p. 204.

23. Heidegger, *The Metaphysical Foundations of Logic*, p. 205.

24. Heidegger, *The Metaphysical Foundations of Logic*, p. 205.

25. Heidegger, *The Metaphysical Foundations of Logic*, p. 206.

26. Heidegger, *The Metaphysical Foundations of Logic*, p. 208.

27. Heidegger, *The Essence of Reasons*, pp. 36–39. This is a bilingual edition.

28. Heidegger, *The Essence of Reasons*, p. 127.

29. Heidegger, *The Essence of Reasons*, pp. 128–129.

30. Heidegger, "Letter on Humanism," p. 208.

31. Heidegger, "Letter on Humanism," p. 207.

32. Krell, *Intimations of Mortality*, p. 35. Since it is far from clear how the footnote apparatus works in Krell's text, I'm assuming the reference is to *Frühe Schriften* (Frankfurt am Main: Vittorio Klostermann, 1978).

33. Derrida, *Margins of Philosophy*, p. 128.

34. Derrida, *Margins of Philosophy*, p. 130.

35. Derrida, *Margins of Philosophy*, p. 127.

36. Derrida, *Margins of Philosophy*, p. 133.

37. Derrida, *Margins of Philosophy*, p. 134.
38. Derrida, *Margins of Philosophy*, p. 135.
39. Derrida, *Margins of Philosophy*, p. 136.

Chapter Three

1. Heidegger, *Heraklit*, p. 223.
2. Heidegger, *Heraklit*, p. 266.
3. Heidegger, "Letter on Humanism," p. 193 ("Brief Über den 'Humanismus,'" p. 145).
4. Ricoeur, "Heidegger and the Subject," in *Conflict of Interpretations*, p. 224.
5. Erasmus Schöfer in Kockelmans, *On Heidegger and Language*, p. 298. Schöfer comes close to recognizing that it is by means of paronomasia that Heidegger breaks the hermeneutic circle, that metalepsis is key.
6. Notice the analysis in chapter 1 on the Anaximander seminar given by Heidegger in 1941 in which the paronomasic slippage of *aletheia, apeiron,* and *arché* have special significance for a theory of temporality and how this seminar approaches the question of "man" posed in the Heraclitus seminars we have been considering here.
7. Heidegger, *Being and Time*, p. 226.
8. Heidegger, *Heraklit*, p. 276.
9. Roudinesco, *Histoire de la psychanalyse en France*, vol. 2, p. 309.
10. Blanchot, *Le livre à venir.*
11. Blanchot, *La part du feu*, p. 115.
12. Blanchot, *La part du feu*, p. 116.
13. Blanchot, *La part du feu*, p. 116.
14. Blanchot, *La part du feu*, p. 117.
15. Blanchot, *La part du feu*, p. 119.
16. Blanchot, *La part du feu*, pp. 117–118.
17. "Pourquoi le poète pressent-il, pourquoi peut-il exister sur ce mode du pressentiment?" (Blanchot, *La part du feu*, p. 122).
18. Blanchot, *La part du feu*, p. 122.
19. Blanchot, *La part du feu*, p. 123.
20. Blanchot, *When the Time Comes*, p. 71.
21. Blanchot, *La folie du jour*, p. 12.
22. Blanchot, *La part du feu*, p. 125.
23. Blanchot, *La part du feu*, p. 126.
24. Blanchot, *La part du feu*, p. 127.
25. Blanchot, *La part du feu*, p. 129.
26. de Man, *Blindness and Insight*, 2nd ed., p. 265. This revised edition generously includes earlier pieces from the 1950s.

27. Heidegger, "Logos," in *Early Greek Thinking*, p. 72.

28. Blanchot, *Le livre à venir*, p. 335.

29. Blanchot, *Le livre à venir*, p. 346.

30. Derrida, "Mes chances," p. 17.

31. Blanchot, *Le livre à venir*, p. 330.

32. Derrida, "Mes chances," p. 18.

33. Blanchot, *Le pas au-delà*, p. 58.

34. Blanchot, *Le pas au-delà*, p. 64.

35. Nancy, *Le partage des voix*.

36. Heidegger, *The Essence of Reasons*, pp. 37–39.

37. Blanchot, *Le pas au-delà*, pp. 48–49.

38. Blanchot, *Le pas au-delà*, p. 49.

39. Blanchot, *Le pas au-delà*, p. 8. "Temps, temps: le pas au-delà qui ne s'accomplit pas dans le temps conduirait hors du temps, sans que ce dehors fût intemporel, mais là où le temps tomberait, chute fragile, selon ce 'hors temps dans le temps' vers lequel écrire nous attirerait, s'il nous était permis, disparus de nous, d'écrire sous le secret de la peur ancienne."

40. Blanchot, *Le pas au-delà*, p. 70. Italics mine.

41. Heidegger, *On Time and Being*, p. 15 ("Zeit und Sein," p. 16).

42. Heidegger, *On Time and Being*, pp. 21–22 ("Zeit und Sein," pp. 22–23). "Denn, indem wir dem Sein selbst nachdenken und seinem Eigenen folgen, erweist es sich als die durch das Reichen von Zeit gewährte Gabe des Geschickes von Anwesenheit. Die Gabe von Anwesen ist Eigentum des Ereignens. Sein verschwindet im Ereignis. In der Wendung: 'Sein als das Ereignis' meint das 'als' jetzt: Sein, Anwesenlassen geschickt im Ereignen, Zeit gereicht im Ereignen. Zeit und Sein ereignet im Ereignis. Und dieses selbst? Lässt sich vom Ereignis noch mehr sagen?" (Heidegger, "Zeit und Sein," pp. 22–23).

43. Heidegger, *The End of Philosophy*, p. xii.

44. Blanchot, *Le pas au-delà*, p. 13.

45. Blanchot, *When the Time Comes*, pp. 59–60.

46. Heidegger, *Identity and Difference*, pp. 72–73.

47. Heidegger, *Identity and Difference*, p. 73.

48. Vattimo, *Les aventures de la différence*, p. 138.

49. Derrida, *Parages*, p. 27.

50. Derrida, *Parages*, p. 21.

51. Derrida, *Parages*, p. 23.

52. Derrida, *Parages*, p. 25.

53. Derrida, *Parages*, pp. 27–28.

54. See Derrida, *Otobiographies*. In examining Nietzsche's ears,

Derrida will notice that they hear everything together as well as apart or distanced. The treatment of the conjunction "and" in the *Declaration of Independence* is also reminiscent of the sort of particle analysis carried out in "Pas."

55. "To make 'deconstruction in America' a theme or the object of an exhaustive definition . . . defines the enemy [Wellek, Bate, etc.] of deconstruction—someone who . . . would like to wear deconstruction out, exhaust, it, turn the page" (Derrida, *Memoires for Paul de Man*, p. 17).

56. Derrida, *Parages*, p. 30. "[La lenteur] accomplit, accélère et retarde à la fois infiniment un étrange déplacement du temps, des temps, des pas continus et des mouvements enroulés autour d'un axe invisible et sans présence, passent l'un dans l'autre sans rupture, d'un temps dans l'autre, en gardant la distance infinie des moments. Ce déplacement se déplace lui-même, dans toute la complexité de son réseau, á travers *L'attente l'oubli*. Le récit récite toujours, d'abord, le déplacement de ces déplacements. Il les é-loigne d'eux-mêmes."

57. Derrida, *Parages*, pp. 36–37.

58. Ibid.

59. Heidegger, *Poetry, Language, Thought*, p. 182.

60. Derrida, *Parages*, pp. 36–37.

61. Gasché, "Joining the Text," p. 157.

62. Derrida, "The Retrait of Metaphor," p. 10.

63. Derrida, "The Retrait of Metaphor," p. 17.

64. Derrida, *Margins of Philosophy*, p. 226.

65. Derrida, "The Retrait of Metaphor," p. 16.

66. "Restitutions of Truth to Size," in *Research in Phenomenology*, vol. 8, 1978, p. 13. The translation, by John P. Leavey, Jr., accounts for only a portion of the original essay which appears in *La verité en peinture* (Paris: Flammarion, 1978). Yet I am using this text in the present chapter, because it captures much better than the recent translation by Geoff Bennington and Ian McLeon, *The Truth in Painting*, some of the textual undertones which Derrida has produced.

67. "Restitutions of Truth to Size," p. 17.

68. Heidegger, "The Self-Assertion of the German University," p. 470.

69. Derrida, *De l'esprit*, p. 119.

70. Derrida, *De l'esprit*, p. 53.

71. Heidegger, *Introduction to Metaphysics*, pp. 31–32. The publication date (1953) of the German, *Einführung in die Metaphysik*, is significant in that Derrida will consider the temporal proximities between this text and "Die Sprache im Gedicht" from *Unterwegs zur*

Sprache, which was also first given out in 1953. The coincidence of these texts—the *Introduction,* of course, was composed in the 1930s—is itself metaleptic.

72. Derrida, *De l'esprit,* pp. 89–90.

73. Derrida, *De l'esprit,* p. 32.

74. Derrida, *De l'esprit,* p. 47.

75. Derrida, "*Fors*: The Anglish Words of Nicolas Abraham and Maria Torok," p. xiv.

76. Derrida, "*Fors*: The Anglish Words of Nicolas Abraham and Maria Torok," p. xxxvi.

77. Derrida, "*Fors*: The Anglish Words of Nicolas Abraham and Maria Torok," pp. xxxv, xxxi.

78. Derrida, *De l'esprit,* pp. 118–119.

79. Derrida, *De l'esprit,* p. 129.

80. Heidegger, *On the Way to Language,* p. 179 (*Unterwegs zur Sprache,* p. 60). It is interesting that in the English translation the essay on Trakl is placed last, as if it represented to the translators Heidegger's furthest reaching thoughts on language.

81. See Derrida, *The Ear of the Other.* In this text, Derrida speaks of signing Nietzsche's writings with "the ear of the other." "When, much later, the other will have perceived with a keen-enough ear what I will have addressed or destined to him or her, then my signature will have taken place." And, "politically *and* historically . . . it is we who have been entrusted with the responsibility of the signature of the other's text which we have inherited" (p. 51). More important, given our context, one notes the following, "if therefore, one writes not only for those who are yet to live but also for the dead or for the survivors who have gone before us, then things get very complicated. I'm going to end by going very quickly here: I think one writes also for the dead. [. . .] Now if the other who signs in my place is dead, that has a certain number of consequences" (p. 53). The implication here for a text like *De l'esprit* is that not only does Derrida hear with the ears of the Other, but that these ears sign for Heidegger, and that these ears belong not only to Derrida but to the dead, that this hearing deconstitutes the difference between those who have survived and those who have not. The significance of such a hearing of a Nietzschean discourse is worked out in terms of that discourse's fascist destiny, and it might be said that in *De l'esprit* an analogous reading of Heidegger is taking place. Of course, this analogy goes far beyond the scope of my study, but acknowledgment of it is imperative, nevertheless.

82. Derrida, *Of Grammatology,* pp. 23, 47.

83. Derrida, *Of Grammatology,* p. 47.

84. Derrida, *Of Grammatology*, p. 62.
85. Derrida, *Of Grammatology*, p. 47.
86. Derrida, *De l'esprit*, p. 144.
87. Derrida, *De l'esprit*, p. 143.
88. Derrida, *De l'esprit*, p. 150.
89. Derrida, *De l'esprit*, p. 179.
90. Derrida, *De l'esprit*, p. 167.
91. Derrida, *Glas*, pp. 240a–242a.

Chapter Four

1. Derrida, *The Post Card*, p. 37.
2. Kockelmans, *On the Truth of Being*, p. 67.
3. Kockelmans, *On the Truth of Being*, pp. 67–68.
4. Kockelmans, *On the Truth of Being*, p. 70.
5. Sallis, "Towards the Showing of Language," p. 82.
6. Derrida, *Edmund Husserl's Origin of Geometry*, p. 150.
7. Derrida, *Edmund Husserl's Origin of Geometry*, p. 151.
8. Derrida, *Edmund Husserl's Origin of Geometry*, p. 151.
9. Derrida, *Edmund Husserl's Origin of Geometry*, p. 151.
10. Derrida, *Edmund Husserl's Origin of Geometry*, pp. 151–152.
11. Derrida, *Edmund Husserl's Origin of Geometry*, p. 153.
12. Derrida, *Edmund Husserl's Origin of Geometry*, p. 153.
13. Derrida, *Edmund Husserl's Origin of Geometry*, p. 153.
14. Derrida, *Edmund Husserl's Origin of Geometry*, p. 153.
15. Heidegger, *On the Way to Language*, p. 106.
16. Heidegger, *On the Way to Language*, p. 107.
17. Derrida, "La Différance," in *Margins of Philosophy*, p. 9.
18. Derrida, *Parages*, p. 12.
19. Heidegger, *On the Way to Language*, pp. 96–97.
20. Heidegger, *On the Way to Language*, p. 98.
21. Heidegger, *On the Way to Language*, p. 101.
22. Levinas, "Beyond Intentionality," pp. 110–111.
23. Heidegger, *On the Way to Language*, p. 104.
24. Heidegger, *On the Way to Language*, p. 104.
25. Heidegger, *On the Way to Language*, p. 101.
26. Heidegger, *On the Way to Language*, p. 106.
27. Heidegger, *On the Way to Language*, p. 122.
28. Heidegger, *On the Way to Language*, pp. 122–123.
29. Derrida, *The Post Card*, p. 65.
30. Derrida, *The Post Card*, p. 65.
31. Derrida, *The Post Card*, p. 66.

32. Derrida, *The Post Card*, p. 191.
33. Lukacher, *Primal Scenes*, p. 113.
34. Lukacher, *Primal Scenes*, p. 62.
35. Lukacher, *Primal Scenes*, p. 24.
36. Derrida, *The Post Card*, p. 194.
37. Derrida, "Of an Apocalyptic Tone," p. 87.
38. Levinas, *Totality and Infinity*, p. 195.
39. Derrida, "Of an Apocalyptic Tone," p. 70.
40. Derrida, "Of an Apocalyptic Tone," p. 81.
41. Derrida, "Of an Apocalyptic Tone," p. 84.
42. Derrida, "Of an Apocalyptic Tone," p. 84.
43. Derrida, "Of an Apocalyptic Tone," p. 86.
44. Derrida, "Of an Apocalyptic Tone," p. 87.
45. Derrida, "Of an Apocalyptic Tone," p. 87.
46. Derrida, "Of an Apocalyptic Tone," p. 93.
47. Derrida, "Of an Apocalyptic Tone," p. 94.
48. Derrida, "Of an Apocalyptic Tone," p. 94.
49. Derrida, "Of an Apocalyptic Tone," p. 95.
50. Derrida, *Writing and Difference*, p. 153.
51. Levinas, *En découvrant l'existence avec Husserl et Heidegger*, p. 188.
52. Derrida, "Of an Apocalyptic Tone," p. 83.
53. Derrida, "Of an Apocalyptic Tone," p. 85.
54. Derrida, "Of an Apocalyptic Tone," p. 86
55. Derrida, "Of an Apocalyptic Tone," p. 86.
56. Derrida, "Of an Apocalyptic Tone," p. 85.
57. Levinas, *Ethics and Infinity*, p. 50.
58. Levinas, "La trace de L'autre," in *En découvrant l'existence avec Husserl et Heidegger*, pp. 198–201.
59. Levinas, *Otherwise Than Being or Beyond Essence*, p. 117.
60. Derrida, "Of an Apocalyptic Tone," p. 94.
61. Derrida, "Two Words for Joyce," pp. 145–146.
62. Derrida, "Two Words for Joyce," p. 149.
63. Derrida, "Two Words for Joyce," pp. 153–154.
64. See, for example, Kockelmans, *On the Truth of Being*, p. 68.
65. Derrida, "Two Words for Joyce," p. 154.
66. Derrida, "Two Words for Joyce," p. 154.
67. Derrida, "Two Words for Joyce," p. 155.
68. Derrida, "Two Words for Joyce," p. 158.
69. See Blanchot, *L'écriture du désastre*.
70. Another important complement to this group of writings is Derrida's lecture on negative theology entitled, "Comment ne pas parler: Dénégations." The ending of the lecture discusses Heidegger's

affinities with the metaphysics of Pseudo-Dionysius, wherein the concept of God is thought in terms of the beyond of Being. At one point Derrida asks whether Heidegger in acknowledging the announcement of God from within Dasein's experience of Being is not already a theological meditation and whether the sign of the cross that crosses out Being (its erasure) in "The Question of Being" is not, in fact, a familiar theological emblem? Throughout the remarks on Heidegger, Derrida takes his distance by assigning to Heidegger a very metaphysical recovery, i.e., a theological project. See *Psyché*, pp. 589–594.

71. Derrida, "Shibboleth," p. 311.
72. Derrida, "Shibboleth," p. 312.
73. Derrida, "Shibboleth," p. 313.
74. Derrida, "Shibboleth," p. 315.
75. Derrida, "Shibboleth," pp. 334–335.
76. Derrida, "Shibboleth," p. 336.
77. Derrida, "Geschlecht II," p. 169.
78. Derrida, "Geschlecht II," p. 166.
79. Derrida, "Geschlecht II," pp. 175 and 182.
80. Derrida, "Geschlecht II," p. 166.
81. Celan, "Engführung."
82. Levinas, *Ethics and Infinity*, p. 87.
83. Levinas, *De dieu qui vient a l'idée*, p. 187.
84. Levinas, *Face to Face with Levinas*, p. 21.
85. Levinas, *De dieu*, p. 185.
86. Levinas, *De dieu*, p. 186.

Chapter Five

1. Derrida, "The Time of the Thesis," p. 34.
2. Derrida, "The Time of the Thesis," pp. 34–35.
3. Derrida, "The Time of the Thesis," p. 41.
4. Derrida, "The Time of the Thesis," p. 42.
5. Carnap, *The Logical Structure of the World*, p. 19.
6. Derrida, *Speech and Phenomena,*, p. 52.
7. Derrida, *Speech and Phenomena*, p. 52.
8. Derrida, *Speech and Phenomena*, pp. 52–53.
9. Derrida, *Speech and Phenomena*, p. 54.
10. Derrida, *Speech and Phenomena*, p. 99.
11. Derrida, *Speech and Phenomena*, pp. 101–102.
12. Derrida, *Speech and Phenomena*, p. 102.
13. Derrida, *Truth in Painting*, p. 198.
14. Derrida, *Truth in Painting*, pp. 291–292.

15. Derrida, *Truth in Painting,* p. 296.

16. Derrida, *Truth in Painting,* p. 297.

17. Derrida, *Truth in Painting,* p. 298.

18. Kant, *Critique of Pure Reason,* p. 181.

19. Derrida, *Truth in Painting,* p. 299.

20. Heidegger, *What Is a Thing?* p. 36.

21. Heidegger, *What is a Thing?* pp. 46, 38.

22. Kant, *Critique of Pure Reason,* p. 185.

23. Kant, *Critique of Pure Reason,* p. 185.

24. Derrida, *The Post Card,* p. 259.

25. Derrida, *The Post Card,* pp. 260–261.

26. Birault, *Heidegger et l'expérience de la pensée,* p. 553.

27. Levinas, *Le temps et l'autre,* p. 10. This text was originally presented as lectures during the years 1946–1947.

28. Habermas, *Philosophical Discourse,* p. 162.

29. Marcuse, *Negations,* p. 24.

30. Marcuse, *Negations,* p. 35.

31. Habermas, *The Philosophical Discourse,* p. 179.

32. Habermas, *The Philosophical Discourse,* p. 163.

33. Habermas, *The Philosophical Discourse,* p. 181.

34. Habermas, *The Philosophical Discourse,* p. 157.

BIBLIOGRAPHY

Aquinas, St. Thomas. *Commentary on Aristotle's "Physics."* Trans. R. J. Blackwell, R. J. Spath, and W. E. Thirkel. New Haven: Yale University Press, 1963.

Aristotle. *The Metaphysics.* Trans. Richard Hope. Ann Arbor: University of Michigan Press, 1968.

———. *The Physics.* Trans. H. G. Apostole. Bloomington: Indiana University Press, 1969.

Beaufret, Jean. *Dialogue avec Heidegger.* 3 vols. Paris: Minuit, 1973–1974.

Birault, Henri. *Heidegger et l'expérience de la pensée.* Paris: Gallimard, 1978.

Blanchot, Maurice. *Au moment voulu.* Paris: Gallimard, 1951.

———. *L'écriture du désastre.* Paris: Gallimard, 1980.

———. *L'entretien infini.* Paris: Gallimard, 1969.

———. *La folie du jour.* Bilingual ed. Trans. Lydia Davis. Barrytown, N.Y.: Station Hill Press, 1981. Published in French under same title (Paris: Fata Morgana, 1973).

———. *Le livre à venir.* Paris: Gallimard, 1959.

———. *La part du feu.* Paris: Gallimard, 1949.

———. *Le pas au-délà.* Paris: Gallimard, 1973.

———. *When the Time Comes.* Trans. Lydia Davis. Barrytown, N.Y.: Station Hill Press, 1985. Published in French as *Au moment voulu.*

Boeckaert, Luk. "Ontology and Ethics: Reflections on Levinas' Critique of Heidegger." *International Philosophical Quarterly* 10 (1970).

Carnap, Rudolf. *The Logical Structure of the World.* Trans. R. A. George. Berkeley: University of California Press, 1967.

Celan, Paul. "Engführung" in *Sprachgitter.* Frankfurt Am Main: S. Fischer, 1959.

Chalier, Catherine. *Judaisme et alterité.* Paris: Verdier, 1982.

Clark, Timothy. "Being in Mime: Heidegger and Derrida on the Ontology of Literary Language." *Modern Language Notes* 101, no. 5 (1986).

Deleuze, Gilles. *Différence et répétition.* Paris: P.U.F., 1968.

de Man, Paul. *Blindness and Insight,* 2nd edition. Minneapolis: University of Minnesota Press, 1983.

279

Derrida, Jacques. "Comment ne pas parler: *Dénégations.*" In *Psyché.* Paris: Galilée, 1987.

――――. "Deconstruction in America: An Interview with Jacques Derrida." *Society for Critical Exchange,* no. 17 (Winter 1985).

――――. *De l'esprit: Heidegger et la question.* Paris: Galilée, 1987.

――――. "Différance." In *Margins of Philosophy.* Trans. Alan Bass. Chicago: University of Chicago Press, 1982. Published in French as "La différance," in *Marges de la philosophie* (Paris: Minuit, 1972).

――――. *Dissemination.* Trans. Barbara Johnson. Chicago: University of Chicago Press, 1981. Published in French as *La dissémination* (Paris: Seuil, 1972).

――――. *The Ear of the Other: Otobiography, Transference, Translation.* Ed. C. Lévesque and C.V. McDonald. Trans. Peggy Kamuf. New York: Schocken, 1975. Published in French as *L'Oreille de l'autre: Textes et débats avec Jacques Derrida* (Montreal: Vlb, 1982).

――――. *Edmund Husserl's Origin of Geometry: An Introduction.* Trans. John P. Leavey, Jr. Ed. David B. Allison. Stony Brook, N.Y.: Nicolas Hays, 1978. Published in French as *L'origine de la géométrie,* translation of and introduction to Edmund Husserl's "Origin of Geometry" (Paris: Presses Universitaires de France, 1962).

――――. "En ce moment même me voici." In *Psyché.* Paris: Galilée, 1987. Original version published in *Textes pour Emmanuel Levinas* (Paris: J.M. Place, 1980).

――――. "The Ends of Man." In *Margins of Philosophy.* Trans. Alan Bass. Chicago: University of Chicago Press, 1982. Published in French as "Les fins de l'homme," in *Marges de la philosophie* (Paris: Minuit, 1972).

――――. *Eperons.* Paris: Flammarion, 1976.

――――. *Feu la cendre.* Paris: Des Femmes, 1987.

――――. "*Fors*: The Anglish Words of Nicolas Abraham and Maria Torok." Trans. Barbara Johnson. In *The Wolf Man's Magic Word.* Minneapolis: University of Minnesota Press, 1986. Published in French as "Fors," preface to *Le verbier de l'homme aux loups,* by Nicolas Abraham and M. Torok (Paris: Flammarion, 1976).

――――. "*Geschlecht*: différence sexuelle, différence ontologique." In *Psyché.* Paris: Galilée, 1987.

――――. "Geschlecht II: Heidegger's Hand." In *Deconstruction and Philosophy,* ed. J. Sallis. Chicago: University of Chicago Press, 1986. Published in French as "La main de Heidegger (*Geschlecht II*)," in *Psyché* (Paris: Galilée, 1987).

――――. *Glas.* Trans. John P. Leavey, Jr., and Richard Rand. Lincoln: University of Nebraska Press, 1986. Published in French as *Glas* (Paris: Galilée, 1974).

————. "How To Avoid Speaking: Denials." Lecture, Cornell University, 1986.

————. *Margins of Philosophy*. Trans. Alan Bass. Chicago: University of Chicago Press, 1982. Published in French as *Marges de la philosophie* (Paris: Minuit, 1972).

————. *Memoires for Paul de Man*. New York: Columbia University Press, 1986.

————. "Mes chances." In *Taking Chances*, ed. J. Smith and W. Kerrigan. Baltimore: Johns Hopkins University Press, 1984.

————. "Of an Apocalyptic Tone Recently Adopted in Philosophy." Trans. John P. Leavey, Jr. *Semeia* 23 (1982). Published in French as *D'un ton apocalyptique adopté naguère en philosophie* (Paris: Galilée, 1983).

————. *Of Grammatology*. Trans. G. C. Spivak. Baltimore: Johns Hopkins University Press, 1976. Published in French as *De la grammatologie* (Paris: Minuit, 1967).

————. *Otobiographies: L'enseignement de Nietzsche et la politique du nom propre*. Paris: Galilée, 1984.

————. "Ousia and Gramme." In *Margins of Philosophy*, trans. Alan Bass. Chicago: University of Chicago Press, 1982. Published in French as "Ousia et grammè: Note sur une note de Sein und Zeit," in *Marges de la philosophie* (Paris: Minuit, 1972).

————. *Parages*. Paris: Galilée, 1986.

————. "Pas." In *Parages*. Paris: Galilée, 1986.

————. *Positions*. Trans. Alan Bass. Chicago: University of Chicago Press, 1981. Published in French as *Positions* (Paris: Minuit, 1972).

————. *The Post Card*. Trans. Alan Bass. Chicago: University of Chicago Press, 1987. Published in French as *La carte postale*: *De Socrate à Freud et au-delà* (Paris: Flammarion, 1980).

————. "The Retrait of Metaphor." *Enclitic* 2, no. 2 (1978). Published in French as "Le retrait de la métaphore," in *Psyché* (Paris: Galilée, 1987). Originally published in *Poesie* 7 (1978).

————. "Shibboleth." In *Midrash and Literature*. New Haven: Yale University Press, 1986. Published in French as *Shibboleth* (Paris: Galilée, 1986).

————. *Signéponge*. Trans. Richard Rand. New York: Columbia University Press, 1984.

————. *Speech and Phenomena and Other Essays on Husserl's Theory of Signs*. Trans. D.B. Allison. Evanston, Ill.: Northwestern University Press, 1973. Published in French as *La voix et le phénomème* (Paris: Presses Universitaires de France, 1967).

————. "The Time of the Thesis: Punctuations." In *Philosophy in France Today*. London: Cambridge University Press, 1983.

———. *The Truth in Painting*. Trans. G. Bennington and I. McLeod. Chicago: University of Chicago Press, 1987. Published in French as *La vérité en peinture* (Paris: Flammarion, 1978).

———. "Two Words for Joyce." In *Post-Structuralist Joyce*. London: Cambridge University Press, 1984. Published in French in *Ulysse gramophone: Deux mots pour Joyce*. Paris: Galilée, 1987.

———. "The White Mythology." In *Margins of Philosophy*. Trans. Alan Bass. Chicago: University of Chicago Press, 1982. Published in French as "La mythologie blanche: La métaphore dans le texte philosophique," in *Marges de la philosophie* (Paris: Minuit, 1972).

———. *Writing and Difference*. Trans. Alan Bass. Chicago: University of Chicago Press, 1978. Published in French as *L'écriture et la différence* (Paris: Seuil, 1967).

Diels, Hermann. *Die Fragmente der Vorsokratiker*. Berlin: Weidmannsche Verlagsbuchhandlung, 1951.

Donato, Eugenio. "Ending/Closure: On Derrida's Edging of Heidegger." *Yale French Studies* 67 (1984).

Faye, J.-P. "Attaques nazis contre Heidegger." *Critique* 234 (1962).

Fynsk, Christopher. *Heidegger: Thought and Historicity*. Ithaca: Cornell, 1986.

Gadamer, Hans Georg. *Philosophical Hermeneutics*. Ed. David E. Linge. Berkeley: University of California, 1976.

Gasché, Rodolphe. "Joining the Text: From Heidegger to Derrida." In *The Yale Critics: Deconstruction in America*, ed. J. Arac, W. Godzich, W. Martin. Minneapolis: University of Minnesota Press, 1983.

———. *The Tain of the Mirror: Derrida and the Philosophy of Reflection*. Cambridge: Harvard University Press, 1986.

Habermas, Jürgen. *The Philosophical Discourse of Modernity*. Trans. F. Lawrence. Cambridge: MIT Press, 1987.

Halliburton, David. *Poetic Thinking*. Chicago: University of Chicago Press, 1981.

Hartman, Geoffrey. *Saving the Text*. Baltimore: Johns Hopkins University Press, 1980.

Heidegger, Martin. "Aletheia (Heraklit, Fragment 16)." In *Vorträge und Aufsätze*. Pfullingen: Günter Neske, 1961.

———. "The Anaximander Fragment." In *Early Greek Thinking*. New York: Harper and Row, 1975. Published in German as "Der Spruch des Anaximander," in *Holzwege* (Frankfurt am Main: Vittorio Klostermann, 1950).

———. *Basic Problems of Phenomenology*. Trans. Albert Hofstadter. Bloomington: Indiana University Press, 1982. Published in German as *Die Grundprobleme der Phänomenologie* (Frankfurt am Main: Vittorio Klostermann, 1975).

———. *Being and Time.* Trans. J. Macquarrie and E. Robinson. New York: Harper and Row, 1962.

———. "Das Ding." In *Vorträge und Aufsätze.* Pfullingen: Günter Neske, 1961.

———. *Early Greek Thinking.* New York: Harper and Row, 1975.

———. *The End of Philosophy.* Trans. J. Stambaugh. New York: Harper and Row, 1973.

———. *The Essence of Reasons.* Evanston, Ill.: Northwestern University Press, 1969. Published in German as *Vom Wesen des Grundes* (Frankfurt am Main: Vittorio Klostermann, 1928).

———. *Gelassenheit.* Pfullingen: Günter Neske, 1959.

———. *Grundbegriffe.* Ed. Petra Jaeger. Frankfurt am Main: Vittorio Klostermann, 1981.

———. *Heraklit.* In *Gesamtausgabe,* vol. 55. Frankfurt am Main: Vittorio Klostermann, 1979.

———. *History of the Concept of Time.* Trans. Theodore Kiseil. Bloomington: Indiana University Press, 1985.

———. *Holzwege.* Frankfurt am Main: Vittorio Klostermann, 1950.

———. *Identity and Difference.* Bilingual ed. Trans. Joan Stambaugh. New York: Doubleday, 1961. Published in German as *Identität und Differenz* (Pfullingen: Günter Neske, 1957).

———. *An Introduction to Metaphysics.* Trans. Ralph Mannheim. New York: Doubleday, 1962. Published in German as *Einführung in die Metaphysik* (Tübingen: Max Niemeyer, 1953).

———. "Language in the Poem." Trans. Peter Hertz in *On the Way to Language.* New York: Harper and Row, 1971. Published in German as "Die Sprache im Gedicht: Eine Erörterung von Georg Trakls Gedicht," in *Unterwegs zur Sprache* (Pfullingen: Günter Neske, 1959).

———. "The Letter on Humanism." In *Martin Heidegger: Basic Writings,* ed. D. Krell, trans. F. Capuzzi, G. Gray, and D. Krell. New York: Harper and Row, 1977. Published in German as "Brief über den 'Humanismus,'" in *Wegmarken* (Frankfurt am Main: Vittorio Klostermann, 1967).

———. "Logos (Heraklit, Fragment 50)." In *Vorträge und Aufsätze.* Pfullingen: Günter Neske, 1961.

———. *The Metaphysical Foundations of Logic.* Trans. Michael Heim. Bloomington: Indiana University Press, 1984. Published in German as *Die Metaphysische Anfangsgründe der Logik im Ausgang von Leibniz* (Frankfurt am Main: Vittorio Klostermann, 1978).

————. *Nietzsche*. 2 vols. Pfullingen: Günter Neske, 1961.

————. *On the Way to Language*. Trans. Peter Hertz and Joan Stambaugh. New York: Harper and Row, 1971. Published in German as *Unterwegs zur Sprache* (Pfullingen: Günter Neske, 1959).

————. *On Time and Being*. Trans. J. Stambaugh. New York: Harper and Row, 1972. Published in German as "Zeit und Sein," in *Zur Sache des Denkens* (Tübingen: Max Niemeyer, 1969).

————. "The Origin of the Work of Art." In *Poetry, Language, Thought*. New York: Harper and Row, 1971. Published in German as "Der Ursprung des Kunstwerkes," in *Holzwege* (Frankfurt am Main: Vittorio Klostermann, 1950).

————. *Prolegomena Zur Geschichte Des Zeitbegriffs*. Frankfurt am Main: Vittorio Klostermann, 1979.

————. *The Question concerning Technology and Other Essays*. Trans. W. Lovitt. New York: Harper and Row, 1977. Published in German as *Die Technik und die Kehre* (Pfullingen: Günter Neske, 1962).

————. *The Question of Being*. Trans. J. Wilde and W. Kluback. New Haven: College and University Press, 1958. Published in German as *Zur Seinsfrage* (Frankfurt am Main: Vittorio Klostermann, 1956).

————. *Sein und Zeit*. 15th ed. Tübingen: Max Niemeyer, 1979. Originally published in *Jahrbuch für Philosophie und phänomenologische Forschung*, vol. 8, 1927.

————. "The Self-Assertion of the German University." Trans. Karsten Harries in *Review of Metaphysics* 38, no. 3 (March 1985). Published in German as *Die Selbstbehauptung der deutschen Universität* (Breslau: Korn, 1933).

————. "Überwindung der Metaphysik." In *Vorträge und Aufsätze*. Pfullingen: Günter Neske, 1961.

————. *Vorträge und Aufsätze*. Pfullingen: Günter Neske, 1961.

————. "Das Wesen der Sprache." In *Unterwegs zur Sprache*. Pfullingen: Günter Neske, 1959.

————. "Der Weg zur Sprache." In *Unterwegs zur Sprache*. Pfullingen: Günter Neske, 1959.

————. *What Is a Thing?* Trans. W. B. Barton and V. Deutsch. New York: Regnery, 1967. Published in German as *Die Frage Nach Dem Ding* (Pfullingen: Günter Neske, 1962).

————. *What Is Philosophy?* Trans. W. Kluback and J. T. Wilde. New York: Twayne, 1958. Published in German as "Was ist das—die Philosophie?" (Pfullingen: Günter Neske, 1956).

————. "Who Is Nietzsche's Zarathustra?" Trans. Bernd Magnus. In *The New Nietzsche*, ed. D. B. Allison. New York: Dell, 1977. Published in German as "Wer ist Nietzsches Zarathustra," in *Vorträge und Aufsätze*. (Pfullingen: Günter Neske, 1961).

———. "Das Wort." In *Unterwegs zur Sprache*. Pfullingen: Günter Neske, 1959.

———. "Zeit und Sein." In *Zur Sache des Denkens*. Tübingen, Max Niemeyer, 1969.

Holland, Nancy J. "Heidegger and Derrida Redux." In *Hermeneutics and Deconstruction*, ed. H. J. Silverman and D. Ihde. Albany: State University of New York Press, 1985.

Kant, Immanuel. *Critique of Pure Reason*. Trans. N. K. Smith. New York: St. Martin's Press, 1965.

Kettering, Emil. *Nähe: Das Denken Martin Heideggers*. Pfullingen: Neske, 1987.

Kirk, C. S. and Raven, J. E. *The Presocratic Philosophers*. London: Cambridge University Press, 1957.

Kockelmans, Joseph J. *On the Truth of Being*. Bloomington: Indiana University Press, 1984.

———, ed. *On Heidegger and Language*. Evanston, Ill.: Northwestern University Press, 1972.

Kofman, Sarah. *Lectures de Derrida*. Paris: Galilée, 1984.

Kolb, David. *The Critique of Pure Modernity: Hegel, Heidegger, and After*. Chicago: University of Chicago Press, 1986.

Krell, David. *Intimations of Mortality: Time, Truth, and Finitude in Heidegger's Thinking of Being*. University Park: Pennsylvania State University Press, 1986.

———. "The Perfect Future: A Note on Heidegger and Derrida." In *Desconstruction and Philosophy*, ed. J. Sallis. Chicago: University of Chicago Press, 1987.

Krüger, Lorenz. "Why Do We Study the History of Philosophy?" In *Philosophy in History*, ed. R. Rorty, J. B. Schneewind, and Q. Skinner. London: Cambridge University Press, 1984.

Lacoue-Labarthe, P., and Nancy. J.-L, eds. *Les fins de l'homme: A partir du travail de Jacques Derrida*. Paris: Galilée, 1981.

———. *Le sujet de la philosophie: Typographies I*. Paris: Flammarion, 1979.

Leavey, J. P. "Destinerrance: The Apotropocalyptics of Translation." In *Deconstruction and Philosophy*, ed. J. Sallis. Chicago: University of Chicago Press, 1987.

Levesque, Claude. *L'étrangeté du texte: Essai sur Nietzsche, Freud, Blanchot, et Derrida*. Paris: U.G.E. 1978.

Levinas, Emmanuel. *L'au-delà du verset*. Paris: Minuit, 1982.

———. "Beyond Intentionality." In *Philosophy in France Today*. London: Cambridge University Press, 1983.

————. *De dieu qui vient à l'idée*. Paris: Vrin, 1982.

————. *En découvrant l'existence avec Husserl et Heidegger*. Paris: Vrin, 1982.

————. *Ethics and Infinity*. Trans. R. Cohen. Pittsburgh: Duquesne University Press, 1985.

————. *Face to Face with Levinas*. Ed. R. A. Cohen. Albany: State University of New York Press, 1986.

————. *Humanisme de l'autre homme*. Paris: Fata Morgana, 1972.

————. *Otherwise Than Being or Beyond Essence*. Trans. A. Lingis. The Hague: Martinus Nijhoff, 1981. Published in French as *Autrement qu'etre ou au-delà de l'essence* (The Hague, Martinus Nijhoff, 1978).

————. *Le temps et l'autre*. Paris: P.U.F., 1985.

————. *Totality and Infinity*. Pittsburgh: Duquesne University Press, 1969.

Lukacher, Ned. *Primal Scenes*. Ithaca: Cornell University Press, 1986.

Marcuse, Herbert. *Negations*. Trans. J. J. Shapiro. Boston: Beacon Press, 1968.

Marx, Werner. *Heidegger and the Tradition*. Trans. T. Kisiel and M. Greene. Evanston, Ill.: Northwestern University Press, 1971.

Megill, Allan. *Prophets of Extremity: Nietzsche, Heidegger, Foucault, Derrida*. Berkeley: University of California Press, 1986.

Nancy, Jean-Luc. *Le partage des voix*. Paris: Galilée, 1982.

Nietzsche, Friedrich. "Rhétorique et langage: Texts traduits, présentés et annotés par Philippe Lacoue-Labarthe et Jean-Luc Nancy." *Poétique* 5 (1971).

Olafson, Frederick A. *Heidegger and the Philosophy of Mind*. New Haven: Yale University Press, 1987.

Olkowski, Dorothea. "If the Shoe Fits—Derrida and the Orientation of Thought." In *Hermeneutics and Deconstruction,* ed. H. J. Silverman and D. Ihde, Albany: State University of New York Press, 1985.

Pöggler, Otto. *Der Denkweg Martin Heideggers*. Pfullingen: Neske, 1963.

————. *Heidegger und die Hermeneutische Philosophie*. Fribourg: Alber, 1983.

————. "Sein als Ereignis." In *Zeitschrift für philosophische Forschung* 13 (1959).

Rey, Jean-Michel. *L'enjeu des signes: Lecture de Nietzsche*. Paris: Seuil, 1971.

Richardson, W. J. *Heidegger: Through Phenomenology to Thought*. The Hague: Martinus Nijhoff, 1963.

Ricoeur, Paul. *The Conflict of Interpretations*. Evanston, Ill.: Northwestern University Press, 1974.

————. *Temps et récit.* 3 vols. Paris: Seuil, 1983–1985.

Rosales, Alberto. *Transzendenz und Differenz. Ein Beitrag zum Problem der ontologischen Differenz beim frühen Heidegger.* The Hague: Martinus Nijhoff, 1970.

Rose, Gillian. *Dialectic of Nihilism: Post-Structuralism and Law.* London: Blackwell, 1984.

Rosenzweig, Franz. *The Star of Redemption.* Trans. W. W. Hallo. Boston: Beacon Press, 1972.

Roudinesco, Elizabeth. *Histoire de la psychanalyse en France.* 2 vols. Paris: Editions du Seuil, 1986.

Said, Edward. "Abecedarium Culturae." In *Modern French Criticism.* Chicago: University of Chicago Press, 1972.

Sallis, John. *Delimitations: Phenomenology and the End of Metaphysics.* Bloomington: Indiana University Press, 1986.

————, ed. *Heidegger and the Path of Thinking.* Pittsburgh: Duquesne University Press, 1970.

————. "Towards the Showing of Language." In *Thinking about Being,* ed. R. W. Shahan and J. N. Mohanty. Norman: University of Oklahoma Press, 1984.

Schneeberger, Guido. *Nachlese Zu Heidegger.* Bern: Suhr, 1962.

Schöfer, Erasmus. "Heidegger's Language: Metalogical Forms of Thought and Grammatical Specialities." In *On Heidegger and Language,* ed. J. Kockelmans. Evanston, Ill.: Northwestern University Press, 1974.

————. *Die Sprache Heideggers.* Pfullingen: Neske, 1962.

Schweppenhäuser, Hermann. "Studien über die Heideggersche Sprachtheorie." *Archiv für Philosophie* 7 (1957) and 8 (1958).

Serres, Michel. *The Parasite.* Trans. L. R. Schehr. Baltimore: Johns Hopkins University Press, 1982. Published in French as *Le parasite* (Paris: Grasset, 1980).

Sheehan, Thomas. "Derrida and Heidegger." In *Hermeneutics and Deconstruction,* ed. H. J. Silverman and D. Idhe, Albany: State University of New York Press, 1985.

————. "Heidegger's Philosophy of Mind." In *Contemporary Philosophy,* ed. G. Floistad. The Hague: Martinus Nijhoff, 1983.

————. "'Time and Being,' 1925–27." In *Thinking about Being,* ed. R. W. Shahan and J. N. Mohanty. Norman: University of Oklahoma Press, 1984.

Shürmann, Reiner. *Le principe d'anarchie: Heidegger et la question de l'agir.* Paris: Seuil, 1982.

Steiner, George. *Martin Heidegger.* New York: Viking, 1979.

Sweeney, Leo. *Infinity in the Presocratics.* The Hague: Martinus Nijhoff, 1972.

Ulmer, Gregory. *Applied Grammatology*. Baltimore: Johns Hopkins University Press, 1986.
Vattimo, Gianni. *Les aventures de la différence*. Paris: Minuit, 1985.
Warminski, Andrzej. *Readings in Interpretation: Hölderlin, Hegel, Heidegger*. Minneapolis: University of Minnesota Press, 1987.

INDEX

Anaximander, 18, 27, 29, 30, 36, 45, 55, 67, 71, 76, 79, 205, 233, 235
Aristotle, 3, 22, 36, 41, 43, 45, 48, 66, 69, 70, 169, 170, 173, 196; *The Metaphysics,* 76, 77, 78, 121; *The Physics,* 49, 71–79, 85

Barthes, Roland: "Death of the Author," 118
Bass, Alan, 150
Beaufret, Jean, 110
Beckett, Samuel, 144
Birault, Henri: *Heidegger et l'expérience de la pensée,* 258
Blanchot, Maurice, 11, 12, 16, 93, 103, 110, 111, 202, 203, 210, 211, 212, 217, 218, 230, 233, 247; *Au moment voulu,* 119, 137, 138; "L'absence de livre," 129; *L'arrêt de mort,* 102, 140; *L'attente l'oubli,* 215; *Le dernier homme,* 101, 206; *L'entretien infini,* 11; *La folie du jour,* 102, 119; *Le livre à venir,* 112, 117, 123, 124, 126; "Où va la littérature?" 123–27; "La parole 'sacrée' de Hölderlin," 112, 115–23; *La part du feu,* 19, 112, 123, 124, 130; *Le pas au-delà,* 113, 129–33, 136–37, 138, 228
Burch, George, 48

Carnap, Rudolf, 249; *The Logical Structure of the World,* 248
Celan, Paul, 234, 236–38; "Engführung," 241–43
Char, René, 110
Chase, Cynthia, 198
Cherniss, Harold, 49
Culler, Jonathan, 198

Deleuze, Gilles, 43; *Différence et répétition,* 88–89
De Man, Paul, 71, 121; *Blindness and Insight,* 123
Derrida, Jacques: "Of An Apocalyptic Tone Recently Adopted in Philosophy," 16–